Feminist Dilemmas in Fieldwork

FEMINIST DILEMMAS IN FIELDWORK

---

edited by
DIANE L. WOLF

with a Foreword by
CARMEN DIANA DEERE

WestviewPress
A Division of HarperCollinsPublishers

For our students

Copyright © 1996 by Westview Press, Inc., A Division of HarperCollins Publishers, Inc., except Chapter 4, which is copyright © Carol B. Stack

Published in 1996 in the United States of America by Westview Press, Inc., 5500 Central Avenue, Boulder, Colorado 80301-2877, and in the United Kingdom by Westview Press, 12 Hid's Copse Road, Cumnor Hill, Oxford OX2 9JJ

Library of Congress Cataloging-in-Publication Data
Feminist dilemmas in fieldwork / edited by Diane L. Wolf.
    p. cm.
  Includes bibliographical references.
  ISBN 0-8133-8496-6 (hc)—ISBN 0-8133-8499-0 (pbk)
    1. Women's studies—Field work. 2. Feminism—Research. I. Wolf,
Diane L.
HQ1180.F45 1996
305.42'072—dc20
                                        95-42688
                                                CIP

10   9   8   7   6   5   4   3   2

Contents

Foreword

This collection of essays on feminist dilemmas in fieldwork should be mandatory reading for students about to undertake fieldwork for the first time. The volume is not a manual on "how to do fieldwork," nor does it offer definitive answers to the conundrums feminist researchers have faced in the field. Rather, taken as a whole, the individual chapters introduce prospective field researchers to a broad variety of concrete problems and ethical dilemmas they are apt to face in the field, whether carrying out research among women in the Third World or women of color in the United States. While the majority of essays are written by anthropologists and sociologists, the volume includes contributions from the disciplines of economics, history, and geography, giving it a rather unique multidisciplinary perspective on the fieldwork experience.

The central focus of the volume is its concern with pursuit of "research by women, with women, and for women." As Diane Wolf argues, considerable progress has been made on the first count over the past two to three decades. The challenge still lies in the other part of the equation: that research "with" women replace research "on" women and that feminist research practice realize its transformative potential.

This collection should be as thought-provoking to those of us who went into the field in the 1970s and early 1980s as it is to students. Fueled by the emancipatory discourse of making "women's work visible," my generation often assumed that the common bond of sisterhood was sufficient to allow us to capture and interpret the experience of women in heterogeneous cultural settings. Although many of us in this generation were clearly aware that women's experience could not be universalized and that field research required attention to the diverse effects of class, race, and ethnicity (among other factors) in defining gender roles, we rarely questioned the process of our own interventions in defining the kind of knowledge that we produced.

Moreover, for my generation, making women's work visible was implicitly assumed to be liberating for those whom we studied. By gathering women's life histories, enumerating their hours of work, and illustrating the unequal burden of the gender division of labor, we implicitly assumed that we were involved in a process of feminist consciousness-raising among those whom we studied. All too often we assumed that this process itself was potentially transformative of gender relations. In addition, we tended to assume that the data we gathered would provide the basic building blocks for the formation of national and international policies to benefit women. The next generation of feminist field researchers, as seen in this volume, has shattered many of these assumptions.

Issues regarding representation—of the researcher and the researched—and of positionality—of the researcher to the researched—have become central in recent feminist scholarship. At the heart of the matter, as argued by Diane Wolf, is the issue of power relations: the unequal hierarchy between the researcher and those researched in defining the research agenda, the research process, and the research outcome.

In her introductory essay, Wolf questions whether feminist research is, indeed, possible, given the thorny issues raised in this volume, particularly as regards the transformative element. At the same time, she and many of the other authors conclude that the point is not to discourage future feminist researchers from carrying out fieldwork but rather to encourage them to continue confronting the feminist dilemmas of fieldwork without naïveté.

Carmen Diana Deere

Preface

Since the 1970s, feminist scholars have spent considerable time focusing upon the power relations between men and women in society. Recently, feminists have begun to turn the academic lens upon themselves, examining the power relations in which they are involved as researchers. Fieldwork as a research method poses particular challenges for feminists because of the power relations inherent in the process of gathering data and implicit in the process of ethnographic representation. The challenges of fieldwork and representation become even more complicated when the research focus is on women in the Third World or women of color in the United States, since in most cases this research entails "studying down," that is, studying women who are poor, powerless, or marginalized.

In 1983, when I returned from my first major period in the field in Java, Indonesia, I was relieved to have finished my dissertation research but, at the same time, upset and disturbed by the contradictions of the situation. There had been wonderful moments during fieldwork; there had been difficult moments. I recall lying on my bamboo bed, under my mosquito net with a flashlight under my chin, re-reading several dissertations from U.S. and Australian universities based on Javanese rural fieldwork, trying to get a clue about how others before me had solved some of the problems and dilemmas I confronted. There were no hints. It was as though such problems did not exist or they were a secret topic that could not enter a political economy text.

Creating and negotiating my identity in the field posed one particular challenge and dilemma. I felt forced to lie about the same topics about which I hoped for honesty from my respondents. I lied about my religious affiliation, my marital status, and my finances at the same time that the focus of my research was on young women's finances, family finances, and marriage. This particular representation of myself made me feel dishonest and uncomfortable, but I could not see another way out.

My discomfort intensified during certain moments; for example, one evening when my research assistant and our village hosts were sitting and talking and the Ibu (the mother of the family) asked me to describe my wedding. This was a wedding I had supposedly had with a fellow Cornell graduate student researcher with whom I was involved who was off doing his fieldwork in another part of Java. I

This is a revised version of an article that originally appeared in *Frontiers: A Journal of Women Studies* 8, no. 3 (1993). Reprinted with permission of the publisher.

was dying to discuss this problematic relationship with my assistant and with others, but instead, I had to make up the scene of our wedding. Although many villagers would not have been shocked at our cohabiting but nonmarried state, since some rural Javanese people live in consensual unions, our urban-educated sponsors would not have supported our situation, and we were forced to lie.

I contemplated the risk of telling my assistant the truth, since we often talked about her marriage. I think that she would have been shocked initially but would then have rationalized it as "modern" and "Western." Her husband, however, would have been less amused and probably would have made her quit. I already knew from her that he was wary of me and feared that I was influencing her as she tried to cope with her recent discovery that her husband had another wife and two other children. The result was that although my research was an attempt to analyze gender inequality and poverty, I exacerbated the inequalities between me and my respondents by not telling the truth.

I was also increasingly disturbed in the field by the structural elements of the villagers' poverty. The better I got to know some of the young factory workers and their families, the more I saw the depths of their poverty and the enormous constraints facing them. My research was an attempt to analyze and depict their lives, their situation, and the grueling work of factory jobs (Wolf, 1992). I would go on to finish my dissertation, get a Ph.D., get a job based on a talk about this research, make enough money in one month to sustain an entire village for several, publish, and, I hoped, make a career. The money I gave to people or the organizations I contribute to will not be able to change much in the lives of those I worked with. Despite my good intentions, I was making a situation for myself based on the structures of poverty and gender inequality.

In his book *A Fortunate Man: The Story of a Country Doctor,* John Berger writes about the bitter paradox confronting the doctor as he treats his poor, rural English patients. The contrast between the doctor and his patients makes him feel his own inadequacy; this is closely related to the study of poorer, more marginal groups, or "studying down":

> He must recognize that what he can do, if one considers the community as a whole, is absurdly inadequate. He must admit that what needs to be done is outside his brief as a doctor and beyond his power as an individual. Yet he must then face the fact that he needs this situation as it is: that to some extent, he chose it. It is by virtue of the community's poverty that he is able to practice as he does. .Their poverty enables him to follow his cases through all their stages, grants him the power of his hegemony, encourages him to become the "consciousness" of the district, allows him unusually promising conditions for achieving a "fraternal" relationship with his patients, permits him to establish almost entirely on his own terms the local image of his profession (Berger, 1967:144).

Although many of us do not see ourselves as doctors or our subjects as patients, there are some common and troubling themes in this quote that resonate for those of us who work with poorer people.

There was little room for discussion of such issues in my dissertation or in other academic settings. In 1989 I decided to write a paper on "Dilemmas of Fieldwork." The twenty or so pages I thought would take a weekend to write came out in only a few hours, quickly, without cessation, as these stories had been bottled and stored for years. I gave the paper to a friend and colleague to read, someone who got his degree in my department at Cornell years earlier. The following week he said, "Well, Diane, this is important stuff and all very true, but you know, these aren't just the dilemmas of fieldwork, these are the *secrets* of fieldwork, things that people don't talk about. I'm not sure that you should publish this before you have tenure; it will make you vulnerable." Clearly, discussing some of these issues makes us vulnerable; I am sure there are issues that we choose to keep secret, to not discuss in a conference setting, or not to publish because of the political or personal nature of such conflicts, confrontations, or dilemmas.

In 1990 I organized a roundtable at the Asian Studies Association meetings on "Feminist Dilemmas of Fieldwork: Negotiating and Renegotiating Identities," in which white women who had worked in Asia and Asian women who had returned to their home countries from U.S. universities spoke about how they had formulated their identities and the challenges to them. When I called people to begin organizing the roundtable, I found many others who also had a paper on fieldwork they had written, filed away, and never published. It was clearly a topic that aroused enthusiasm and one that people were eager to discuss but, until recently, did not have much of a forum in which to do so.

Recent writings by postcolonial feminists and critical anthropologists have problematized not only the representation of Third World women by Western feminists but also the entire fieldwork endeavor. The issues that have been stirred up strike at the very core of how we do our research, why we do it, and how we present our work to the world; they challenge some feminists to confront difficult, uncomfortable, and threatening territory, particularly in the case of white feminists working abroad with Third World women. In fact, one might argue that the practice of academic feminism, particularly as it relates to women in Third World societies and women of color in the United States, is experiencing a deep and far-reaching crisis of identity, purpose, and practice. This volume, however, does not espouse a politics of despair but rather a politics of often uncomfortable self-conscious questioning and a critical questioning of the field and the motives underlying what we do.

Contemporary feminist writings and the chapters in this volume raise epistemological concerns that are bound up with and generated by the practice of fieldwork. They compel us to consider how we as feminist researchers are constituted as culturally, socially, and historically specific subjects within a particular global configuration of economic and political powers. The authors address some critical questions of our times: What kinds of dilemmas arise from attempting to shape field relations and a field project in a more feminist manner? What kinds of strategies have researchers developed to deal with these dilemmas? Can we legitimately and ethically study and represent women who are different from us? How does the researcher's identity affect the kinds of dilemmas that arise and how she deals with them? Do these dilemmas differ when we are studying our own culture from when we are studying another (an Other)?

The contributors to this volume occupy different positionalities vis-à-vis those they researched. Since they are feminist scholars caught in webs of insiderness, outsiderness, and both and neither, simultaneously, their perspectives will enrich the literature with experientially based dilemmas and challenges. Some studied populations in a familiar, "native" home, some were in a familiar but not native home, and others worked in unfamiliar places. Some authors focused on Third World populations abroad, some focused on minority populations in the United States, and two authors did both. The geographical locations of the studies in this volume range from Alabama, rural California, and Harlem to the Sudan, Lebanon, Taiwan, and Guyana.

Günseli Berik, Suad Joseph, Ping-Chun Hsiung, Valerie Matsumoto, Jayati Lal, Patricia Zavella, and Brackette Williams did research on an ethnic/cultural/national group to which they are connected through their own background, although class or educational differences may exist, whereas Cindi Katz, Carol Stack, and Brackette Williams worked with an ethnic, cultural, racial, or national group different from their own. Margery Wolf, to whom I am most unfortunately not related, has written a final reflection for the volume, as a longtime fieldworker and feminist. Multiple disciplines are also very deliberately represented in this volume—anthropology, sociology, history, economics, and geography.

The common thread that links these diverse backgrounds, geographical locales, and disciplinary differences is concern with how the researcher constructs and reconstructs her identity and deals with her positionality vis-à-vis the researched. By bringing together those who work in the geographical Third World and those who work with women of color in the United States, we wish to blur some of the traditional divisions among those who study these groups and draw out the common threads so that we may build bridges and coalitions for future collaboration.

Diane L. Wolf

REFERENCES

Berger, John. 1967. *A Fortunate Man: The Story of a Country Doctor.* New York: Pantheon Books.
Wolf, Diane Lauren. 1992. *Factory Daughters: Gender, Household Dynamics, and Rural Industrialization in Java.* Berkeley: University of California Press.

Acknowledgments

Someone once told me that we end up teaching the courses we wished we had as graduate students; in this case, I wanted to put together the kind of book I had wished for as a student trying to make sense of fieldwork and of the post-fieldwork experience.

I wish to thank all those graduate students and faculty who participated in, attended, and volunteered their labor for "Feminist Dilemmas in Fieldwork," a lively conference sponsored by the Gender and Global Issues group at the University of California, Davis in 1992. Several of the conference participants' papers are in this volume and other authors were since added. The graduate students at U.C. Davis involved in the Gender and Global Issues group and the Third World women activists who come to our program every spring continue to be a source of inspiration.

Among the authors in this volume, we have experienced the gamut of life transitions during this book's evolution, including struggling with cancer, cross-country moves, new jobs, promotions, the deaths of parents and grandparents, and the births of little ones. I wish to thank the contributors for their adherence to deadlines despite these life changes.

Throughout this project, I have benefited from the support of Barbara Ellington at Westview Press and from the unflagging encouragement of Frank Hirtz, Christine D.F. Di Stefano, and Margery Wolf. I wish to thank Jane Raese at Westview, who has helped this book through the production process, and an anonymous reviewer for helpful comments. I also wish to thank Cindi Katz for last-minute editorial advice. I am extremely grateful to Jennifer Bickham Mendez and Estee Neuwirth, who cheerfully, conscientiously, and creatively assisted with the production of this book. I hope that one day they will be inspired to write the book that they were missing during their graduate education.

D.L.W.

1

Situating Feminist Dilemmas
in Fieldwork

DIANE L. WOLF

I prefer fieldwork; I suspect we all do. If I'd wanted to spend my days in an office, I'd have studied to be an underwriter for the insurance company next door. Their work seems boring 80 percent of the time, while mine only bores me about one hour out of every ten.

—Sue Grafton, *"D" Is for Deadbeat*

FEMINIST DILEMMAS in fieldwork are "as much ethical and personal as academic and political" (Hale, 1991: 121); they gnaw at our core, challenging our integrity, our work, and at times, the raison d'être of our projects. Feminist dilemmas in fieldwork revolve around power, often displaying contradictory, difficult, and irreconcilable positions for the researcher. Indeed, the power dimension is threaded throughout the fieldwork and postfieldwork process and has created a major identity crisis for many feminist researchers.

This chapter is meant to contextualize feminists' dilemmas in fieldwork over time and geographical spaces with a particular focus on research on women in "Third World"[1] countries and among women of color in the West.[2] I have written it and provided an extended bibliography with the interested but uninitiated reader in mind, perhaps as a way to offer some of the guidance and background I had wished I had as a neophyte fieldworker.

The questions that informed this chapter are: What kinds of dilemmas, quandaries, and contradictions have feminists confronted and grappled with in the process of fieldwork or its aftermath? What kinds of contradictions have feminists uncovered during fieldwork? How have these challenges and contradictions changed over time, and what do these changes imply for current and future fieldwork? Indeed some of these shifts could easily change the topic of this chapter and book from "feminist dilemmas in fieldwork" to "should we do fieldwork at all?"

1

Why *feminist* dilemmas in fieldwork? Without a doubt, nonfeminist women or men, particularly those with a political commitment to social change, may also experience some of the dilemmas or challenges I discuss here. However, the important difference for feminists is that many of these dilemmas and contradictions directly challenge the underlying tenets of their beliefs, because feminists "are among the few who articulate commitments and political priorities" that invoke a "better model of human behavior that is as yet nowhere to be found" (Patai, 1991: 137).

Feminists may raise more questions about the ethics of research because they often (although certainly not always) "are moved by commitments to women" rather than merely pursuing their "own careers and adding knowledge to the world" (Patai, 1991: 138). These commitments create moral and ethical crises because of the inherent power hierarchies that perpetuate women of color or "Third World" women as "subjects" in subordinate positions to "First World" feminist researchers, most of whom are white.[3] Such seemingly irreconcilable contradictions pierce and potentially subvert the goals of many feminist researchers who start out meaning well. This crisis, I believe, has directly resulted in a recent avalanche of feminist writings on the topic, resulting in what Carol Warren (1988: 8) terms "methodological feminocentrism" in the literature, a term she coined in contrast to the androcentrism of substantive and theoretical concerns.[4]

The Issue Is Power

Feminist dilemmas in fieldwork have changed over time, reflecting shifts in feminist theory and epistemology.[5] The most central dilemma for contemporary feminists in fieldwork, from which other contradictions are derived, is power and the unequal hierarchies or levels of control that are often maintained, perpetuated, created, and re-created during and after field research.[6] Power is discernible in three interrelated dimensions: (1) power differences stemming from different positionalities of the researcher and the researched (race, class, nationality, life chances, urban-rural backgrounds); (2) power exerted during the research process, such as defining the research relationship, unequal exchange, and exploitation; and (3) power exerted during the postfieldwork period—writing and representing.

The first dimension of power difference cannot be altered if one is studying marginalized or poor peoples. Whereas white women from the "First World" may experience multiple levels of difference that boost their privileged position when working in Third World countries, postcolonial feminist scholars working in their own country, or scholars of color working with their racial-ethnic group in the United States, experience their class and educational privilege, at the very least. "Studying up"—studying those with more power than the researcher—is perhaps one way to subvert this particular power hierarchy.

The second and third dimensions result from feminist researchers tending to maintain control over their research agenda, the research process, and their results. Although feminist researchers may use methods that "give research subjects more power" (Cancian, 1992: 627), it is not clear that they have succeeded. Maguire notes that the research process has the greatest potential for feminist process but is the "weakest link in feminist research" (1987: 35). Activist or action-research demands that the researcher give up some of these controls and share them with others, and it is still rare in feminist academic writings (Cancian, 1992). The few examples that exist tend to be from research conducted in Western countries. Although feminists have been at the forefront of experimenting with strategies of co-authoring, polyvocality, and representation as a way of confronting or changing power differences, academic feminists have tended to maintain control over research projects and "knowledge creation," as have conventional nonfeminist researchers, rarely empowering the women they study (Maguire, 1987). By maintaining this control and distance, most feminist scholars end up benefiting the researcher more than those studied and furthering the gap between the researcher and the researched. This behavior undercuts some of the goals set forth by feminist researchers and reproduces aspects of mainstream academic research.

There is now a great deal of research about women by women, but there is not much academic feminist research "with" and "for" women. I am not blaming feminist scholars, however. It is difficult to change power differences during and after fieldwork without radically changing the kind of research that is done and, therefore, without confronting and challenging the structure of academia: how products are judged acceptable and by whom, how progress is viewed, how "theory" is understood, how Ph.D.s are awarded, how tenure is granted, and how women's studies is regarded.

> For it is a fact that we are confronted by dual allegiances. On the one hand, we are obligated to our academic disciplines and institutions, within which we must succeed if we are to have any impact on the academy (and this in itself involves us in numerous contradictions, as part of our project entails transforming those very disciplines and institutions). On the other hand, if we take feminism seriously, it commits us to a transformative politics. In other words, most of us do not want to bite the hand that feeds us; but neither do we want to caress it too lovingly (Patai, 1991: 138–139).

Despite my conclusion that truly feminist research based on certain feminist principles may not be possible, it is *not* time to abandon ship. Fieldwork is still a useful and important process that challenges fieldworkers to witness, record, and try to understand vastly different and often harsh conditions; it opens vistas to their readers and students, worlds to which they/we would not otherwise be exposed. Confronting and understanding the multiple and often irreconcilable contradictions therein constitutes an important step in approaching projects with a political awareness and consciousness that will not be devastated when such dilemmas arise. Recognizing and accepting the imperfections within feminist fieldwork and research constitutes a necessary step if we are to refocus our gaze beyond ourselves.

Feminist Methods, Methodology, and Epistemology

Feminist Epistemology and Positivism

One of the major challenges of feminist epistemology[7] to mainstream science and social science has been a powerful critique of positivism and its underlying assumptions. In a rather dwarfed nutshell, positivist science is based on the tenet of value-free objectivity that can, should, and must be attained by the scientist or social scientist in order to seek and uncover "facts" and "the truth." Research must be completely replicable by others, and this entire endeavor is thought to further our knowledge of universal truths. This view of science entails and encourages distance and noninvolvement between the researcher and researched and assumes that the researcher can objectively see, judge, and interpret the life and meanings of his/her subjects. This contrasts sharply with the ways feminist research has been described: "contextual, inclusive, experiential, involved, socially relevant, . . . complete but not necessarily replicable, inclusive of emotions and events as experienced" (Nielsen, 1990: 6).

Feminist critiques of positivism have been located in three main areas: (1) philosophical critiques of positivism and its pretense of value-free science, (2) moral critiques of objectification and exploitation of subjects, and (3) practical critiques of the way positivism opposes the interest of the researcher and the researched (Gorelick, 1991: 460). Political critiques underlie all three of these areas.

Feminists (and others) have argued that being objective and value-free is not only impossible, since we all carry experiences and values that shape our vision and interpretations and since, by virtue of our presence as outsiders, we intervene in the normal flow of life, but it is also *undesirable* (see Cancian, 1992). The kinds of relationships positivism requires between researchers and the researched struck many feminists as simply a reflection of male forms of interpersonal dynamics—distant, "rational," uninvolved, hierarchical, and unrelated. Indeed, Pat Caplan (1988) suggests that objectivity is simply a form of male subjectivity. At the same time, however, some feminist scholars are reappraising the relationship between feminist inquiry and the norms of objectivity (Antony and Witt, 1993).

Feminist scholars oriented toward qualitative fieldwork in particular often have encouraged relationships between the researcher and researched that defy the tenets of positivism and objectivity. They have sought to break down the hierarchical and potentially exploitative relationship between researcher and researched by cultivating friendship, sharing, and closeness that, it was felt, would lead to a richer picture of women's lives. Many feminists heeded the call of "passionate scholarship" (Du Bois, 1983), joining their methods with their political sympathies. Indeed, German feminist Maria Mies argued that any truly feminist research must involve some kind of change through activism and consciousness-raising (1983: 124–126). Clearly, these stances constitute a far cry from the neutrality desired in positivism.

Many feminists have argued for an approach that focuses on process (Gorelick, 1991: 461), one that uses rather than denies one's intuition, feelings, and viewpoint as part of the research relationship and process. For example, some have found it fruitful to engage in "intersubjectivity," a dialectical relationship that allows the researcher to compare her work with her own experience as a woman and scientist and share it with her subjects, who then add their opinion (Duelli Klein, 1983: 94). This not only challenges the splitting of researcher and researched and of subject and object but encourages the researcher to put herself into the research and writing as part of the experience.

Uma Narayan questions whether the Anglo-American feminist epistemological project of posing positivism as the main enemy holds equally for non-Western feminists and women in non-Western societies. She insightfully points out that feminists' focus on positivism should not lead us to assume that all nonpositivist frameworks are therefore acceptable and that positivism is "our only enemy" (1989: 260). However, we must be wary about generalizations concerning *the* Anglo-American feminist project as well, since it is not unitary and since some Anglo feminists work in a positivist tradition (Sprague and Zimmerman, 1989). Basically, the challenges to feminism by Third World feminists, feminists of color, and those in cultural studies and postmodernism encourage a conceptualization of feminist epistemology as a heterogenous enterprise with multiple strands. "Its practitioners differ both philosophically and politically in a number of significant ways. But an important theme on its agenda has been to undermine the abstract, rationalistic, and universal image of the scientific enterprise by using several different strategies" (U. Narayan, 1989: 257).

Contemporary Theoretical Challenges

Some of the greatest challenges to feminist epistemology have been developed by women of color in the United States and feminists from Third World countries, often from Asia, educated and teaching in the United States. These critiques have unsettled the "notion of feminism as an all-encompassing home" for all women and feminists (Martin and Mohanty, 1986: 192).

Mohanty asks and encourages us to ask: "Who/what is the Third World? Do Third World women make up any kind of a constituency? On what basis? Can we assume that Third World women's political struggles are necessarily 'feminist'? How do they define feminism?" (1991a: 2–3). She challenges feminist scholars with important questions about power and location: "Who produces knowledge about colonized peoples and from what space/location? What are the politics of the production of this particular knowledge?" (Mohanty, 1991a: 3). Mohanty unsettles not only the category of "Third World woman" but also the assumptions of unity underlying "women" as a central category of analysis (Mohanty, 1991b). She encourages critical scrutiny of the linkages between the power and location of First World feminists, with epistemological questions concerning knowledge—what knowledge is produced, under what conditions, about whom, and for whom.

The postmodernist turn in theorizing has challenged, unsettled, and inspired feminists and other researchers.[8] Feminist scholars are divided about the merits and shortcomings of postmodernist theorizing. Some have found useful the sensitivity postmodernism demonstrates toward a greater multiplicity of power relations. Postmodernist theorizing has created opportunities for further innovation in research methods and the post-fieldwork process, particularly representation and writing.

Still, a number of feminists argue that postmodernism poses certain obstacles to feminism (McDowell, 1992; Mascia-Lees, Sharpe, and Cohen, 1989; Hekman, 1990; Hartsock in Hekman, 1990: 154; Fardon, 1990; Gewertz and Errington, 1991). Some wonder why the often inaccessible abstract and hypertheoretical language of postmodernism happened to evolve at a time when more women and minorities had gained positions in academia (Di Stefano, 1990; Hekman, 1990). Others are concerned that the overly textual focus of postmodernism renders the lived realities of women irrelevant (Gewertz and Errington, 1991: 81; Lazreg, 1988; Udayagiri, 1995); on the other hand, that argument can be made about academic writings in general.

Just as we cannot talk about *the* feminist research method (Harding, 1987), we must also recognize multiple feminist epistemologies and multiple feminist projects. We are living in a time when the substantial challenges faced by those doing fieldwork among Third World women or women of color, particularly if the researcher is Anglo or foreign, are increasingly recognized. The epistemological uncertainty that exists can be unsettling and may discourage some from beginning or continuing the fieldwork endeavor, guiding them to the safer position of textual analysis; others, however, will feel at home in and challenged by such uncertainty.[9] This book is meant to encourage future feminist scholars to enter the field with their eyes open so that they can confront these contradictions and challenges without naïveté, and so that they can move on to the many compelling questions that still beg for research.

Fieldwork

Fieldwork, "that brash, awkward, hit-and-run encounter of one sensibility with others" (Kumar, 1992: 1), connotes very different practices for different disciplines. Although fieldwork is often assumed to be synonymous with ethnography and anthropology, such assumptions should be suspended in this volume.

In the social sciences, fieldwork involves varying degrees of participant-observation and may include structured or semistructured interviews. A majority of the authors in this volume gathered mostly qualitative data, although some sought quantitative data as well. Although fieldwork can include extensive survey interviews in which quantitative data is sought, the kinds of fieldwork and the resultant dilemmas discussed here focuses more on intensive methods with fewer subjects.

The meaning of fieldwork is discipline-specific and is bound up with different disciplinary histories. Anthropologists have inherited the burden of the linkages between early fieldwork and the colonialist effort (Asad, 1973). Until recently, fieldwork in social or cultural anthropology has been considered a "natural" and normal part of the discipline's rite de passage. Fieldwork has had an almost "macho mystique" (Scheper-Hughes, 1983: 114) about it as students of anthropology go off to sink or swim, usually without any course preparation in field methods. The politicization of anthropology and its history has generated an internal critique of fieldwork and of "the field" (Huizer, 1979), and feminists have been an important part of that discussion (Visweswaran, 1994). These critiques have spawned fieldwork "at home" and a turn to textual analysis among some anthropologists.

In the 1920s and 1930s, while anthropologists went abroad to remote places to conduct fieldwork, the North American sociologists known as the Chicago School stayed at home, using the techniques of participant-observation to focus on urban-based topics such as gangs, the dance hall, and hobos, later turning to rural and community studies (see Burgess, 1982). Whereas most sociologists who do fieldwork focus on issues in the United States, a small number of sociologists, usually those in the sociology of development, go to Third World countries. But because of different disciplinary heritages, such fieldwork has been less politically charged than in anthropology. Fieldwork does not carry the same sink-or-swim mystique in sociology, and some departments offer intensive courses on fieldwork (see Burawoy et al., 1991).

Although non-anthropologists may use the tools of participant-observation and sometimes do ethnography, the content and duration of their fieldwork may differ from that of anthropologists. Rather than embarking on long, extended stays in one site, sociologists (and other social scientists) may engage in shorter periods of fieldwork that could include several research sites (e.g., villages, factories, cities). Rather than becoming familiar with a small number of people, the sociologist or economist may interview larger numbers. As Günseli Berik, an economist, points out in Chapter 2, it is rare for economists to engage in fieldwork, particularly in Third World countries. In order to be taken seriously within her discipline, she had to interview over 130 women to get sufficient quantitative data. Although fieldwork, particularly fieldwork in a Third World country that focuses on women, could be considered a political act for an economist, she still needs to toe the quantitative line.

As Cindi Katz explains in Chapter 9, the history of fieldwork in human geography is linked to expeditions and conquering frontiers, actions that conjure up questionable images in today's more politically conscious academic environment. Those in human geography working in development studies, political ecology, and more recently, urban social geography tend to do fieldwork, ranging from in-depth ethnographic case studies to large-scale surveys, covering such topics as land use practices and socioeconomic relations. Recently, feminist geographers have been turning their attention to fieldwork.[10]

Historians have turned to oral histories, which are directly linked to the rise of social history and have become more prevalent since the late 1960s and 1970s, when the civil rights, ethnic pride, and women's movements began. Oral histories are a way to capture the pasts of less literate and more marginalized groups whose histories might not otherwise be transcribed (see Matsumoto, Chapter 8) and have been especially utilized by feminist historians.

Thus, fieldwork—conventional and assumed for anthropologists—may constitute an unusual or even a political act for others, depending upon the discipline. However, it is important to understand that the politicization of fieldwork's history in anthropology has forced contemporary critical anthropologists to engage in it with more deliberate political considerations; anthropologists, particularly feminist anthropologists, have been at the forefront of experimenting with more ethical and less exploitative methods.

Feminists and Fieldwork

Feminist Politics of Entering the Field

What happens to women, particularly feminist researchers, as they attempt to enter a culture and society?[11] Entering the field is always difficult and may pose particular challenges for women because of their gender. There are many stories, such as those in Peggy Golde's (1970) classic, about how white women were treated in the field—sometimes as androgynous, as honorary males, as children, or as feebleminded beings that needed protection. Carol Warren points out, however, that although white females may have secondary status because of gender, they acquire authority and privilege through race, class, and Western culture (Warren, 1988: 26). This led Daphne Patai (1988a), in her research with poor Brazilian women, to be painfully aware that although gender united her with her subjects, race and class divided them.

Some believe that women researchers, regardless of race, are pressured more than men to conform to local gender norms, which may create difficulties and dilemmas for feminist researchers working in highly patriarchal settings. Although foreign women may gain more license and flexibility to cross gender boundaries (Papanek, 1964) because of their foreign "otherness," they may indeed receive and feel more pressure than men to adhere to gender role behaviors. Women who have worked in the Middle East or South Asia write about adopting local dress, wearing a veil, and not looking at or speaking to men in some cases. This may feel strange at first, but eventually, for some, it becomes "natural" (Schenck-Sandbergen, 1992; Pettigrew, 1990; Abu-Lugod, 1986).[12] Although some feminist researchers resist some aspects of patriarchally based dress codes, they end up having to acquiesce in certain circumstances.

Dress is not the only pressure point for women; those who have done research in caste-based societies discuss difficulties in adapting to what they cannot do—for example, clean their houses or their bathrooms, cook, eat with people from certain castes—in order to remain acceptable to certain local people (Kumar, 1992; Schenk-Sandbergen, 1992); these constrictions pertain to men as well (Srinivas, 1979). Elizabeth Enslin (1990), an American anthropologist married to a Nepali, did her research in her husband's village while they lived with his Brahmin family. Although she resisted most pressures to wear a sari, she found it extremely difficult to deal with the way she was treated as polluted when she was pregnant.

Unmarried female fieldworkers may feel pressures to be (or to claim to be) married or may be encouraged to marry someone in the field. Veena Dua (1979), a single Indian anthropologist, was advised by her respondents in India to go home and get married; in the meantime, she received unwanted marriage proposals and sexual advances. Married women researchers more than married men researchers are sometimes chastised for doing fieldwork and not being home taking care of their children (Myerhoff, 1978; Gupta, 1979).

In some highly patriarchal societies, several feminist scholars describe being introduced and gaining entry through male privilege—through the connections of their father, husband, or brother (Gupta, 1979). Lila Abu-Lughod, an Arab-American anthropologist who researched Bedouin women, was brought to the field by her Arab and anthropologist father who lives in the United States, who introduced her to and entrusted her into the care of a Bedouin patriarch, whose daughter she became. During her second fieldwork venture, she was accompanied by her father and her new husband (Abu-Lughod, 1993).

In Chapter 2, Günseli Berik, a Turkish feminist and economist, describes the importance of her husband's presence during her fieldwork; indeed, most villagers continued to think that it was his research that brought them there (see also Oboler, 1986). Because male villagers felt more comfortable talking with him, a Turkish male, his input and assistance constituted a crucial contribution to his wife's project as he distracted husbands while Günseli interviewed their wives at home.

Clearly, many feminist researchers have drawn upon patriarchal relations to gain access and, at times, have played upon their race, their class position, and/or their status as women when it was useful. Despite resistance to essentialist thinking or writing, feminists have often used essentialist notions of womanhood in a strategic manner during fieldwork, to gain access and acceptance.[13]

Anthropologists often use the technique of immersion when doing ethnography. Immersion into a culture provides one way to downplay one's privilege and difference, and it may provide a less intrusive and obtrusive methodology. Lila Abu-Lughod became a Bedouin daughter who conformed more strictly to gender norms than other Bedouin young women. Dorinne Kondo, a Japanese American who did research in Japan, describes the complexity and shock of total immersion and the withdrawal and distance that came from it (1986). In a wonderfully rich ethnography, Karen McCarthy Brown (1991) describes her total immersion in the culture of voodoo as she studies a voodoo priestess in New York and then goes to Haiti with her to convert to voodooism.

Despite partial or complete immersion that can render the researcher feeling unempowered and dependent, inequality may still persist between the researcher and her subjects. This is particularly evident because the fieldworker has the ability and privilege to leave the field location once the research is over. Thus, immersion may be a useful strategy to attempt to view a culture from within, and it may position the researcher in a way that differs from a more distant participant-observer, but it does not basically alter the researcher's positionality, which remains part of her in the field and to which she returns in full when she is finished. Changing locations does not fundamentally alter one's positionality or the situatedness of one's knowledge. And the researcher's positionality tends to reflect inequality between her and her subjects. Such differences may temporarily be unimportant or may be buffered by the researcher's sincere attempts to become part of that culture. Successful immersion may create more sensitive researchers and ethnographies but cannot change where we come from and where we return to.

The Limits of Gender in Fieldwork

It is important to challenge a tendency in the feminist literature to focus solely on the effects of the researcher's gender on field relations at the expense of other important axes of power. Race may dominate the kinds of social interactions that occur in the field, rather than gender or class (Johnson-Odim, 1991); however, this dynamic may not be obvious in the text, since some white fieldworkers tend not to acknowledge that they too bear race (Harding, 1991: 215; Mohanty, 1991a).

Sandra Harding draws on Maxine Baca Zinn's observations to delineate three different feminist approaches. One approach views race and class as secondary to female subordination. Another views the inequalities of gender, class, and race as having created different experiences, and believes that "women have a race-specific and a class-specific relation to the sex-gender system." A third focuses on describing the problems and lives of women in subordinated race and class groups (Harding, 1991: 213). It is significant that much feminist analysis has fallen into the first category and those in the second and third categories tend to focus more on class oppression rather than race. The difficulties of focusing on race, particularly for white researchers, has created silences and gaps that need to be addressed, despite the discomfort (for exceptions see Lugones and Spelman, 1983; Stack, Chapter 4; Frankenberg, 1993).

Lynn Bolles's (1985) experiences in Jamaica and Brackette Williams's comparative experiences in Alabama and Guyana (Chapter 3) suggest that there is greater fluidity in what barriers appear important, depending upon the axes of power and difference in the society being studied and where the researcher is located in such axes. Sharing a common racial/ethnic background will be binding in some circumstances and irrelevant in others. Carol Stack's (Chapter 4) comparative experiences in doing research as a white woman with urban African Americans during the 1960s and with African Americans in the South in the 1980s suggest that historical time, generational location, and geography affected the importance of racial difference and distance in these two settings.

Finally, even when the researcher's gender, language, culture, nationality, and race match those of her subjects, class differences usually prevail if the researcher is studying rural poor or urban working-class people (see Lal, Chapter 10). Yet some women working in highly patriarchal societies corroborate Shahrashoub Razavi's (1993) findings that her "superior position" due to class was "somewhat redressed" by her inferior gender position (see also Berik, Chapter 2; Morsy, 1988). This redressing may tend to equalize relations in the field, but it does not alter basic differences in class background and social status. Finally, although there has been little written about this in the feminist literature, in some societies, age may be a more important determinant of status than gender (Wax, 1986).

The Researcher and Her Persona: Representing One's Self

Although we cannot hide our race or gender, there are other aspects of our identity that may be less obvious. Feminists have struggled with presenting and representing their selves and the problems, dilemmas, and contradictions of engaging in deception (Daniels, 1983). This is one area in which our power and control offers us the choice to construct and (re)shape our selves to our subjects, playing on the different positionalities of the researcher and the researched. This is particularly the case when researchers are far enough from home that their research subjects do not encounter many of their family members or friends, whereas our respondents are usually surrounded by kin and friends and cannot similarly withdraw, hide, and alter aspects of their identity.

Feminist fieldworkers have lied about their marital status, stating that they were married when they were not (Dua, 1979; D. Wolf, Preface; Katz, Chapter 9), about their national identity or ethnic/religious background (Fawzi El-Solh, 1988), about divorce and former marriages (Schrijvers, 1993), and about their class background, among other factors. In her study of domestic workers in the United States, Judith Rollins (1985), an African American sociologist, did not inform her employers for whom she cleaned house that she was a student doing research on them, and even wrote her own letters of reference. She altered her speech, her demeanor, and her posture in order to be convincing. Although she spends considerable time in her introduction justifying this deception, it is also clear from the number of pages she wrote on the topic that the deception created a difficult and unsolvable quandary (1985: 11–16). Because she believed the Bedouin could not imagine an unmarried woman living on her own, Lila Abu-Lughod (1988: 148) let people believe that Harvard University was in Chicago, where they knew her father lived.

In most of these cases, the harm is minimal, but the guilt for those deceiving their respondents with whom they are attempting to create a bond of empathy may cause considerable anguish. Although many nonfeminist fieldworkers may deceive their subjects and feel bad about it, feminists have expressed considerable distress over this dilemma, because lying directly contradicts attempts at a more feminist approach to fieldwork, which includes attempts to equalize a relationship and create more of a friendship. Fawzi El-Solh struggled with her guilt and fear over lying about her national identity and states that most fieldworkers "will at some point in their research find a measure of dishonesty unavoidable. The crucial question should be how much harm we thereby cause those we seek to study" (1988: 101). Indeed, the guilt I felt about lying about my marital status, income, religion, and the other basics about which I hoped for honesty from my respondents and the contradictions between this lying and the kind of rapport I tried to attain created years of unease and most likely was the raison d'être of this book (see Preface).

A few researchers found that exposing some of these hidden truths ended up being far less problematic than they expected. And researchers have noted that keeping secrets is much more difficult when one's children are in the field (Cassell, 1987). When Joke Schrijvers's (1993: 148) young son kept referring to his father and his stepfather, Schrijvers finally explained her divorce and remarriage to one woman, who quickly spread the gossip. Villagers found the situation amazing and wonderful rather than scandalous, as Schrijvers had feared, because they could not understand how a stepfather could be so kind to his stepchild.

After my second fieldwork stint was over, I nervously told my research assistants that I was not and had never been married and was no longer even involved with the man I still claimed was my husband. To my surprise, they were delighted rather than scandalized and found it "really cool" that I was a career woman. However, the joke was on me, because they then confessed that they had something to tell me as well—that they were not friends, as they had claimed, but actually sisters. They had not wanted to tell me for fear that I would not have hired them or felt free to criticize one of them if she had not done her work well. Having the tables turned on me was almost a relief but also a sign that I probably could have been somewhat more open and honest without fear, at least in some contexts. I think that the villagers would also have easily accepted my previous single but cohabiting status, since they were much less formal about such liaisons than were my urban middle-class colleagues and sponsors. However, I also believe that some villagers would have been less than delighted with my Jewishness, since my fieldwork overlapped with the highly visible Israeli invasion of Lebanon, and the few nonacademic Indonesians to whom I confessed that I was Jewish conflated my being Jewish with being an Israeli and a Zionist.

It is not simply coincidental that I have not found anything written by a feminist researcher working in a Third World context who says that while she was in the field she concealed her sexual preference for other women. Clearly, there are and have been feminist and lesbian researchers who remained closeted while doing fieldwork, posing as either married or single heterosexual women. However, it is still too risky to speak out and write about such a topic, as I discovered when I unsuccessfully sought papers for this volume from those who could discuss this topic. Coming out as a lesbian in a field setting could endanger the researcher, affecting her research relations, and possibly put her in a dangerous situation not only in the field but in her career once she returned home.

Feminist Standpoints and Approaches

According to feminist standpoint theory (Hartsock, 1987; Smith, 1974; Harding, 1991) one's positionality as a woman is crucial in gaining knowledge and understanding of other women. Drawing on Marxist theory, Nancy Hartsock (1987) argued that due to women's position within the sexual division of labor and sexist oppression, in general, women would have greater insights as researchers into the lives of other women. In other words, one's position in the social hierarchy vis-à-vis other groups potentially "limits or broadens" one's understanding of others. Members of the dominant group will have viewpoints that are "partial and perverse" in contrast to those from subordinated groups, who have greater potential to have fuller knowledge (Nielson, 1990: 10; Hartsock, 1987). Sociologist Dorothy Smith (1987: 107) believed that the only way one can know a socially constructed world is to know it from within. The epistemological contribution of women researchers is their "embodied subjectivity"—their own knowledge and experiences are crucial for creating knowledge and for determining how fully they can understand a phenomenon.

Although feminist scholars might easily accept that only women can fully and truly understand other women (Kremer, 1991), this "epistemology of insiderness" (Reinharz, 1992: 260) and somewhat essentialist view overlooks questions of difference (Epstein Jayaratne and Stewart, 1990). "Shouldn't there be an 'ex-colonial' epistemological standpoint for reasons analogous to those advanced for a feminist standpoint? What should be the relationship between the two?" (Hartsock, 1987: 158). As awareness of class, racial, and ethnic diversity has increased, the discussion has broadened to "standpoints," since there clearly is no single standpoint for women of racially and ethnically diverse backgrounds.

If the argument is that knowing oppression firsthand helps one more fully understand (an)Other's oppression, then standpoint theory raises questions about epistemic privilege, or whether it "takes one to know one" (Shapiro in Moore, 1988: 5). Taking feminist standpoint theory one step further might lead to a claim that only those who are of a particular race or ethnic group can study or understand others in a similar situation, or that only those who are women of color or lesbian can generate antiracist or antihomophobic insights (Harding, 1991: 278). To some extent then, as Nielsen (1990: 25) points out, standpoint theory implies that "one group's perspective is more real or better than others; it implies that the greater the oppression, the greater one's potential knowledge" (see Margery Wolf, Chapter 11). But as Nancy Tuana (1993: 283) points out, why assume that the perspectives of those on the margin are less distorted rather than simply different from those not on the margin? And as Jayati Lal argues (Chapter 10), this notion of epistemic privilege essentializes "insiders" while reducing them to homogeneous entities.

The notion of standpoint and positionality led to concepts that drew on the researcher's own identification vis-à-vis those she researched and the social situatedness of knowledge. The terms "double consciousness," "outsiders within," and "double vision" (Collins in Harding, 1991: 131) describe the position of academics of color who study their own group, being and seeing in two different, often incompatible, worlds (see Zavella, Chapter 7; Hsiung, Chapter 6). These concepts suggest that because of double or multiple positions, these academics gain and offer particular insights into their own group that may not be experienced by an outsider. Common and shared positions due to race, class, gender, or nationality do not always, or do not necessarily, lead to common understandings, however (Tedlock, 1991; Bolles, 1985; Williams, Chapter 3; Kumar, 1992).

Uma Narayan (1989: 263–264) views this problematic thoughtfully and in terms of probabilities rather than absolutes, without excluding multiple views. She argues against any "metaphysical presumption" that experiencing oppression will enable an individual to understand others but believes that those who have experienced the oppression of the group they do research on are more likely to have critical insights than will outsiders. Yet she does not exclude the possibility that those with a different social location can gain some understanding and insight.

Some feminist scholars have found Donna Haraway's "politics and epistemology of location" (1991: 195) a useful alternative to feminist standpoint theory (Rofel, 1993; Enslin 1990; Mani, 1990). This politics and epistemology is based on situating, location, and positioning, "where partiality and not universality" is the basis for knowledge claims. "Situated knowledges" are "marked knowledges" that produce "maps of consciousness" reflecting the various categories of gender, class, race, and nationality of the researcher (Haraway, 1991: 111). They reflect our locationality (historical, national, generational) and positionality (race, gender, class, nationality, sexuality), acknowledging how the dynamics of where we are always affects our viewpoint and the production of knowledge without privileging one particular position over another, as in standpoint theory. Our positionality is not fixed, but relational, a "constantly moving context that constitutes our reality and the place from which values are interpreted and constructed" (Geiger, 1990: 171).

"Feminist objectivity is about limited location and situated knowledge" (Haraway, 1991: 188), which allows for a multiplicity of viewpoints. This perspective not only allows and encourages feminist researchers to bring their own particular location and position into the research, to acknowledge and build on their partial perspective, but makes it imperative for them to do so before any discussion of another's reality can be introduced (see Bhavnani, 1991: 97–98). This approach goes beyond a binary discussion of the "haves" (insiders) and the "have-nots" (outsiders), which is a natural outcome of standpoint theory and encourages us to think in terms of multiple perspectives and mobile subjectivities, of forging collaborations and alliances and juxtaposing different viewpoints.

Insiders/Outsiders/Both/Neither

I found that those who studied a group to which they belonged often claimed to have an advantage that led to a privileged or more balanced view of the people/society under study (Abu-Lughod, 1988; Altorki, 1988; Baca Zinn, 1979; Caufield, 1979; Collins, 1990; Kondo, 1986; Kumar, 1992; Ladner, 1987; Obbo, 1990). This perspective includes arguments that native or indigenous researchers would offer a critique of colonialist, racist, ethnocentric, and exploitative anthropology (Caufield, 1979: 311), balance the distortions presented by white or Anglo researchers (Baca Zinn, 1979), creatively use their special standpoint or double consciousness (Collins, 1990; Obbo, 1990), or be privileged to a more intimate view (Abu-Lughod, 1988).[14] Many of these researchers explicitly state that they are not suggesting that "outsiders" should not engage in such research or cannot produce insightful results.

Far fewer "outsiders" make a similar claim, but those who do offer reasons similar to those asserted by "insiders." Some believe that as outsiders, they have better access to local secrets because of their neutrality (Berninghausen and Kerstan, 1992), greater objectivity, and an enhanced ability to see patterns in which insiders would be immersed (Fonow and Cook, 1991: 3), or greater role flexibility in a highly patriarchal setting (Papanek, 1964).

There is only one study that "tests" this relationship: Tixier y Vigil, a Chicana researcher, and Elsasser, an Anglo researcher (Tixier y Vigil and Elsasser, 1976), interviewed the same Chicana women, asked the same questions and did an intensive textual analysis of what was said to whom, how much, and when. They found that the Chicana subjects were much more open about sex and bodily functions such as menstruation with the Anglo interviewer, whereas they were much more tight-lipped about these issues with the Chicana. Yet with the Chicana, they spoke much more freely about discrimination than with the Anglo researcher. Their article makes a compelling case for multiple perspectives, in that each researcher, because of her positionality vis-à-vis the community under study, received important but different information.

Many more insiders than outsiders mentioned problems they experienced during research due to their positionality. Some examples of insiders' problems include the concealment of information (Altorki, 1988: 57), crossing caste lines (Dua, 1979; Kumar, 1992; Srinivas, 1979), the restricting expectations of others (Altorki, 1988: 59; Gupta, 1979), and overidentification and merging and the resultant lack of privacy (Joseph, 1988 and Chapter 5; Kondo, 1986). Suad Joseph's (Chapter 5) immersion in and identification with Lebanese culture created epistemological quandaries, as she later found that her close relationship to her respondents and key informant affected her ability to see certain of their political views with which she disagreed.

A number of feminist researchers reject this simplistic dichotomy of insider-outsider and the "idea of the monolithic 'indigenous' anthropological orientation" (Morsy, 1988: 70). Some feminists say they felt they were neither an insider or outsider but both simultaneously, in large part due to either their complicated position of having a dual identity (e.g., Arab American, Asian American) or to their position as an academic, trained in the West (Abu-Lughod, 1988 and 1991; Kondo, 1986; Hsiung, Chapter 6; Zavella, Chapter 7). Indigenous fieldworkers are often "marginal natives" (Freilich in Altorki, 1988: 16) and often feel they are both insiders and outsiders due to class, cultural, rural/urban backgrounds, or language, in addition to having spent years in Western universities. It is difficult, therefore, and perhaps less than useful, to argue that there are indeed any pure insiders as opposed to outsiders. Whereas some have felt torn between their perspective as a woman of color on the one hand and a social science approach on the other (Ladner, 1987), others may feel positively challenged by their multiple positions (Uma Narayan, 1989: 266). Jayati Lal (Chapter 10), returning "home" to India where she spent much of her childhood and went to university, explores her multiple positionings during fieldwork—being more of an insider with the Indian women she researched than a westerner, yet also an outsider with tremendous differences due to her more privileged class position.

In Chapter 3 Brackette Williams writes about how shared race created very different bonds in two different national settings—Alabama, where the African Americans with whom she spoke were constantly trying to place her possible kinship connections to them, and Guyana, where she was very much outside Afro-Guyanese culture. Both Williams and Hsiung (Chapter 6) illustrate how their identities shifted as the research site shifted. In Hsiung's case, she felt an uncomfortable shift when talking with factory workshop bosses, hoping her connections with workers would not be affected.

Although seemingly an insider, Patricia Zavella (Chapter 7) studied Chicana working mothers, women from the same ethnic, gender, and class background as her own. Yet she found that she did not sufficiently problematize her own ethnic identity and was unable to see nuances among her subjects' ethnic identities. She carries no illusions of female solidarity from her subjects with her research—the women with whom she worked were cooperative, but she constantly felt differences between them.

Valerie Matsumoto's (Chapter 8) research in a Japanese American rural community provides yet another insider-outsider complexity. Although not from that community, Matsumoto was accepted and welcomed as a Japanese American daughter, and her work was greatly appreciated by a community that wanted to have its history documented.

Recent reflections on this topic have further complicated the simplistic dichotomy of insider-outsider (Karim, 1993a). Abu-Lughod (1993: 41) writes about her position as a "halfie" (half Palestinian, half American), one who moves between worlds and identities, disrupting traditional anthropological boundaries between Self and Other, a position that allows her writings to "work against the grain" of Western hegemonic discourses (Ong, forthcoming). Abu-Lughod also believes that her project can "convey a sense of the common everyday humanity of an Arab community" within the context of Western hostility toward Middle Eastern peoples (Abu-Lughod, 1991: 159; Ong, forthcoming). But how similar or different is Abu-Lughod's Palestinian half from those she is studying? Couldn't the privilege stemming from class differences further bifurcate that half? Kirin Narayan (1993) first coined the term "halfie" in a personal communication with Abu-Lughod (Abu-Lughod, 1991: 161, n. 1); however, she contests Abu-Lughod's use of this self-description, arguing that "two halves cannot adequately account for the complexity of an identity in which multiple countries, regions, religions and classes may come together" (1993: 673).[15]

Assumptions about understandings that arise from being a halfie or having some kind of mutual self-identification as members of an oppressed group overlook or perhaps skirt the issue of the ethnographer's personality, openness, willingness to listen, and ability to empathize. Assuming that such personality traits arise naturally or are naturally present in a context where identity is shared suggests a kind of essentialism similar to the one concerning women making better fieldworkers by nature of their feminine traits. It also brings us back to critiques of earlier feminist works— do we need to identify with all our subjects? What if we don't like them, or vice versa?

Finding her position as a "native anthropologist" uncomfortable and essentializing, Kirin Narayan argues that other important factors, such as gender, class, sexual orientation, race, and duration of contacts, may "outweigh the cultural identity we associate with insider or outsider status" (1993: 672). Her critique of the entire insider-outsider paradigm traces the initial distinction between the "native" and the "real" (now more diplomatically called the "insider"/"outsider") anthropologist to colonialist times (1993: 672). She asks, "How native is a native anthropologist? How foreign is one from abroad?" (1993: 671). She argues for a greater focus on the "quality of relations" with those we represent in our texts and for the "enactment of hybridity" in writing that "depicts authors as minimally bicultural in terms of belonging simultaneously to the world of engaged scholarship and the world of everyday life" (1993: 671).

She rejects the overused binary of insider-outsider and also considers important the kinds of relationships formed by "non-native" anthropologists who return every year to the same community, acknowledging that even so-called insiders are at times drawn into a particular context and at other times experience the distance of an outsider. Drawing on Rosaldo, she argues that every anthropologist exhibits a " 'multiplex subjectivity' with many cross-cutting identifications," such that each context may force us to choose or accept different facets of our subjectivity (1993: 676). "We are all incipiently bi- (or multi-) cultural in that we belong to worlds both personal and professional, whether in the field or at home" (1993: 681).

Aihwa Ong, who self-identifies as an "expatriate ethnographer" (forthcoming), contends that "positionality on the basis of mixed heritage does not necessarily predispose one to produce a politically correct ethnography of the Other." She suggests that feminists should shift their concerns and focus from the "politics of positionality" to the "politics of intercultural perception and interaction in ethnography." "I suggest that postcolonial feminists can develop their own intercultural self-understanding as a meeting-ground for dialogue with other postcolonial informants. . . . we have the capacity to reinscribe ourselves in different cultural narratives" (forthcoming). She argues that this can create "an inter-referencing modality" that is pivotal in offering a "sympathetic point of entree into an ethnographic relationship between postcolonials." Furthermore, she contends that this could create a "different dynamic of listening, telling and representation that avoids recreating the inequalities of conventional ethnography" (forthcoming).

In her interviews with Chinese immigrant women in California, Ong's Chinese identity and the desire she shared with the immigrant women to alter Western views of Chinese women provided a bridge for some subjects to share poignant stories they had not told before. Other respondents found her position as a female professor more daunting and distancing. In this setting, a sense of "shared marginalization in Chinese culture, history and in Western society . . . creates a different ethnographic situation than that of an ethnographer from a privileged Western country descending into a village in some Third World country" (forthcoming), creating a situation of "telling and listening" between "fellow travelers." This "lessening of the personal and pedagogical distance" between the ethnographer and her subject allows for "an intimacy that nurtures trust and increases the informants' power to influence the ethnographic product" (forthcoming). This view echoes Uma Narayan's view (1989: 263) that shared positionalities as members of an oppressed group create a greater probability of sharing and understanding.

At the same time, Ong and others suggest that a shared positionality can potentially bring with it another way of understanding, seeing, listening, telling, and retelling. It is very probable, but not necessarily automatic, that such commonalities can produce different insights. It is also very possible that such a position may make it difficult for the researcher to critically "air the dirty laundry" (See Hsiung, Chapter 6; Zavella, Chapter 7) due to her bonds and allegiances. Although we have much to learn from these different sights, sounds, and vistas, we must also take care not to make automatic assumptions about solidarity, empathy, and understanding or to assume that those who do not share such positionalities cannot offer important and critical insights into the workings of a culture or group. Indeed, the Tixier y Vigil and Elsasser (1976) study of the same women encourages researchers with shared and nonshared positionalities to undertake research, because subjects are likely to discuss only certain subjects with individual researchers, depending upon the researcher's positionality.

This topic continues to stir up considerable feeling on all sides of the debate and continues simultaneously to encourage some while discouraging other feminist scholars. We now turn from the position and voices of fieldworkers to how feminists have tried to deal with the positionality and voices of their research subjects.

Attempts to Deal with Power: Friendship and Confronting Exploitation

Earlier feminist works suggested a natural and comfortable congruence between the feminist researcher and women subjects (Oakley, 1990; Finch, 1984). As feminists began to confront and unravel the power relations underlying their research and confront the exploitative aspects that had previously seemed possible only under a positivist regime (Patai, 1991; Stacey, 1991), they stimulated a long-term identity crisis for feminist fieldworkers. Naming the exploitation inherent in research relationships meant having to explicitly acknowledge that serious power differentials exist between the researcher and her subjects, an issue that previously had not seemed apparent or problematic. By naming these power differentials and possibly exploitative interactions and bringing them into feminist discourse, feminists shattered the original tenets of early feminist work. What was previously seen as natural and easy has been problematized as one of the greatest dilemmas of feminist field research.

The power differentials between the researcher and the researched and the resultant possibilities for exploitation, reciprocity, and egalitarian ties cover the three dimensions of power delineated earlier: power in positionality, power during the research process, and power in the post-fieldwork stage; however, most of the attention has focused on the research process itself.

In terms of the power hierarchies inherent in different positionalities, some argue for or attempt downplaying differences to reach a more egalitarian relationship (Mies 1982, 1983, 1990; Bronstein in Reinharz, 1992: 29), but others believe that such attempts are disingenuous, since the relationship can never be egalitarian or reciprocal (Reinharz, 1992). Sherry Gorelick finds that an ideology of equality between the researcher and her subjects "reintroduced the notion of value free science in a new guise, obscuring the differences of their roles and the power complexities of their relationship" (1991: 469). Sondra Hale (1991: 133) argues that because of differences that privilege the researcher, it is not appropriate for a researcher to want equal time or expect to be equally affirmed.

Feminists may not have seen these power differentials because of their assumptions about the commonality of womanhood and about mutual self-identification that avoids race and class differences (Edwards, 1990). Furthermore, Kum-Kum Bhavnani (1988) argues that often these power relations are hidden, because the researcher's power is often "transparent, unspoken." But as long as the researcher makes the decisions about the topic of research and how to conduct it and write it up, she holds that power, and most feminists do hold those reins of power, from conceptualization to writing.

Although one initial goal of feminist research was to change the traditional research relationship into one of friendship, equal footing, and reciprocity, these goals have been called into question. Attempts to create a more "friendship-like" rapport include having the researcher talk about herself, having the researched ask questions of the researcher or take the lead, and having more of a dialogic interaction rather than a forced, unnatural, and formal question-and-response format. Although many feminists utilize this approach and view it as feminist, it is not a specifically or exclusively feminist method.

Feminist scholars have long hoped for egalitarian relationships and friendships during the research process and have engaged in techniques such as sharing information about themselves as a way to confront distance (Matsumoto, Chapter 8; Gluck, 1977; Oakley, 1990) and to assure themselves that the relationship is not exploitative. Shulamit Reinharz does not mince words on this topic: "Purported solidarity is often a fraud perpetuated by feminists with good intentions" (1992: 265). Furthermore, as Jane Ribbens points out, volunteering information about oneself can often be the opposite of reciprocity. When she did so in her research, she felt that she was a "nuisance" (1989: 584); others may experience such unloading as a burden.

Shulamit Reinharz contends that feminist scholars' striving for empathy and intimacy should not be confused with friendship. Longer-term relationships in which there is a transformation, such as that experienced by Karen McCarthy Brown in her study of Mama Lola, a voodoo priestess, or by Nancy Scheper-Hughes with Brazilian women she knew for twenty years, may result in friendship, but this is the exception rather than the norm (Reinharz, 1992: 68). Indeed, because of distance and time, most friendships cultivated during field research are short-lived (see Hendry, 1992).

Judith Stacey (1991: 114), in her now classic piece "Can There Be a Feminist Ethnography?" argues that the friendship that may develop between a feminist researcher and her subject could end up being *more* manipulative than traditional positivist methods in which there is no guise of solidarity, empathy, or friendship. Friends end up knowing more about each other than do conventional researchers and their subjects; Stacey was privy to extremely private information about her informants and felt that she was using and betraying them by transforming that information into data.[16]

Thus, the closeness that many feminist researchers seek and the manipulation that may result could expose subjects "to far greater danger and exploitation than do more positivist, abstract, and 'masculinist' research methods. And the greater the intimacy . . . . the greater is the danger" (1991: 114). Thus, the kind of rapport feminists developed in an effort to reject cold, distanced, exploitative, and "male" methods may have backfired and produced a more intense version of what was being rejected.

One exploitative dilemma inherent in the research process that has received little attention pinpoints a pivotal problem in the social sciences: the crises and tragedies we see occurring to our respondents or study population—for example, death, illness, and natural disasters—may enhance our own research by exposing basic relationships or social processes that we would not have observed otherwise. The death of Stacey's key informant (1991: 113–114) gave her further research opportunities and allowed her to use some of the information the now-deceased person had given her. As tragedies kept unfolding in the life of one of her key informants, Stacey decided to end that portion of her research. Through the death of the Haj's uncle and Abu-Lughod's participation in the ritual lamenting with the deceased man's sister, Abu-Lughod gained greater acceptance from this important woman in the community, who previously had been somewhat reserved toward her (1986: 21).

In terms of attempting less exploitative and more egalitarian methods during the research process, Acker, Barry, and Esseveld (1990) found that research subjects didn't necessarily want to lead the discussion; they also thought, like Stacey, that research relationships layered with friendship can be even more exploitative. In her research in a Chicano community, Maxine Baca Zinn (1979) believed that her relationships with those she researched were neither exploitative nor egalitarian.

Daphne Patai (1991), in "U.S. Academics and Third World Women: Is Ethical Research Possible?" responds with an unequivocal "no" in the first sentence of her essay. She points to the inherent hierarchy and inequalities that exist between First World feminist researchers and their Third World subjects, despite the efforts of the former to do research *for* women. "Is it possible," she asks, "to write about the oppressed without becoming one of the oppressors?" (1991: 139). She thinks not, due to inequities based on race and class and the subject-object split which leads, despite good intentions, to the researchers using (and exploiting) others for their own ends (1991: 139). She reminds us that "merely engaging in the discourse of feminism" does not protect or exclude feminists from exploiting their subjects, particularly "when routine research practices are embedded in a situation of material inequality" (1991: 139). Yet Patai seems to exclude activist research, considering only more conventional academic research.

Others contend that their subjects had at least as much power as they did, if not more. Dorinne Kondo (1986: 80) felt her research subjects assert their power over her, engaging in " 'symbolic violence' trying to dominate the anthropological encounter" through their control of her behavior. Kondo argues that research informants are not only objects but active subjects who have the power "to shape and control the ethnographer and the ethnographic encounter" (1986: 80). In Chapter 6 Ping-Chun Hsiung argues that there are other players with power who must be configured in the researcher-subject relationship. As an insider, she was perhaps more vulnerable to exploitation, as workshop bosses took advantage of her free labor.

Whereas Patai, Stacey, and others write about the power of the researcher, Lila Abu-Lughod writes about the other end of the power continuum—being powerless in her role as a researcher/Bedouin daughter (see also Berik, Chapter 2). Abu-Lughod could not force people to discuss issues that did not interest them; she writes about being part of the backdrop and being dependent (1986; 1988: 153).

Susan Abbott (1983) writes about her powerlessness in an East African context when the Kikuyu woman who headed the women's committee, out of anger at not being approached first and out of dislike for Abbott's African assistant, told other committee members not to grant Abbott an interview. Finally, after agreeing to an interview with Abbott, the woman refused to grant her the interview when Abbott arrived at her home. In the end she agreed to an interview, but this power struggle and those described in Karen McCarthy Brown's rich book about Mama Lola offer examples of situations in which the researcher is not in full control.

Yet to claim complete powerlessness on behalf of the researcher seems disingenuous. It is clear that subjects can resist and subvert the researcher's efforts, making some interviews difficult or even impossible. But it is important to differentiate between the power plays during the microprocesses of interpersonal dynamics, which may render the researcher quite helpless, and her locationality and positionality within a global political economy. In other words, the powerlessness a researcher may feel when her subjects won't talk to her or won't share the full story does not mean the researcher is a powerless person.

Too few feminist researchers admit or discuss power struggles with their subjects, particularly when they disagreed with their research subjects (McCarthy Brown, 1992; Mbilinyi, 1982; Briggs, 1970). Acker, Barry, and Esseveld (1990) did not always agree with their research subjects; the conflict led to their excluding the subjects as active participants in the research analysis. When Rebeka Kalindile, a Tanzanian peasant woman interviewed by Marjorie Mbilinyi, shocked Mbilinyi by stating that she was against colonialists being replaced by Africans, Kalindile challenged Mbilinyi to prove that the position of women had improved with independence.

Sondra Hale (1991: 127–131) admits to disliking the elitist and classist attitudes of the Sudanese leader of the women's union, whose attitudes Hale found unfeminist in the Western sense of feminism. This was particularly painful because of her important role in Sudanese history and the immense respect Hale felt for her. Hale describes her conflict about whether to publish this woman's views—whether to censor the interview or publish it and betray the union's cause. She decided not to follow her own agenda but to publish the narrative and to simultaneously acknowledge different agendas and multiple feminisms. The problem with this approach for someone interested in decentering Western hegemony, Hale insightfully found, was that such self-reflexivity puts the white researcher in the center of discourse and marginalizes the Third World woman narrator.

In descriptions of research on Third World women, with a few exceptions (Hale, 1991; M. Wolf, 1968; Shostak, 1981), few feminist researchers admit to not liking some of their subjects. This omission may be due in part to the pressure to have a more feminist (read friendly and empathic) relationship with informants. But even if we reject the notion of common identification through shared sisterhood, surely there are times when the researcher experiences alienation from and dislike of some subjects. Claudia Koonz (1987) describes her fantasy of strangling

Gertrud Scholtz-Klink, the former Nazi women's leader, as Koonz interviewed her, realizing that the woman had never given up her Nazi ideology. But clearly that admission is understandable in light of Scholtz-Klink's past and current ideology.

There is also insufficient attention to feminist fieldworkers' interactions with those with power in the community or region—for example, local government officials, army and police officials, and capitalists—most of whom tend to be male (see Wolf, 1985; ch. 2). In order to conduct research in many postcolonial settings, it is necessary not only to receive approval and clearance from various state levels but also to seek the tacit, if not explicit, approval of officials in the area. These kinds of relationships may be uncomfortable in highly patriarchal settings or in settings with authoritarian state rule and strong military control. The ways in which feminists have navigated these necessary and often problematic relationships is not usually discussed, particularly in settings where those responsible for perpetuating systems of inequality and injustice must be appeased in order for the research to be conducted. In some cases, as Margery Wolf has pointed out to me, the omission may be deliberate and politically strategic for the sake of future researchers; in other cases the omissions are not politically related.

Jayati Lal (Chapter 10) describes an interview with a factory manager who called in two factory workers to demonstrate with one woman the quickness he looks for in hiring and in the other, the less desirable trait of slowness or lethargy, all the while talking about the women in front of them to Lal. These kinds of painful moments may be difficult to avoid, and they end up aligning the researcher with management, irrespective of the researcher's desire to be closer to the workers. Despite the researcher's sympathies with workers, these moments also signify the undeniable—that the researcher's class position is closer to that of the manager than of the workers.

Working with research assistants also touches on power differentials. With a few exceptions, I rarely came across any mention of how feminist fieldworkers dealt with their research assistants. Regina Oboler (1986) wrote about how her field assistants sought guidance from her husband and about her difficulty in establishing authority with a male field assistant. Nita Kumar (1992: 116) mentions her anger about her research assistant's laziness, but again, this is a rare admission.

Perhaps some of these omissions are due to the level of funding feminist researchers may receive; they may not get enough funding to hire others. It may also be related to the kind of research that some feminist fieldworkers, particularly ethnographers, tend to conduct. Some feminist ethnographers won't hire assistants, not because they are feminists, but because ethnographers tend to do all the interviewing themselves. All the same, I am quite sure that more than two of those whose work I read employed research assistants, and that these relationships often require considerable negotiation. For example, researchers often discover that their translators are not translating everything, or that they change what they translate.

Reciprocity

One way that feminist researchers have attempted to deal with their guilt concerning their superior privilege compared with that of their research subjects and the "predatory nature" of research has been to engage in acts of reciprocity (Razavi, 1993: 157; Scheper-Hughes, 1992), realizing all the while that such acts do not counter the inequalities that remain and are reproduced. This is in keeping with a general feeling that for research to be truly feminist, someone other than the researcher should benefit (Geiger 1990: 178).[17] Feminist scholars write about helping out those in need, an activity that can often take much of their research time. The help often takes the form of giving out medicines, lending money, and driving people to doctor's appointments or to visit family members. Other attempts at reciprocity include giving gifts of money or other goods as a way to express gratitude. Schenk-Sandbergen (1992) thinks that women researchers feel more compelled than do male researchers in general to repay their informants in some manner. Many, however, have found that the high level of reciprocity expected and demanded was simply exhausting (Joseph, 1988). At the same time, feminists have realized that such acts of reciprocity, although important, still do not lead to any kind of equality between middle-class Westerners and their poorer subjects, particularly in Third World settings.

Oral histories, or life histories in particular, have been a method preferred by some feminists (Abu-Lughod, 1993; Behar, 1993; Patai, 1988a; Personal Narratives Group, 1989; Shostak, 1981; see also Watson and Smith, 1992; K. Caplan, 1992) as a way to transmit women's words and lives, often with as little editorial intervention as possible. Some feminists have contended that the interview process or an oral history may benefit those interviewed, making them feel important and increasing their sense of self-worth (Langellier and Hall, 1989). However, this conclusion is usually assumed by the researcher, who does not ask the research subjects if they feel any benefit. Daphne Patai challenges the notion of equal benefits and reciprocity to research subjects who are listened to and given a chance to talk. Even if they "got something too," this doesn't challenge the unequal relationships on which the research process is based (1991: 142).

Many feminists, particularly those who have engaged in long and intense ethnographic research or oral histories, ask themselves what their subjects have gained and who their work benefits, often honestly admitting that their subjects may not greatly appreciate the photos or the texts produced about them (Abu-Lughod, 1993; Behar, 1993). After her long relationship with Nisa, a !Kung woman, Marjorie Shostak (1989) concluded that Nisa may have experienced a small gain through interviews which were done during the emotionally stressful time of menopause. Nisa chose the name Nisa for publication and bought cows with Shostak's book royalties, but Shostak is honest about her conclusion that she played a minor, although positive, role in Nisa's life.

Interestingly, I found few discussions about post-research or post-book relationships that offer models of how feminist scholars deal with reciprocity after the articles or the book written about the research have brought merit (and therefore salary) increases or promotions. Judith Stacey (personal communication) shares her book royalties with her two main informants, and as mentioned earlier, Marjorie Shostak gave money and gifts to Nisa from her royalty payments. Valerie Matsumoto (Chapter 8) was in the unique and enviable position of returning to the Japanese American rural community she researched, after her book was out, as a keynote speaker during their reunion. She recounts looking down from the podium to see many smiling faces and seeing teenagers read her book to find out about their families (personal communication). Clearly, her experience was very unusual. Patai (1991) asks us to consider how the research is returned to the community, to whom, and in what form it is available, questions that those interested in feminist or activist research need to address and confront. But again, Patai tends not to see activist research as a possibility and splits it off from academic research.

Feminist fieldworkers have not found solutions to the ethical problems in field research, especially the issue of exploitation, probably because no solutions exist. Rina Benmayor argues that we should "privilege the dynamics of reciprocity," keeping people and politics "at the center of our research" (1991: 172). It is fitting to end an irreconcilable dilemma on that note.

Empowering Methods?

Feminists have preferred using qualitative methods and have found that life histories and oral histories are particularly compelling and unobtrusive ways to study unempowered women (Abu-Lughod, 1993; Behar, 1993; Geiger, 1986; Patai, 1988a; Personal Narratives Group, 1989; Shostak, 1989; Tsing, 1993).[18] Darling (1987) and Etter-Lewis (1991) argue that oral narratives may be the best method to use when studying women of color, who tend to be marginalized and unempowered. They view oral narratives as an empowering corrective that uniquely allows us to understand women's lives and view.

Several feminist ethnographers discuss their techniques, which may include a "speaker-centered approach" (Patai, 1988: 10), letting the subjects define the topics and discuss them with few or no questions asked by the ethnographer (Abu-Lughod, 1986; Behar, 1992; Tsing, 1993). Several feminists argue that a phenomenological approach, represented by symbolic interactionism and ethnomethodology, is preferable, in part because such an approach best reveals women's standpoint (Farrell, 1992; Stanley and Wise, 1990; Langellier and Hall, 1989). Gluck (1977) goes so far as to argue that through affirming the subject's self-worth during the interview, oral histories can increase a woman's self-esteem.

Although some researchers have claimed that "giving voice" to women is empowering, other feminists contest that conflation (Patai, 1991; Bhavnani, 1988), maintaining that this assumption may mask unequal power relations in and beyond the research process and the appropriation that is taking place. In her talk at the University of California–Davis conference on feminist dilemmas in fieldwork,

Chicana sociologist Beatriz Pesquera raised questions about whose empowerment is being discussed: "Are we concerned with the empowerment of the women
whose voices we will record and analyze, or are we empowering ourselves, our
colleagues, and university students through the use of other women's voices who
are often less privileged than ourselves?" (Pesquera in Scott and Shah, 1993: 97).
Sherry Gorelick (1991: 463) contends that just giving voice to women without
analysis conceals "contradictory and multiple oppressions" in women's lives.
Indeed, the language of "letting" women speak suggests that First World feminists
are once again wielding their hegemonic power to allow Third World subjects an
audience (Spivak, 1988).

For some, consciousness-raising has been part and parcel of their feminist
qualitative methods, particularly during intensive interviews or life histories
(Bernick, 1991; Mies, 1982, 1983, 1990). For Maria Mies, consciousness-raising is
the primary motivator of feminist research. However, over time, this idea has
tended to give way to other feminists critically asking, who are we to change or
raise the consciousness of others? This question becomes even more politicized
when it is First World white feminist researchers attempting to raise the consciousness of Third World women research subjects. Consciousness-raising implies that someone, usually the researched, is less than fully conscious and needs
to have her consciousness raised by someone else, the researcher, whose true and
superior consciousness is already raised and who therefore knows what the researched needs to know about her life (see Gorelick, 1991: 467). This may be a too
cynical exaggeration of the point, but consciousness-raising that is instigated ex-
ogenously by a well-meaning outsider who suddenly appears and later disappears
is no longer politically tenable. It is quite another issue when local women initiate
the process and learn from each other's experiences, even if they invite an outsider
or foreigner to help facilitate the process (see Enslin, 1990).

Participatory and Action-Research

Participatory research is, ideally, conceptualized and planned jointly by the researcher and those to be researched, with the possibility of those being researched
conducting some of the research and with a joint process of analysis and writing
up. Participatory research is interactive (Cancian, 1992: 628), but it can entail very
disparate levels of input from the research subjects. In practice, action-research is
one kind of participatory research, with the greatest participation stemming from
engaging in a joint activity that has a social, economic, or political goal—for example, literacy or stopping domestic abuse. Action-research does not necessarily
include joint participation in analysis and writing up, although it may include aspects of participation in those processes. In either case, the researcher may enter a
community and stimulate the idea for the project, or a group of people may invite
in a researcher or practitioner to help them with a particular task or goal. Many of
the examples of feminist action-research draw on First World–based research
(Cancian, 1992; Mies, 1983; Spalter-Roth and Hartman, 1995).

Because action and participatory research are guided by locally constituted needs and because the subjects define the research agenda, there is much greater potential for some meaningful change to occur for those involved. Whereas conventional research leaves research subjects passive and powerless in defining the research topic or the mode of research, there is greater potential for research subjects involved in a participatory project to be empowered by the process.

In light of some feminist scholars' desire to create meaningful change as part of their research and to do research for women and with women, not simply on women, action-research holds a particular appeal. Although research with participatory elements is extremely appealing to many feminists, it is difficult to enact and is rarely done. Cancian notes that feminists avoid these methods in practice while applauding them in principle (1992: 629). The explanation for this curious discrepancy may be found in logistics and timing, but it may also be found in the domain of power and control.

Projects that entail a more collective, consensual approach must rely on a more interactive process to define the terms, goals, and procedures of the project, and this can be complicated and problematic (Cancian and Armstead, 1992). It is rare that a group comes together, articulates a need for a social scientist to aid in working on a particular issue or project, and then invites one in. Perhaps this is because academics are not available. Analysis and writing up, although enriched by multiple perspectives, can be extremely time-consuming due to the need to reach consensus when there are contested views. Feminist researchers attached to a graduate program, to a department in which they are attempting to be promoted, or to an organization that wants to see results are under time and monetary pressures to start and complete a project within a reasonable period. Additionally, because of different needs and different personal investments, if a project falls apart because of disagreement, a researcher may be left in a precarious situation. All of these issues, however, are linked to the way the academy values certain kinds of research and research products and tends to devalue or even punish a more egalitarian rather than a top-down approach to research (see Cancian, 1992; Katz, Chapter 9).

Chicana sociologist Beatriz Pesquera pinpoints the push and pull of conflicting demands that result in a political and academic dilemma for her as a scholar and a woman of color. She received an invitation to participate in a set of conferences run by a local organization seeking to bring activists and academics together to focus on issues for women of color. One goal of the conference was to match grassroots women's organizations with academics who could help them with their research needs. Pesquera discussed the anxieties she experienced because of possible conflicting demands between her commitment to her community and the academic standards to which she would be held at work. Although drawn to developing empowering methodologies to study Third World women, she struggles to empower herself in an institution that renders her "powerless and oftentimes invisible." Thus, although she is "challenged and held accountable for her position within the academy by her community, she fears losing the relatively little power and privilege she has acquired" in the academy (Pesquera in Scott and Shah, 1993: 99).

Participatory research can be "time consuming, demanding, and troublesome," with small-scale accomplishments and rewards (Maguire, 1987: 37). There aren't many such projects in the feminist literature, and although they are admirable and difficult to do, the benefits seem to be limited to a few people and a short period of time. Margery Wolf (1992) notes that in descriptions of such projects, as much (or more) attention is given to the process as to the outcome, which is often not a long-term change. Nevertheless, participatory research and action-research offer possibilities that cohere with feminist goals much more than conventional research methods. Ideally these methods could unsettle the typical power relations between researcher and subjects, empower the subjects who participate to change their own lives, and instigate meaningful and needed change that is defined endogenously. Research with a more participatory component challenges feminist scholars to practice what they believe and may preach: more egalitarian approaches to empowerment that are *with,* and not simply for, the researched population. Yet feminist fieldworker-scholars have tended not to take up the call of more participatory research and have held on to the reins of research and writing. While this is deeply connected to the structure of power and privilege in the academy, it nonetheless points to a highly problematic contradiction among feminist scholars.

Maria Mies is most frequently cited and lauded in North American feminist works that discuss action-research because of her project with battered women in Germany. She makes strong arguments for feminist research that is action-oriented, calling on researchers to get involved and engaged in "struggles for women's emancipation" (1983: 124; see also Rutledge Shields and Dervin, 1993). She argues for the "view from below" (1983: 123), which stems from what she terms "conscious partiality"—partial identification of the researcher with the researched. This may entail symbolically "dropping down in class" for the researcher (1990: 69). German feminists have criticized many of Mies's assumptions. Can we truly offer the view from below when we are far above it, looking down? Can middle-class women actually "drop down" in class status, even temporarily? (see Berninghausen and Kerstan, 1992). Her approach may emphasize activism and may point to certain differences between the researcher and the researched, but the assumption is still that such differences can be bridged in a meaningful manner. The power differentials that exist in the research hierarchy are not problematized as posing an insurmountable problem. Finally, the role of the researcher as an initiator or catalyst for change in the lives of disadvantaged women is encouraged by Mies rather than critically questioned as a foreign, neocolonialist intrusion.

Although she did not speak their language (Telugu), Mies engaged in an activist project in India in which rural women went on a weekend retreat, and she states that language barriers are not problematic in "this form of reciprocal event" (1990: 7). She describes the weekend retreat as a situation where the women were, in her words and certainly not theirs, which she did not understand anyway, "unmolested by children and husbands" (1990: 72). North American feminists have praised her work and have been remarkably accepting of most of what Mies postulates; she has received more critical attention and scrutiny from German feminists.[19] Furthermore, since hers was one of the few action-research projects based in a Third World country, Mies's inability to directly communicate with the Indian women is disturbing.

In the United States, Rina Benmayor (1991) has been involved with a literacy project among Puerto Ricans in New York City, in which people came together and learned how to write through testimonies and writing their life histories. Patti Lather (1988), in a highly problematic article, gives the example of a project in South Carolina in which low-income women were trained to research their own economic circumstances "in order to understand and change them," but she does not explain whose idea it was to do this project. She seems to assume that she understands the women's conditions but they don't, and in a maternalistic manner (which Opie [1992] terms a "missionary approach") will "help" them acquire this understanding or consciousness.

After doing ethnographic fieldwork on children in the Sudan and after working for CARE on a social and agroforestry project, Cindi Katz decided to work where she lives. In Chapter 9 she offers examples of two different action-research projects in New York in which she has been engaged. These projects— one initiated from a school district committee and the second more collectively designed by researchers and community residents—involve very different modes of community participation in different phases of the project. Her dilemmas focus on the tension between political activism and academic research, and she is keenly aware that the ethnography of children's everyday lives in East Harlem that she had thought about doing will not help them (and may possibly hurt them). Furthermore, in her chapter she discusses the politics of doing activist work in the academy, where it has little currency and may even be detrimental to one's career.

In a Third World setting, Barroso and Bruschini (1991) worked with Brazilian women in a grassroots movement. The Brazilian women requested information about sex education and gender relations, which led to drawings and discussions about sex, sexuality, and domestic relations. Barroso and Bruschini used a "participatory methodology" (1988: 160) but do not explain what it entailed.

Joke Schrijvers (1986), a Dutch anthropologist, worked on a Sri Lankan research action project that was part of a three-country project. Poor, landless women were empowered by the project, which created a women's farm for the landless. In an encounter with rich landowners who tried to keep the women tied to them, the landless women resisted and walked away from their employers, demonstrating that the project had helped to empower them.

Nancy Scheper-Hughes's ethnography on poor women and children in northeastern Brazil started off as an academic project; however, the women in Bom Jesus demanded that Scheper-Hughes get involved with their local activities and needs. In other words, although she came to do an academic study, she was presented with no choice but to get involved. She had lived there years earlier, as a young Peace Corps volunteer who began to do medical work, helped organize a crèche, and tried to save some of the children who were starving to death. Scheper-Hughes views herself as a "militant anthropologist" who brings theory and practice to bear on real-life problems, helping others to understand their situation or to act on it. However, she is firm in her belief that it must be their project, not her conception of what their project should be. She views her activism as taking a rhetorical form—writing and teaching—that reaches audiences who might not otherwise be aware of the dimensions of Third World poverty, hunger, and food politics (Scheper-Hughes, personal communication, 1993).

In her Nepali research, Elizabeth Enslin had to get involved with local village women who were demanding their own public space. They also wanted "development" and were dubious about Enslin and her husband's encouragement of a literacy project. She got involved in their literacy classes, and the confidence they gained from their activities led them to confront domestic abuse in the village. If a local woman was badly beaten, the women would embarrass her husband with such tactics as sitting outside his house. Like Benmayor, Enslin sees changes in education and training as having the greatest potential for challenging local politics. Like Nancy Scheper-Hughes, she realized early on that her feminist sympathies "would have meant very little if I had not participated in meetings and mobilization efforts" (1990: 6). Eventually, the women got land to build their center and created a tree nursery.

In an article that came out as this book went to press, Enslin reflects further on her multiple and at times conflicting roles as ethnographer, activist, wife, and daughter-in-law during her research, in light of her niece's letter from Nepal: "You looked, you saw, you wrote a book. But that book won't do anything if not accompanied by work, by practice. Right?" (Enslin, 1994: 537).

Did these projects result in empowerment or meaningful political change? Or perhaps that is the wrong question, the wrong litmus test under conditions of right-wing hegemony, oppressive military-run regimes, poverty, and powerlessness. Perhaps the appropriate question is this: has action-research brought us farther along than other methods?[20]

The Brazilian women who worked with Barroso and Bruschini felt the project had been positive for their personal growth, but Barroso and Bruschini note that the women's new consciousness had not been translated into a sustained commitment to engage in collective efforts for change. However, they were holding discussion groups on their own after the researchers ended their participation in the project, and the women had shared the booklets they made with thousands of

Brazilian women (Barroso and Bruschini, 1991). Benmayor's participants in the literacy project felt the process had been therapeutic. She turned down my invitation to contribute to this volume because of a book the group is now writing. The women's farm in Sri Lanka continued for at least five years after the Western researchers departed (Schrijvers, 1986: 115). From her correspondence with her Nepali mother-in-law, who lives in the village where she did her research, Enslin found that the women continued to intervene in domestic violence cases after she departed.

These projects appear to empower women temporarily, or at least in the "medium run," but due to their necessarily small scale, they do not seem to create political or economic change that would truly transform poor women's difficult lives. And, to be fair, a significant transformation that affects everyday life would require substantial time from the researcher-activist. However, as Cindi Katz pointed out to me, while some feminists may be doing politicized research, we're not "storming the barricades." Furthermore, however limited these projects were, they were useful for the women involved and cohere with feminist goals.

Perhaps the small-scale and sometimes short-run effects of such projects are connected to the kinds of populations being addressed. Although action-research is defined by "local needs," local needs and interests are not homogeneous and vary by the major axes of stratification present in a society—for example, gender, class, and caste. Since action-research tends to be conducted with the poorest populations, the need being fulfilled may not cohere, and may often conflict, with those of better-off locals, such as the large landowners Schrijvers describes. It is possible that the small-scale and short-term nature of these projects, then, is not only related to conflicting interests but results from the wish of nonparticipants to see the project ended, which becomes easier once the researcher/activist is gone.

Most of the authors mentioned meshed their activism with their research projects rather than running the two as parallel activities. In Scheper-Hughes's ethnography, a delicate equilibrium is struck between the two as she tries to balance soliciting information from women about breastfeeding, illness, child mortality, and the like with trying to convince them to change their child care patterns.

Rina Benmayor (1991) argues that feminist researchers must decenter themselves from the "ivory tower" and create more participatory research practices; the question remains as to why this has not happened more frequently. To answer the question we should not only focus attention on feminist scholars' tendencies to engage in research with a fairly conventional form but should also examine the general marginalization of feminist and women's studies in the academy.

Finally, some feminists may engage in policy-oriented research as an effort to make their research more politically useful to others (Cancian, 1992; Spalter-Roth and Hartman, 1995). Although such projects are neither participatory research nor action-research, they represent a form of activism, albeit from a safer distance, which can be useful for women whose lives are debated and affected vis-à-vis welfare or poverty.

Postfieldwork Conundrums

Sharing Results, Co-authorship, and Writing

The problems of hierarchy, exploitation, appropriation and empowerment do not end with the fieldwork encounter—in some sense, they only begin there. Feminist and other critical scholars problematize these issues in terms of authorship, authority, and representation of the Other. Even with action-research, the processes of writing, interpreting, representing, and authoring run into the same problems as conventional research: "afterwards, once we write, regardless of methods, the critiques associated with the politics of representation apply with little distinction" (C. Hale, 1992: 5). The discomfort feminists and other researchers, usually postmodernists or critical anthropologists, have felt during the post-fieldwork process has led to experimentation with sharing results, co-authorship, decentering the authorship of the researcher, and an increased sense that texts are "constructed domains of truth" and "serious fictions" (Clifford, 1988: 10; Geiger, 1990: 178). These topics deserve and have received enormous attention that cannot be done justice in this chapter, but I will attempt to touch on some of the problems encountered.

Of the authors mentioned earlier on action-research, I do not think that most shared their draft texts with the participants. Nancy Scheper-Hughes had parts of her draft translated, and when she returned to the village she found that people were angry with her for her portrayal of them or for leaving things out. At a talk she gave at U.C.–Davis, she jokingly stated that the rules of anonymity for anthropological research were probably created to protect the anthropologist in such circumstances, rather than the population studied.

A number of authors have attempted to share their results and writing with research subjects, usually northern Americans, with varying reactions. Valerie Matsumoto got feedback on her dissertation before she turned it into a book and experienced a nonconflictual (and unusual) process. Although Katherine Borland suggests playing back oral history tapes and discussing them with the subject, she did not do this when interviewing her grandmother, whose response to Borland's written interpretive text became the title of Borland's article: "That's not what I said!" (1991). The grandmother castigates her granddaughter for misconstruing her history and doing what pleased Borland: "The story is no longer *my* story at all . . . but has become your story" (1991: 70). Playing back a tape of an interview or an oral history may work in some cultural settings but not in others. Furthermore, while it may allow for corrections or amendments, it does not deal with the interpretation in the written text, which is exactly the problem Borland confronted (see also Acker, Barry, and Esseveld, 1990).

"It's your story . . . it's your baby," states one of Judith Stacey's (1990) main informants after reading a draft of her text. Neither of the two main informants were enthusiastic about the way she was represented in the text, and Stacey published the transcript of a conversation with one of the women, who was rather critical. The book ends on this note, without Stacey attempting to explain, justify, or defend her position.

Feminist researchers have struggled with decentering their own power by listing (or offering to list) the subjects as coauthors of their texts (Billson, 1991; Mbilinyi, 1989). Others have found this kind of interaction impractical, impossible, and politically risky (Opie, 1992; Wolf, 1992). When there is considerable geographical distance between the author and her informants, she must somehow return the text to them. If she has worked in another culture and language, the text must be translated. Due to the geographical inaccessibility of some groups, problems with mail delivery, potential political risks in mailing such a text, and the problem of illiteracy, the sharing can often only be done in person, which may take considerable time and expense if the site is thousands of miles away. Even then, Margery Wolf is hesitant to implicate her Chinese subjects in her texts due to the potential risks for them in an unstable political climate.

Kim England (1994) remains skeptical of the viability of these attempts to decenter the researcher's authority in academic texts, arguing that the researcher ultimately chooses what to quote, and these quotes often reflect responses to unsolicited questions from the researcher. Sherry Gorelick also remains dubious of attempts to decrease the power differentials and to increase equality through dialogues and the "contrapuntal duet," as long as "the vast majority of researchers (or interpreters) remain predominantly white and privileged" (1991: 469).

Representation

Chandra Mohanty's now classic piece, "Under Western Eyes: Feminist Scholarship and Colonial Discourses," republished in 1991(b), along with Aihwa Ong's (1988) article in a similar vein, were meant to confront and contest the ways in which Third World women have been conceptualized and represented by First World (usually Anglo) feminist scholars. Both authors point to the false binary oppositions that have been utilized to conceptualize and represent Third World women (e.g., uneducated, illiterate, poor, powerless), which implicitly use the First World feminist researcher as the reference point (e.g., educated, literate, better-off, in control). First World feminist researchers, however, remain transparent in this process—their presence and power is unnamed and unstated (Bhavnani, 1988: 42). Mohanty challenged generalized notions of "Third World women" as "a singular monolithic subject" (1991b: 53).[21] Ong points out how the preferences and priorities of First World academic feminists, rather than those of the researched, have set the agenda for what has been studied—work and labor have been a more major focus than family, children, and friendships (see also Lazreg, 1988; Visweswaran, 1994)

Those involved in subaltern studies have focused on the impossibility of representing oppressed postcolonial subjects, arguing that such representations continue to mirror historical and contemporary exploitative relations between colonizers and the colonized, reflecting more about the former than the latter (Spivak, 1988). Daphne Patai, a feminist and a fieldworker, staunchly and passionately challenges such arguments from armchair critics, focusing to some extent on the privilege of intellectuals in this argument—for example, deciding what kind of speech "counts as authentic speech," overvaluing researchers and undervaluing the researched, and writing in a "mode that is inaccessible" to most, particularly to the subalterns being discussed. She challenges the position that only manipulation, disingenuousness, mystification, or lack of self-awareness are possible. She argues for recognition of our own limits in our research and for attempts to combat "our own complicity and privilege where they exist" (1988b: 24–25).

Feminist scholars continue to experiment with different strategies of representation (see Lal, Chapter 10). A few contemporary feminist ethnographers have focused on the life or oral history of one individual woman (Abu-Lughod, 1993; Behar, 1993; Tsing, 1993), attempting to represent her through her own voice and story, which are edited as little as possible and may not be guided by the researcher's questions. By publishing the oral histories they gathered with as little doctoring as possible, Lila Abu-Lughod (1993) and Ruth Behar (1993) attempt to avoid the problem of imposing their editing and interpretation. Behar acknowledges that because of national and international power differences, her oral history cannot be a "co-production of knowledge," but it is, instead, a "translation of power" (1993: 229). She negotiated the terms by which she would use Esperanza's story. Yet Behar has the last word in her book and unsuccessfully (and rather embarrassingly) attempts to demonstrate the parallels between her life and the life of Esperanza.

Whereas experimenting with strategies of representation has produced some alternatives, it is doubtful that these forms of representation are distinctly different from others, since the end product does not necessarily appropriate less and does not shift the balance of power or the benefits. Despite important efforts to experiment with strategies of representation and authorship, the basic power differences and the distribution of benefits from research remain the same. Few practical changes that have been attempted translate into radically transforming the researcher's privileged position. While more theorizing on these contradictions is needed, perhaps an acknowledgment of their irreconcilability is also necessary.

Self and Positionality

How then can and should feminist researchers locate themselves in their research, in the process of doing research and writing texts? A greater focus on self and positionality and on Self and Other has encouraged and allowed feminist researchers to pursue the politics of positionality in their texts (Enslin, 1990). Because one's "biography, politics and relationships become part of the fabric of the field" (Bell, 1993b: 41), this must be confronted and considered in a conscious manner.

Pat Caplan (1993b: 78) suggests that we ask ourselves "who are we for them? Who are they for us?" as we situate the politics of our research on interpersonal, local, and global levels (Gordon, 1988). In doing so, the researcher may realize that she "is also the 'other' which is being subject to observation and analysis by the local community." Researchers then must deal with two kinds of reflexivity—"the 'self' as both 'object' and 'subject' and the 'other' as 'observed' and 'observer'"

(Karim, 1993b: 89). Patricia Zavella (1991) argues for locating ourselves as positioned subjects and drawing on these social locations as data; indeed, the politics of location and the ways in which it situates knowledge have been integrated in many feminist texts based on fieldwork (Enslin, 1990; Bolles, 1985; Rofels, 1993; Schrijvers, 1986).

There are drawbacks and risks, however, to the process of situating oneself. Rather than being drawn into questions about epistemology, the politics of research, and writing, Daphne Patai finds that the tendency to situate oneself instead often leads to tropes that sound like apologies, which are then "deployed as badges." They are assumed to pay "one's respect to 'difference,' but do not affect any aspect of the research or the interpretive text" (1991: 149; see also Bhavnani, 1993; Scheper-Hughes, 1983; Patai 1994: A52). Self-reflexivity, Daphne Patai asserts, does not change reality. "It does not redistribute income, gain political rights for the powerless, create housing for the homeless, or improve health" (1994: A52). The challenge remains to write a text that does not position the researcher on center stage while marginalizing those being researched (see Moore, 1994, Chapter 6). This challenge becomes a greater dilemma for those writing about people on the margin, attempting to bring their stories and lives into the center.[22]

Although I concur with Patai's views, such positionings are glaringly absent where they are much needed—in the women-and-development literature. These liberal feminists' writings simply assume that the position of the author does not need to be questioned, a problem also found in the political-economy-of-gender literature that focuses on the Third World. In this day and postmodern age, all feminists in the field of "development studies" need to critically and self-consciously examine their positionality, if only to better understand their role in the global arena or their self-appointed "do-gooder" role.

Conclusions

Power

I think it is important to acknowledge and accept that when one is working with poorer and marginalized peoples, power differentials between feminist researchers and their subjects remain as such. Although feminist researchers may attempt to equalize relationships while in the field through empathic and friendly methods, these methods do not transform the researchers' positionality or locationality. The "equality" is short-lived and illusory because the researcher goes home when she is finished, reflecting her privileged ability to leave. This does not mean that attempts at more egalitarian field relationships should be abandoned but rather that they should be seen more realistically.

At the same time, I do not mean to portray research subjects as victims without agency or consciousness. Our subjects affect our research plans if they decide not to interact with us. But these microdynamics do not subvert the hierarchy of power when the positionality of the researcher is considered. Furthermore, our subjects are often fully aware of this differential and the difference in benefits that will result from the research.

Although we may confront the dilemma of power in our positionality, our research processes, and our post-fieldwork practices, many feminists, particularly feminists of color, confront their own sense of marginality when they return to academia. Although being an academic is a privileged position, feminists are usually not in positions of power within the academy. Thus, the dilemma of power in field relations is fraught with further contradictions—although we may be treated as privileged in the field, we have no power to alter policies that may affect our subjects' lives and usually very little power once we return to our own workplace and home.

In Chapter 11, Margery Wolf argues that feminists are not accustomed to having power and are uncomfortable with it. She encourages us to be more realistic, particularly when training our students for the field. At a recent sociology conference on feminist research, Judith Stacey pushed the power dilemma one step further by arguing that feminists need to acknowledge not only that we have power but that we desire it. Feminist researchers, she contends, tend to focus on the dilemmas of power as though they themselves were selfless and virtuous, with little reflexivity and some dishonesty about their desire for power and privilege (Stacey in Naples and Ribet, 1994: 20). Reflecting upon this position and its implications will surely push our discussion to new levels.

The Future Is Now

What are our tasks, as feminist fieldworker-researchers? Can some of the problems outlined earlier be addressed or altered? First, I think it is important to recognize, acknowledge, and accept the imperfections and the incompleteness of feminist research goals. A feminist agenda for the future should include working with and through these critiques, struggling with them, and to some extent, moving on.

On a basic level, a number of anthropologists have encouraged more critical consideration of what we consider "the field": What constitutes the field and where does it begin and end? (Clifford, 1990). Problematizing the dichotomy between "home" and "the field" has encouraged some to examine the notion of working at home, or doing one's homework (Williams, forthcoming; Visweswaran, 1994), which may lead to some uncomfortable and challenging reactions (Obbo, 1990; Williams, Chapter 3). Furthermore, as Anna Tsing points out, we need to examine the ways in which "home" and "the field" are economically, politically, and culturally interdependent (Tsing in Scott and Shah, 1993: 94). Doing research "at home," a notion that also has been problematized, may hold increasing appeal for white, Western feminist researchers who wish to avoid all the colonialist and imperialist implications that are coupled with working in Third World research sites; it also brings us back to sociology.

As a way to avoid some of the pitfalls mentioned, some have argued for a shifting research agenda—"studying up"—studying those with power and control rather than continuing the almost exclusive focus on the powerless and marginalized (Nader, 1972). Sylvia Yanagisako (in Scott and Shah, 1993) encourages this move, not only because it may partially solve the problems of power inequalities and exploitative research relationships but also because we can learn about important social constructions from different perspectives. For example, we learn about social class differently when studying the poor and when studying the upper class; we learn about the social construction of race and racism differently when studying people of color and when studying whites.

In other words, we may better understand the process of marginalization and dominance by studying the dominant, the colonizing, "the center" (Scott and Shah, 1993: 94). Yet Tsing pointed out the dangers in simply "reversing the gaze" to study whites or elites, concerned that this would encourage studying communities and their privilege or exclusion in an isolated rather than a dependent manner. Furthermore, Sandra Harding contends that "the perspective from the lives of the less powerful can provide a more objective view than the perspectives from the lives of the more powerful," until those with less power articulate their life experiences (1991: 270).

One important dilemma mentioned earlier concerns the gap between feminist professed goals and feminist research practices, particularly the lack of action-research and activist research. Deborah Gordon (in Scott and Shah, 1993: 100) encourages more community-based action-research projects such as the one described by Rina Benmayor (1991) in East Harlem, where personal testimony and the migration experience are drawn on in a literacy course; Enslin's research shows how literacy empowered women to engage in political action. Gordon encourages these types of projects, which are less exploitative and actually contribute something to the community. These projects are in some sense ideal for feminist researchers, and they are also difficult to find and to do. At the same time, young feminist scholars need to be aware of the "cost" and the penalty of doing such research, since it will not translate easily into the degrees or promotions they seek within the academy. Indeed, much of our struggle may need to be within academia rather than in the field.

Henrietta Moore envisages a new kind of ethnography based on multiple authorship of texts, representing collaboration in the research process between the feminist researcher and her informants (1988: 194). This brings up the difficult task of collaborative research not only between the researcher and the researched but between feminist scholars from different backgrounds (see Lugones and Spelman, 1983). In other words, there are painfully few interethnic, interracial, and international attempts of scholars to collaborate on feminist research projects. A challenge for our future and the next generation of researchers is to confront this research individualism and attempt dialogues across multiple differences and borders. Other dilemmas that need to be addressed are how a research agenda is established and what topics become our focus, who funds us,[23] writing and representation, and ways of engaging our respondents in our research.

My essay and this book are not meant to encourage future feminist fieldwork-ers to abandon the practice of fieldwork—to the contrary—nor can we offer ways to reconcile these deep contradictions. The book is meant to underscore and ex-emplify dilemmas of power inherent in the fieldwork and post-fieldwork process that plague the most self-conscious and well-meaning researcher. They are also meant to encourage future feminist fieldworkers to continue confronting and in-tegrating these dilemmas without naïveté, to continue rocking the epistemologi-cal boat, to continue challenging conventional notions about what constitutes quality research, and to continue striving for politically meaningful coalitions and projects.

NOTES

A fellowship from the Department of Rural Development of the University of Wageningen allowed me to begin work on this project. I am grateful to Norman Long for his support. A Faculty Development Award from U.C. Davis allowed me to complete this project. I wish to thank Charles Hale, Cindi Katz, Jennifer Bickham Mendez, Aihwa Ong, Judith Stacey, Christine D.F. Di Stefano, Margery Wolf, and an anonymous reviewer for careful readings and helpful comments. None of them is in any way responsible for my errors and argu-ments. Thanks to Raquelle Zachman and Jennifer Bickham Mendez for assistance and Rosemary Powers for providing materials from the ASA conference. My own work on this essay was delayed by my grandmother's stroke and death and has been wonderfully chal-lenged by the birth of my son; this essay is dedicated to Alice Scheuer and Max, two souls who irrevocably changed the course of my life.

1. I will use the terms "Third World" or "postcolonial" to refer to Asia, Africa, and Latin America despite my dissatisfaction with both concepts. "Third World" denotes a normative hierarchy and is increasingly meaningless amid contemporary global shifts that include not only the demise of the former "Second World" but also rates of poverty, disease, and infant mortality in the United States that rival those in Third World countries. The term "postcolonial" obscures neocolonial relationships.

2. Although feminist researchers have focused on gender as a central category of analy-sis, much of the feminist literature on fieldwork focuses on women.

3. Many of the dilemmas discussed in this chapter, particularly those dealing with un-equal power relations and exploitation, also contradict the tenets of socialism and would pose similar dilemmas for progressive researchers. Yet little has been written from the so-cialist perspective that directly claims and acknowledges these problems.

4. Anthropologist Jean-Paul Dumont notes the predominance of women in early field-work accounts and points out that while their husbands were engaged in the "real" work of understanding politics and public life (1978: 8), women (usually wives) were writing up fieldwork accounts of everyday life practices. Indeed women, particularly feminists, have contributed the lion's share of recent writings on fieldwork and its contradictions.

5. The first phases of feminist research, in the 1970s, set out to correct the androcen-trism present in the social sciences, to set the record straight, and to do research by women, for women (Duelli Klein, 1983), but ended up ignoring differences of race, class, ethnicity, and nationality, which were assumed to be subordinate to the common bonds of woman-hood between the researcher and her subjects (Oakley, 1990; Finch, 1984).

6. These dilemmas are based on Western conceptions of power, stemming from the privilege of our economic position and educational backgrounds, differences that usually place the academic researcher in a higher socioeconomic position than her subjects. However, it is important to note that Western notions of the basis of power may differ from those of our subjects—for example, motherhood, age. I am grateful to Cindi Katz for pointing this out to me.

7. Methodology constitutes the theory and analysis of how research should proceed (Harding, 1987a). Methodology is inextricably linked to epistemology, our theory of knowledge—what can be known, by whom, and through what means (Harding, 1987: 3); methodology is based on and guided by what we think we can and should know about a subject.

8. Some feminists have argued that male academic postmodernists appropriated much of what feminists had been saying and doing for years but gained much more attention for it because of their privileged position in academia (Mascia-Lees, Sharpe, and Cohen, 1989; Caplan, 1988; Wolf, 1992). When women engaged in self-reflexivity, Margery Wolf observes, it was dismissed as "self-indulgent"; when men do it, it becomes an experimental and privileged discourse (1992: 50). In their book *Writing Culture,* Clifford and Marcus (see Clifford, 1986: 17–21) do indeed draw on feminist techniques and approaches, but they explicitly marginalize feminist scholarship (Leonardo, 1991; Gordon, 1988), provoking a number of strong reactions from feminists (Gordon, 1988; Mascia-Lees, Sharpe, and Cohen, 1989; Visweswaran, 1988).

9. Clearly, textual analysis has its own dilemmas, such as interpretation, but it avoids the particular epistemological crisis one confronts with face-to-face research and in that sense is "safer."

10. See *The Canadian Geographer,* 1993, vol. 37, number 1, and *The Professional Geographer,* 1994, vol. 46, number 1; both are special issues focusing on feminist geography and fieldwork.

11. Some have argued that women make better fieldworkers and are well suited to qualitative methods because of women's tendency to engage in certain social dynamics—empathy, sharing, emphasis on process, friendship, and desire for equal and nonhierarchical relationships (Scheper-Hughes, 1983). Others may see these kinds of dynamics as part and parcel of a feminist method (Roberts, 1990). One problem with the argument that women make better fieldworkers concerns the essentialism underlying this notion, which naturalizes women's (and also men's) personality traits (see Bell, 1993a). Although women have been socialized to have certain traits that may make such connections and communications easier, it would be wrong to assume that all feminist fieldworkers possess these traits or that all male or nonfeminist fieldworkers do not possess them. Indeed this kind of essentialism is parallel to that found in the argument that "native" anthropologists or "insiders" naturally and organically produce more insightful research.

12. One of the more humorous examples of dress codes comes from anthropologist Ifi Amadiume, who did research in her father's Nigerian village. Once when she wore jeans, people laughed at her, and men called her "Master who does not have a penis" (1993: 188).

13. As Judy Stacey and Cindi Katz have pointed out to me, this may not differ substantially from how we live our non-fieldwork lives, drawing on different aspects of our multiple positionalities when necessary.

14. Nita Kumar, an Indian anthropologist, states, in a similar vein, that an indigenous anthropologist is engaged in more of an activist project and a voyage of self-discovery, but also "a more holistic project, one more generous in its method and more liberal in its scope" (Kumar, 1992: 11). Yet the evidence for greater holism or generosity is not at all clear in the perspective she offers in her book.

15. This notion of incompleteness in dichotomous identities is taken up by Jeff Yang in his review of recent Asian American anthologies. He also contests the simple notion of two halves that has long been utilized to suggest that Asian Americans have a dual personality and two identities—an Asian half that is obedient and industrious, and an American half that challenges the Asian half by being creative and rebellious (1994: 23).

16. Stacey's example of a closeted lesbian relationship provides an instructive case. She was caught between her key informant, now married, who asked Stacey to keep the relationship confidential, and the woman's "spurned" lover, who began to compete for Stacey's sympathy. Furthermore, Stacey was caught in multiple and competing webs of betrayal, between respect for her respondent's confidentiality, collusion "with the homophobic silencing of lesbian experience," and tampering with the ethnographic "truth" (1991: 113–114).

17. Interestingly, Nita Kumar (1992) is one of the rare researchers who writes about (or admits to) refusing to help people out because she felt she had to choose between her work and helping others. "At times it broke my heart to say no, which I learned to do automatically in case I waivered" (1992: 168). The case she describes involved a policeman who had helped them out previously; he came over and asked her to intervene in his impending transfer out of Banaras because of her father's former high position in the police. She responded "No, I can't help you. I never do this on principle" (1992: 169). Kumar does not identify herself as a feminist in her book, nor does she discuss her research in terms of feminism.

18. Geiger warns against the simple assumption that the technique of oral history is inherently and necessarily feminist; what constitutes feminist work is a framework that challenges existing androcentric or partial constructions of women's lives (1990: 169; Bhavnani, 1993).

19. In their Javanese-based research, for example, Berninghausen and Kerstan (1992) found that Mies's postulates for research did not work well. When they tried to exemplify "conscious bias" in favor of their respondents, they had trouble making this clear to the Indonesian women. The Indonesian respondents were not interested in protesting against patriarchal structures. The authors hesitated to engage in consciousness-raising, which they did not feel they had the right to do in another culture, and they finally accepted that the change Mies argues for may not happen, because Western feminist researchers and the women they study have different interests.

20. I wish to thank Charles Hale for his thoughtful input on this question.

21. Margery Wolf contests this generalization, arguing that Mohanty "falls into the same trap she accuses others of, by characterizing First World feminist anthropologists in terms of the writings of a few anthropologists with Zed Press" (1992: 12).

22. It is ironic that Anna Lowenhaupt Tsing's (1993) recent and thoughtful ethnography on marginality will, in the end, put her in "center stage" in terms of the reactions and benefits.

23. There is a surprising dearth of references to funding sources and possible conflicts of interest. Scheper-Hughes mentions receiving funding from the tobacco industry in her acknowledgments, and Günseli Berik (Chapter 2) discusses how her funders—the ILO—wanted results presented in a manner that would obfuscate the problems she observed. These problems may surface more when one is doing a report for an agency or international organization. Since I read more academic works, which would tend not to be sponsored by such organizations, those issues tend not to surface. However, questions about the politics of funding sources remain.

REFERENCES AND SELECTED READINGS

Abbott, Susan. 1983. "In the End You Will Carry Me in Your Car: Sexual Politics in the Field." *Women's Studies* 10: 161–178.

Abramson, Allen. 1993. "Between Autobiography and Method: Being Male, Seeing Myth, and the Analysis of Structures of Gender and Sexuality in the Eastern Interior of Fiji." In *Gendered Fields: Women, Men, and Ethnography,* edited by Diane Bell, Pat Caplan, and Wazir Jahan Karim, 63–77. London: Routledge.

Abu-Lughod, Lila. 1993. *Writing Women's Worlds: Bedouin Stories.* Berkeley: University of California Press.

———. 1991. "Writing Against Culture." In *Recapturing Anthropology,* edited by Richard Fox, 137–162. Sante Fe: School of American Research.

———. 1990. "Can There Be a Feminist Ethnography?" *Women and Performance* 5, no. 1: 7–27.

———. 1988. "Fieldwork of a Dutiful Daughter." In *Arab Women in the Field: Studying Your Own Society,* edited by Soraya Altorki and Camillia Fawzi El-Solh, 139–161. Syracuse: Syracuse University Press.

———. 1986. *Veiled Sentiments: Honor and Poetry in a Bedouin Society.* Berkeley: University of California Press.

Acker, Joan, Kate Barry, and Johanna Esseveld. 1990. "Objectivity and Truth: Problems in Doing Feminist Research." In *Beyond Methodology: Feminist Scholarship as Lived Research,* edited by Mary Margaret Fonow and Judith Cook, 133–153. Bloomington: Indiana University Press.

Agar, Michael. 1986. "Foreword." In *Self, Sex, and Gender in Cross-Cultural Fieldwork,* edited by Tony Larry Whitehead and Mary Ellen Conaway, ix–xi. Urbana: University of Illinois Press.

Alcoff, Linda, and Elizabeth Potter. 1993. "Introduction: When Feminisms Intersect Epistemology." In *Feminist Epistemologies,* edited by Linda Alcoff and Elizabeth Potter, 1–14. New York: Routledge.

Altorki, Soraya. 1988. "At Home in the Field." In *Arab Women in the Field: Studying Your Own Society,* edited by Soraya Altorki and Camillia Fawzi El-Solh, 49–68. Syracuse: Syracuse University Press.

Amadiume, Ifi. 1993. "The Mouth That Spoke a Falsehood Will Later Speak the Truth: Going Home to the Field in Eastern Nigeria." In *Gendered Fields: Women, Men, and Ethnography,* edited by Diane Bell, Pat Caplan, and Wazir Jahan Karim, 182–198. London: Routledge.

Antony, Louise, and Charlotte Witt. 1993. *A Mind of One's Own: Feminist Essays on Reason and Objectivity.* Boulder: Westview.

Appadurai, Arjun. 1986. "Theory in Anthropology: Center and Periphery." *Comparative Studies in Society and History* 28, no. 2: 356–361.

Asad, Talal, ed. 1973. *Anthropology and the Colonial Encounter.* London: Ithaca Press.

Baca Zinn, Maxine. 1979. "Field Research in Minority Communities: Ethical, Methodological, and Political Observations by an Insider," *Social Problems* 27, no. 2: 209–219.

Bar-On, Bat-Ami. 1993. "Marginality and Epistemic Privilege." In *Feminist Epistemologies,* edited by Linda Alcoff and Elizabeth Potter, 83–100. New York: Routledge.

Barroso, Carmen, and Cristina Bruschini. 1991. "Building Politics from Personal Lives: Discussions on Sexuality Among Poor Women in Brazil." In *Third World Women and the Politics of Feminism,* edited by Chandra Talpade Mohanty, Ann Russo, and Lourdes Torres, 153–172. Bloomington: Indiana University Press.

Behar, Ruth. 1993. *Translated Woman: Crossing the Border with Esperanza's Story.* Boston: Beacon Press.

Bell, Diane. 1993a. "Introduction 1: The Context." In *Gendered Fields: Women, Men, and Ethnography,* edited by Diane Bell, Pat Caplan, and Wazir Jahan Karim, 1–18. London: Routledge.

———. 1993b. "Yes, Virginia, There Is a Feminist Ethnography: Reflections from Three Australian Fields." In *Gendered Fields: Women, Men, and Ethnography,* edited by Diane Bell, Pat Caplan, and Wazir Jahan Karim, 28–43. London: Routledge.

Benmayor, Rina. 1991. "Testimony, Action Research, and Empowerment: Puerto Rican Women and Popular Education." In *Women's Words: The Feminist Practice of Oral History,* edited by Sherna Berger Gluck and Daphne Patai, 159–174. New York: Routledge.

Berger, Iris. 1992. "Categories and Contexts: Reflections on the Politics of Identity in South Africa." *Feminist Studies* 18, no. 2: 284–294.

Berger, John. 1967. *A Fortunate Man.* New York: Pantheon Books.

Bernick, Susan E. 1991. "Toward a Value-Laden Theory: Feminism and Social Science." *Hypatia* 6, no. 2: 118–136.

Berninghausen, Jutta, and Birgit Kerstan. 1992. *Forging New Paths: Feminist Social Methodology and Rural Women in Java.* New York: Zed Press.

Bhavnani, Kum-Kum. 1993. "Tracing the Contours: Feminist Research and Feminist Objectivity." *Women's Studies International Forum* 16, no. 2: 95–104.

———. 1988. "Empowerment and Social Research: Some Comments." *Text* 1, no. 2: 41–50.

Billson, Janet Mancini. 1991. "The Progressive Verification Method: Toward a Feminist Methodology for Studying Women Cross-Culturally." *Women's Studies International Forum* 14, no. 3: 201–215.

Blank, Rebecca M. 1992. "A Female Perspective on Economic Man?" In *Revolutions in Knowledge: Feminism in the Social Sciences,* edited by Sue Rosenberg Zalk and Janice Gordon-Kelter, 111–124. Boulder: Westview.

Blauner, Robert, and David Wellman. 1973. "Toward the Decolonization of Social Research." In *The Death of White Sociology,* edited by Joyce Ladner, 310–330. New York: Random House.

Bolles, Lynn A. 1985. "Of Mules and Yankee Gals: Struggling with Stereotypes in the Field." *Anthropology and Humanism Quarterly* 10, no. 4: 114–119.

Borland, Katherine. 1991. "'That's Not What I Said': Interpretive Conflict in Oral Narrative Research." In *Women's Words: The Feminist Practice of Oral History,* edited by Sherna Berger Gluck and Daphne Patai, 63–76. New York: Routledge.

Bowen, Eleanor Smith. 1954. *Return to Laughter.* London: Gollancz.

Briggs, Jean L. 1970. *Never in Anger: Portrait of an Eskimo Family.* Cambridge: Harvard University Press.

Brown, Karen McCarthy. 1991. *Mama Lola: A Vodou Priestess in Brooklyn.* Berkeley and Los Angeles: University of California Press.

———. 1987. "'Plenty Confidence in Myself': The Initiation of White Woman Scholar into Haitian Vodou." *Journal of Feminist Studies in Religion 3,* no. 1:67-76.

Burawoy, Michael, Alice Burton, Ann Arneet Ferguson, Kathryn J. Fox, Joshua Gamson, Nadine Gartrell, Leslie Hurst, Charles Kurzman, Leslie Salzinger, Josepha Schiffman, and Shirori Ui. 1991. *Ethnography Unbound: Power and Resistance in the Modern Metropolis.* Berkeley: University of California Press.

Burgess, Robert G. 1982. "Approaches to Field Research." In *Field Research: A Sourcebook and Field Manual,* edited by Robert G. Burgess, 1–11. London: Allen and Unwin.

Cancian, Francesca. 1995 (forthcoming). "Participatory Research and Alternative Strategies for Activist Sociology." In *Feminism and Social Change: Bridging Theory and Practice,* edited by Heidi Gottfried. Urbana: University of Illinois Press.

———. 1992. "Feminist Science: Methodologies That Challenge Inequality." *Gender and Society* 6: 623–642.

Cancian, Francesca M., and Cathleen Armstead. 1992. "Participatory Research." In *Encyclopedia of Sociology,* edited by Edgar and Marie Borgatta, 1427–1432. New York: Macmillan.

Cannon, Lynn Weber, Elizabeth Higginbotham, and Marianne L.A. Leung. 1990. "Race and Class Bias in Qualitative Research on Women." In *Beyond Methodology: Feminist Scholarship as Lived Research,* edited by Mary Margaret Fonow and Judith Cook, 107–118. Bloomington: Indiana University Press.

Caplan, Karen. 1992. "Resisting Autobiography: Out-Law Genres and Transnational Feminist Subjects." In *De/Colonizing the Subject: The Politics of Gender in Women's Autobiography,* edited by Sidonie Smith and Julia Watson, 115–138. Minneapolis: University of Minnesota Press.

Caplan, Pat. 1993a. "Introduction 2: The Volume." In *Gendered Fields: Women, Men, and Ethnography,* edited by Diane Bell, Pat Caplan, and Wazir Jahan Karim, 19–27. London: Routledge.

———. 1993b. "Learning Gender: Fieldwork in a Tanzanian Coastal Village, 1965–1985." In *Gendered Fields: Women, Men, and Ethnography,* edited by Diane Bell, Pat Caplan, and Wazir Jahan Karim, 168–181. London: Routledge.

———. 1988. "Engendering Knowledge: The Politics of Ethnography." Part 1. *Anthropology Today* 4, no. 5: 8–17.

Carr, Helen, 1988. "In Other Words: Native American Women's Autobiography." In *Life/Lines: Theorizing Women's Autobiography,* edited by Bella Brodzki and Celeste Schenck, 131–153. Ithaca: Cornell University Press.

Cassel, J. 1991. "Subtle Manipulation and Deception in Fieldwork: Opportunism Knocks." *International Journal of Moral and Social Studies* 6, no. 3: 269–274.

Cassell, Joan. 1987. *Children in the Field: Anthropological Experiences.* Philadelphia: Temple University Press.

Caufield, Mina Davis. 1979. "Participant Observation or Partisan Participation?" In *The Politics of Anthropology: From Colonialism and Sexism Toward a View from Below,* edited by Gerrit Huizer and Bruce Mannheim, 309–318. The Hague: Mouton.

Chakravarti, Anand. 1979. "Experiences of an Encapsulated Observer: A Village in Rajasthan." In *The Fieldworker and the Field: Problems and Challenges in Sociological Investigation,* edited by M. N. Srinivas, A. M. Shah, and E. A. Ramaswamy, 38–57. Delhi: Oxford University Press.

Chung, Yuen Kay. 1990. "At the Palace: Researching Gender and Ethnicity in a Chinese Restaurant." In *Feminist Praxis: Research, Theory, and Epistemology in Feminist Sociology,* edited by Liz Stanley. London and New York: Routledge.

Clifford, James. 1990. "Notes on (Field)notes." In *Fieldnotes,* edited by Roger Sanjek, 47–70. Ithaca: Cornell University Press.

———. 1988. *The Predicament of Culture: Twentieth Century Ethnography, Literature, and Art.* Cambridge: Harvard University Press.

————. 1986. "Introduction: Partial Truths." In *Writing Culture: The Poetics and Politics of Ethnography,* edited by James Clifford and George E. Marcus, 1–26. Berkeley: University of California Press.

————. 1983. "On Ethnographic Authority." *Representations* 1, no. 2: 118–146.

Collins, Patricia Hill. 1990. "Learning from the Outsider Within: The Sociological Significance of Black Feminist Thought." In *Beyond Methodology: Feminist Scholarship as Lived Research,* edited by Mary Margaret Fonow and Judith Cook, 35–59. Bloomington: Indiana University Press.

Conaway, Mary Ellen. 1986. "The Pretense of the Neutral Researcher." In *Self, Sex, and Gender in Cross-Cultural Fieldwork,* edited by Tony Larry Whitehead and Mary Ellen Conaway, 52–63. Urbana: University of Illinois Press.

Cook, Judith. 1983. "An Interdisciplinary Look at Feminist Methodology: Ideas and Practice in Sociology, History, and Anthropology." *Humboldt Journal of Social Relations* 10, no. 2: 127–152.

Cook, Judith, and Mary Margaret Fonow. 1986. "Knowledge and Women's Interest: Issues of Epistemology and Methodology in Feminist Sociological Research." *Sociological Inquiry* 56, no. 1: 2–29.

Cooke, Philip. 1990. "Locality, Structure, and Agency: A Theoretical Analysis." *Cultural Anthropology* 5, no. 1: 3–15.

Daniels, Arlene. 1983. "Self-Deception and Self-Discovery in. Fieldwork." *Qualitative Sociology* 6, no. 3: 195–214.

————. 1975. "Feminist Perspectives in Sociological Research." In *Another Voice,* edited by Marcia Millman and Rosabeth Kanter, 340–382. New York: Anchor Press/Doubleday.

Darling, Marsha Jean. 1987. "The Disinherited as Source: Rural Black Women's Memories." *Michigan Quarterly Review* 26, no. 1: 48–63.

Devereux, Stephen, and John Hoddinott, eds. 1993. *Fieldwork in Developing Countries.* Boulder: Lynne Rienner.

De Vita, Philip R., ed. 1990. *The Humbled Anthropologist: Tales from the Pacific.* Belmont, Calif.: Wadsworth.

di Leonardo, Micaela. 1991. "Introduction: Gender, Culture, and Political Economy: Feminist Anthropology in Historical Perspective." In *Gender at the Crossroads of Knowledge: Feminist Anthropology in the Postmodern Era,* edited by Micaela di Leonardo, 1–50. Berkeley: University of California Press.

Di Stefano, Christine. 1990. "Dilemmas of Difference: Feminism, Modernity, and Postmodernism." In *Feminism/Postmodernism,* edited by Linda J. Nicholson, 63–82. New York: Routledge.

Dua, Veena. 1979. "A Woman's Encounter with Arya Samaj and Untouchables: A Slum in Jullundur." In *The Fieldworker and the Field: Problems and Challenges in Sociological Investigation,* edited by M. N. Srinivas, A. M. Shah and E. A. Ramaswamy, 115–126. Delhi: Oxford University Press.

DuBois, Barbara. 1983. "Passionate Scholarship: Notes on Values, Knowing, and Method in Feminist Social Science." In *Theories of Women's Studies,* edited by Gloria Bowles and Renate Duelli Klein, 105–116. London: Routledge.

Duelli Klein, Renate. 1983. "How to Do What We Want to Do: Thoughts About Feminist Methodology." In *Theories of Women's Studies,* edited by Gloria Bowles and Renate Duelli Klein, 88–104. London: Routledge.

Dumont, Jean-Paul. 1978. *The Headman and I: Ambiguity and Ambivalence in the Fieldworking Experience.* Austin: University of Texas Press.

Dyck, Isabel. 1993. "Ethnography: A Feminist Method?" *The Canadian Geographer* 37, no. 1: 52–57.

Edwards, Rosalind. 1990. "Connecting Method and Epistemology: A White Woman Interviewing Black Women." *Women's Studies International Forum* 13, no. 5: 477–490.

Eichler, Margrit. 1988. *Nonsexist Research Methods: A Practical Guide.* Boston: Allen and Unwin.

England, Kim. 1994. "Getting Personal: Reflexivity, Positionality, and Feminist Research." *The Professional Geographer* 45, no. 1: 80–89.

Enslin, Elizabeth Mary. 1994. "Beyond Writing: Feminist Practice and the Limitations of Ethnography." *Cultural Anthropology* 9, no. 4: 537–568.

———. 1990. "The Dynamics of Gender, Class, and Caste in a Women's Movement in Rural Nepal." Ph.D. dissertation, Stanford University.

Epstein Jayaratne, Toby. 1983. "The Value of Quantitative Methodology for Feminist Research." In *Theories of Women's Studies,* edited by Gloria Bowles and Renate Duelli Klein, 140–161. London: Routledge.

Epstein Jayaratne, Toby, and Abigail Stewart. 1990. "Quantitative and Qualitative Methods in the Social Sciences: Current Feminist Issues and Practical Struggles." In *Beyond Methodology: Feminist Scholarship as Lived Research,* edited by Mary Margaret Fonow and Judith Cook, 85–106. Bloomington: Indiana University Press.

Etter-Lewis, Gwendolyn. 1991. "Black Women's Life Stories: Reclaiming Self in Narrative Texts." In *Women's Words: The Feminist Practice of Oral History,* edited by Sherna Berger Gluck and Daphne Patai, 43–58. New York: Routledge.

Eyles, John. 1993. "Feminist and Interpretive Method: How Different?" *The Canadian Geographer* 37, no. 1: 50–52.

Fardon, Richard. 1990. "Localizing Strategies: The Regionalization of Ethnographic Accounts." In *Localizing Strategies: Regional Traditions of Ethnographic Writing,* edited by Richard Fardon, 1–36. Edinburgh: Scottish Academic Press.

Farrell, Susan A. 1992. "Feminism and Sociology. Introduction: The Search for a Feminist/Womanist Methodology in Sociology." In *Revolutions in Knowledge: Feminism in the Social Sciences,* edited by Sue Rosenberg Zalk and Janice Gordon-Kelter, 57–62. Boulder: Westview.

Fawzi El-Solh, Camillia. 1988. "Gender, Class, and Origin: Aspects of Role During Fieldwork in Arab Society." In *Arab Women in the Field: Studying Your Own Society,* edited by Soraya Altorki and Camillia Fawzi El-Solh, 91–114. Syracuse: Syracuse University Press.

Finch, Janet. 1984. "It's Great to Have Someone to Talk To: The Ethics and Politics of Interviewing Women." In *Social Researching: Politics, Problems, Practice,* edited by Helen Roberts and Colin Bell, 70–87. London: Routledge and Kegan Paul.

Fonow, Mary Margaret, and Judith A. Cook. 1991. "Back to the Future: A Look at the Second Wave of Feminist Epistemology and Methodology." In *Beyond Methodology: Feminist Scholarship as Lived Research,* edited by Mary Margaret Fonow and Judith Cook, 1–15. Bloomington: Indiana University Press.

Forster, Peter. 1973. "Empiricism and Imperialism: A Review of the New Left Critique of Social Anthropology." In *Anthropology and the Colonial Encounter,* edited by Talal Asad, 23–38. London: Ithaca Press.

Frankenberg, Ruth. 1993. *White Women, Race Matters: The Social Construction of Whiteness.* Minneapolis: University of Minnesota Press.

Geiger, Susan. 1990. "What's So Feminist About Women's Oral History?" *Journal of Women's History* 2, no. 1: 169–182.

———. 1986. "Women's Life Histories: Method and Content." *Signs* 11, no. 2: 334–351.

Gewertz, Deborah, and Frederick Errington. 1991. "We Think, Therefore They Are? On Occidentalizing the World." *Anthropological Quarterly* 64, no. 2: 80–91.

Giovannini, Maureen. 1986. "Female Anthropologist and Male Informant: Gender Conflict in a Sicilian Town." In *Self, Sex, and Gender in Cross-Cultural Fieldwork,* edited by Tony Larry Whitehead and Mary Ellen Conaway, 103–116. Urbana: University of Illinois Press.

Gluck, Sherna. 1977. "What's So Special About Women? Women's Oral History." *Frontiers* 2, no. 2: 3–17.

Golde, Peggy. 1970. *Women in the Field: Anthropological Experiences.* Berkeley: University of California Press.

Gordon, Deborah. 1988. "Writing Culture, Writing Feminism: The Poetics and Politics of Experimental Ethnography." *Inscriptions* 3, no. 4: 7–24.

Gorelick, Sherry. 1991. "Contradictions of Feminist Methodology." *Gender and Society* 5, no. 4: 459–477.

Gottlieb, Naomi, and Marti Bombyk. 1987. "Strategies for Strengthening Feminist Research." *Affilia* 2, no. 2: 23–35.

Gupta, Khadija Ansari. 1979. "Travails of a Woman Fieldworker: A Small Town in Uttar Pradesh." In *The Fieldworker and the Field: Problems and Challenges in Sociological Investigation,* edited by M. N. Srinivas, A. M. Shah, and E. A. Ramaswamy, 103–114. Delhi: Oxford University Press.

Hale, Charles R. 1992. "Enduring Contradictions: Activist Research and Indian Politics in Latin America." Paper presented at the annual meeting of American Anthropological Association, San Francisco.

Hale, Sondra. 1991. "Feminist Method, Process, and Self Criticism: Interviewing Sudanese Women." In *Women's Words,* edited by Sherna Berger Gluck and Daphne Patai, 121–136. New York: Routledge.

Haraway, Donna. 1991. *Simians, Cyborgs, and Women: The Reinvention of Nature.* New York: Routledge.

Harding, Sandra. 1993. "Rethinking Standpoint Epistemology: What Is 'Strong Objectivity?'" In *Feminist Epistemologies,* edited by Linda Alcoff and Elizabeth Potter, 49–82. New York: Routledge.

———. 1991. *Whose Science? Whose Knowledge? Thinking from Women's Lives.* Ithaca: Cornell University Press.

———. 1987b. "Introduction: Is There a Feminist Method?" In *Feminism and Methodology,* edited by Sandra Harding, 1–14. Bloomington: Indiana University Press.

Harding, Sandra, ed. 1987a. *Feminism and Methodology.* Bloomington: Indiana University Press.

Hartsock, Nancy. 1987. "The Feminist Standpoint: Developing the Ground for a Specifically Feminist Historical Materialism." In *Feminism and Methodology,* edited by Sandra Harding, 157–180. Bloomington: University of Indiana Press.

Hastrup, Kirsten, and Peter Elsass. 1990. "Anthropological Advocacy: A Contradiction in Terms?" *Current Anthropology* 31, no. 3: 301–311.

Hekman, Susan J. 1990. *Gender and Knowledge: Elements of a Post-Modern Feminism.* Boston: Northeastern University Press.

Hendry, Joy. 1992. "The Paradox of Friendship in the Field." In *Anthropology and Autobiography,* edited by Judith Okely and Helen Callaway, 163–174. London: Routledge.

Higginbotham, Elizabeth. 1982. "Two Representative Issues in Contemporary Sociological Work on Black Women." In *All the Women Are White, All the Blacks Are Men, but Some of Us Are Brave,* edited by Gloria Hull, Patricia Bell Scott, and Barbara Smith, 93–98. Old Westbury: Feminist Press.

Huizer, Gerrit. 1979. "Anthropology and Politics: From Naivete Toward Liberation?" In *The Politics of Anthropology: From Colonialism and Sexism Toward a View from Below,* edited by Gerrit Huizer and Bruce Mannheim, 3–41. The Hague: Mouton.

Hutheesing, Otome K. 1993. "Facework of a Female Elder in a Lisu Field, Thailand." In *Gendered Fields: Women, Men, and Ethnography,* edited by Diane Bell, Pat Caplan, and Wazir Jahan Karim, 93–102. London: Routledge.

Jackson, Jean E. 1990. " 'I Am a Fieldnote': Fieldnotes as a Symbol of Professional Identity." In *Fieldnotes: The Makings of Anthropology,* edited by Roger Sanjek, 3–33. Ithaca: Cornell University Press.

James, Wendy. 1973. "The Anthropologist as Reluctant Imperialist." In *Anthropology and the Colonial Encounter,* edited by Talal Asad, 41–69. London: Ithaca Press.

Johnson-Odim, Cheryl. 1991. "Common Themes, Different Contexts: Third World Women and Feminism." In *Third World Women and the Politics of Feminism,* edited by Chandra Talpade Mohanty, Ann Russo, and Lourdes Torres, 314–327. Bloomington: Indiana University Press.

Joseph, Suad. 1988. "Feminism, Familism, Self, and Politics: Research as a Mughtaribi." In *Arab Women in the Field: Studying Your Own Society,* edited by Soraya Altorki and Camillia Fawzi El-Solh, 25–47. Syracuse: Syracuse University Press.

Karim, Wazir Jahan. 1993a. "Epilogue: The 'Nativised' Self and the 'Native.'" In *Gendered Fields: Women, Men, and Ethnography,* edited by Diane Bell, Pat Caplan, and Wazir Jahan Karim, 248–251. London: Routledge.

———. 1993b. "With Moyang Melur in Carey Island: More Endangered, More Engendered." In *Gendered Fields: Women, Men, and Ethnography,* edited by Diane Bell, Pat Caplan, and Wazir Jahan Karim, 78–92. London: Routledge.

Kielstra, Nico. 1979. "Is Useful Action Research Possible?" In *The Politics of Anthropology: From Colonialism and Sexism Toward a View from Below,* edited by Gerrit Huizer and Bruce Mannheim, 281–290. The Hague: Mouton.

Kleiner, Robert J., and Barnabas I. Okeke. 1991. "Advances in Field Theory: New Approaches and Methods in Cross-Cultural Research." *Journal of Cross-Cultural Psychology* 22, no. 4: 509–524.

Kleinman, Sherryl, and Martha A. Copp. 1993. *Emotions and Fieldwork.* Qualitative Research Methods Series, No. 28. Beverly Hills, Calif.: Sage Publications.

Kondo, Dorinne K. 1986. "Dissolution and Reconstitution of Self: Implications for Anthropological Epistemology." *Cultural Anthropology* 1, no. 1: 74–88.

Koonz, Claudia. 1987. *Mothers in the Fatherland.* New York: St. Martin's Press.

Kremer, Belinda. 1991. "Learning to Say No: Keeping Feminist Research for Ourselves." *Women's Studies International Forum* 13, no. 5: 463–467.

Krieger, Laurie. 1986. "Negotiating Gender Role Expectations in Cairo." In *Self, Sex, and Gender in Cross-Cultural Fieldwork,* edited by Tony Larry Whitehead and Mary Ellen Conaway, 117–128. Urbana: University of Illinois Press.

Krieger, Susan. 1985. "Beyond 'Subjectivity': The Use of the Self in Social Science." *Qualitative Sociology* 8, no. 4: 309–320.

Kumar, Nita. 1992. *Friends, Brothers, and Informants: Fieldwork Memoirs of Banaras.* Berkeley: University of California Press.

Ladner, Joyce. 1987. "Introduction to Tomorrow's Tomorrow: The Black Woman." In *Feminism and Methodology,* edited by Sandra Harding, 74–83. Bloomington: Indiana University Press.

Langellier, Kristin, and Deanna Hall. 1989. "Interviewing Women: A Phenomenological Approach to Feminist Communication Research." In *Doing Research on Women's Communication: Perspectives on Theory and Method,* edited by Kathryn Caiter and Carole Spitzack, 193–220. Norwood, N.J.: Ablex Publishing Corporation.

Lather, Patti. 1988. "Feminist Perspectives on Empowering Research Methodologies." *Women's Studies International Forum* 11, no. 6: 569–581.

Lauretis, Teresa de. 1988. "Displacing Hegemonic Discourses: Reflections on Feminist Theory in the 1980's." *Inscriptions* 3, no. 4: 127–144.

Lazreg, Marnia. 1988. "Feminism and Difference: The Perils of Writing as a Woman on Women in Algeria." *Feminist Studies* 14, no. 1: 81–107.

Lockwood, Matthew. 1993. "Facts or Fictions? Fieldwork Relationships and the Nature of Data." In *Fieldwork in Developing Countries,* edited by Stephen Devereux and John Hoddinott, 164–178. Boulder: Lynne Rienner.

LOVA-Nieuwsbrief. 1991. Special Issue on "Veldwerk en Liefde." (Fieldwork and Love) Vol. 12, No. 2. Newsletter from Landelijk Overleg Vrouwenstudies in de Antropologie, Amsterdam.

Lugones, Maria, and Elizabeth Spelman. 1983. "Have We Got a Theory for You! Feminist Theory, Cultural Imperialism, and the Demand for 'The Woman's Voice.'" *Women's Studies International Forum* 6, no. 6: 573–581.

Maguire, Pat. 1987. "Doing Participatory Research: Feminist Approach." *Perspectives* 5, no. 3: 35–37.

Mamak, Alexander F. 1979. "Nationalism, Race-Class Consciousness, and Action Research on Bougainville Island, Papua New Guinea." In *The Politics of Anthropology: From Colonialism and Sexism Toward a View from Below,* edited by Gerrit Huizer and Bruce Mannheim, 447–460. The Hague: Mouton.

Mani, Lata. 1990. "Multiple Mediations: Feminist Scholarship in the Age of Multinational Reception." *Feminist Review* 35: 24–41.

Martin, Biddy, and Chandra Talpade Mohanty. 1986. "Feminist Politics: What's Home Got to Do with It?" In *Feminist Studies, Critical Studies,* edited by Teresa de Lauretis, 191–212. Bloomington: Indiana University Press.

Mascia-Lees, E. Frances, Patricia Sharpe, and Colleen Ballerino Cohen. 1989. "The Postmodernist Turn in Anthropology: Cautions from a Feminist Perspective." *Signs* 15, no. 11: 7–33.

Mbilinyi, Marjorie. 1989. "'I'd Have Been a Man': Politics and the Labor Process in Producing Personal Narratives." In *Interpreting Women's Lives: Feminist Theory and*

Personal Narratives, edited by Personal Narratives Group, 204–227. Bloomington: Indiana University Press.

———. 1982. "My Experience as a Woman, Activist, and Researcher in a Project with Peasant Women." In *Fighting on Two Fronts: Women's Struggles and Research,* edited by Maria Mies, 30–45. The Hague: Institute of Social Studies.

McDowell, Linda. 1992. "Multiple Voices: Speaking from Inside and Outside 'The Project.'" *Antipode* 24, no. 1: 56–72.

Mies, Maria. 1990. "Women's Research or Feminist Research? The Debate Surrounding Feminist Science and Methodology." In *Beyond Methodology: Feminist Scholarship as Lived Research,* edited by Mary Margaret Fonow and Judith Cook, 60–84. Bloomington: Indiana University Press.

———. 1983. "Towards a Methodology for Feminist Research." In *Theories of Women's Studies,* edited by Gloria Bowles and Renate Duelli Klein, 117–139. London: Routledge.

———. 1982a. *The Lace Makers of Narsapur.* London: Zed Press.

———, ed. 1982b. *Fighting on Two Fronts: Women's Struggles and Research.* The Hague: Institute of Social Studies.

Mohanty, Chandra Talpade. 1991a. "Cartographies of Struggle: Third World Women and the Politics of Feminism." In *Third World Women and the Politics of Feminism,* edited by Chandra Talpade Mohanty, Ann Russo, and Lourdes Torres, 1–47. Bloomington: Indiana University Press.

———. 1991b. "Under Western Eyes: Feminist Scholarship and Colonial Discourses." In *Third World Women and the Politics of Feminism,* edited by Chandra Talpade Mohanty, Ann Russo, and Lourdes Torres, 51–80. Bloomington: Indiana University Press.

———. 1987. "Feminism Encounters Locating the Politics of Experience." *Copyright* 1: 30–44.

Moore, Henrietta. 1988. *Feminism and Anthropology.* Minneapolis: University of Minnesota Press.

———. 1994. *A Passion for Difference.* Bloomington: Indiana University Press.

Moore, Lisa. 1993. "Among Khmer and Vietnamese Refugee Women in Thailand: No Safe Place." In *Gendered Fields: Women, Men, and Ethnography,* edited by Diane Bell, Pat Caplan, and Wazir Jahan Karim, 117–127. London: Routledge.

Morsy, Soheir. 1988. "Fieldwork in My Egyptian Homeland: Toward the Demise of Anthropology's Distinctive-Other Hegemonic Tradition." In *Arab Women in the Field: Studying Your Own Society,* edited by Soraya Altorki and Camillia Fawzi El-Solh, 69–90. Syracuse: Syracuse University Press.

Moss, Pamela. 1993. "Focus: Feminism as Method." *The Canadian Geographer* 37, no. 1: 48–49.

Myerhoff, Barbara. 1978. *Number Our Days.* New York: Dutton.

Nader, Laura. 1972. "Up the Anthropologist—Perspectives Gained from Studying Up." In *Reinventing Anthropology,* edited by Dell Hymes, 284–311. New York: Pantheon.

Nakhleh, Khalil. 1979. "On Being a Native Anthropologist." In *The Politics of Anthropology: From Colonialism and Sexism Toward a View from Below,* edited by Gerrit Huizer and Bruce Mannheim, 343–352. The Hague: Mouton.

Naples, Nancy, and Beth Ribet, compilers. 1994. "Ethical, Moral, and Political Dilemmas of Feminist Research." Proceedings of a workshop sponsored by the section on Sex and Gender, American Sociological Association. University of Southern California. Unpublished.

Narayan, Kirin. 1993. "How Native is a 'Native' Anthropologist?" *American Anthropology* 95: 671–686.

Narayan, Uma. 1989. "The Project of Feminist Epistemology: Perspectives from a Nonwestern Feminist." In *Gender/Body/Knowledge: Feminist Reconstructions of Being and Knowing,* edited by Alison M. Jaggar and Susan R. Bordo, 256–269. New Brunswick, N.J.: Rutgers University Press.

Nielsen, Joyce McCarl. 1990. "Introduction." In *Feminist Research Methods: Exemplary Readings in the Social Sciences,* edited by Joyce McCarl Nielsen, 1–37. Boulder: Westview.

Oakley, Ann. 1990. "Interviewing Women: A Contradiction in Terms." In *Doing Feminist Research,* edited by Helen Roberts, 30–61. London: Routledge.

Obbo, Christine. 1990. "Adventures with Fieldnotes." In *Fieldnotes,* edited by Roger Sanjek, 290–302. Ithaca: Cornell University Press.

Oboler, Regina Smith. 1986. "For Better or Worse: Anthropologists and Husbands in the Field." In *Self, Sex, and Gender in Cross-Cultural Fieldwork,* edited by Tony Larry Whitehead and Mary Ellen Conaway, 28–51. Urbana: University of Illinois Press.

Omvedt, Gail. 1979. "On the Participant Study of Women's Movements: Methodological, Definitional, and Action Considerations." In *The Politics of Anthropology: From Colonialism and Sexism Toward a View from Below,* edited by Gerrit Huizer and Bruce Mannheim, 372–394. The Hague: Mouton.

Ong, Aihwa. 1995 (forthcoming). "Women Out of China: Traveling Tales and Traveling Theories in Postcolonial Feminism." In *Women Writing Culture,* edited by Ruth Behar and Deborah Gordon. Berkeley: University of California Press.

———. 1988. "Colonialism and Modernity: Feminist Re-Presentations of Women in Non-Western Societies." *Inscriptions* 3, no. 4: 79–93.

Opie, Anne. 1992. "Qualitative Research, Appropriation of the 'Other,' and Empowerment." *Feminist Review* 40: 52–67.

Ottenberg, Simon. 1990. "Thirty Years of Fieldnotes: Changing Relationships to the Text." In *Fieldnotes,* edited by Roger Sanjek, 139–160. Ithaca: Cornell University Press.

Papanek, Hanna. 1964. "The Woman Fieldworker in a Purdah Society." *Human Organization* 23: 160–163.

Parpart, Jane L. 1993. "Who is the 'Other'? A Postmodern Feminist Critique of Women and Development Theory and Practice." *Development and Change* 24: 439–464.

Patai, Daphne. 1994. "Sick and Tired of Scholars' Nouveau Solipsism." *Chronicle of Higher Education* 40, no. 25: A52.

———. 1991. "U.S. Academics and Third World Women: Is Ethical Research Possible?" In *Women's Words: The Feminist Practice of Oral History,* edited by Sherna Berger Gluck and Daphne Patai, 137–153. New York: Routledge.

———. 1988a. *Brazilian Women Speak.* New Brunswick: Rutgers University Press.

———. 1988b. "Who's Calling Whom 'Subaltern'?" *Women and Language* 11, no. 2: 23–26.

———. 1983. "Beyond Defensiveness: Feminist Research Strategies." *Women's Studies International Forum* 6, no. 2: 177–189.

Personal Narratives Group. 1989. *Interpreting Women's Lives: Feminist Theory and Personal Narratives.* Bloomington: Indiana University Press.

Pettigrew, Joyce. 1990. "Reminiscences of Fieldwork Among the Sikhs." In *Doing Feminist Research,* edited by Helen Roberts, 62–82. London: Routledge.

Picchi, Debra. 1989. "Yare's Anger: Conformity and Rage in the Field." *Anthropology and Humanism Quarterly* 14, no. 2: 65–72.

Rabinow, Paul. 1986. "Representations Are Social Facts: Modernity and Post-Modernity in Anthropology." In *Writing Culture: The Poetics and Politics of Ethnography,* edited by James Clifford and George E. Marcus, 234–261. Berkeley: University of California Press.

———. 1977. *Reflections on Fieldwork in Morocco.* Berkeley and Los Angeles: University of California Press.

Randall, Margaret. 1988. "Power Politics and Gender Awareness: Some Notes on Oral History with Women in Latin America." *Women and Language* 11, no. 2: 30–34.

Rao, Vijay Rukmini. 1982. "My Experience as a Researcher and Activist." In *Fighting on Two Fronts: Women's Struggles and Research,* edited by Maria Mies, 28–29. The Hague: Institute of Social Studies.

Rapp, Rayna. 1992. "Anthropology: Feminist Methodologies for the Science of Man?" In *Revolutions in Knowledge: Feminism in the Social Sciences,* edited by Sue Rosenberg Zalk and Janice Gordon-Kelter, 79–90. Boulder: Westview.

Razavi, Shahrashoub. 1993. "Fieldwork in a Familiar Setting: The Role of Politics at the National, Community and Household Levels." In *Fieldwork in Developing Countries,* edited by Stephen Devereux and John Hoddinott, 152–163. Boulder: Lynne Rienner.

Reinharz, Shulamit. 1992. *Feminist Methods in Social Research.* New York: Oxford University Press.

———. 1983. "Experiential Analysis: A Contribution to Feminist Research." In *Theories of Women's Studies,* edited by Gloria Bowles and Renate Duelli Klein, 162–191. London: Routledge.

Ribbens, Jane. 1989. "Interviewing—an 'Unnatural Situation'?" *Women's Studies International Forum* 12, no. 6: 579–592.

Roberts, Helen. 1990. *Doing Feminist Research.* London: Routledge.

Robertson, Claire. 1983. "In Pursuit of Life Histories: The Problem of Bias." *Frontiers* 7, no. 2: 63–69.

Rofel, Lisa. 1993. "Where Feminism Lies: Field Encounters in China." *Frontiers: A Journal of Women Studies* 8, 3: 33–52.

Rohrlich-Leavitt, Ruby, Barbara Sykes, and Elizabeth Weatherford. 1979. "Aboriginal Woman: Male and Female Anthropological Perspectives." In *The Politics of Anthropology: From Colonialism and Sexism Toward a View from Below,* edited by Gerrit Huizer and Bruce Mannheim, 117–129. The Hague: Mouton.

Rollins, Judith. 1985. *Between Women: Domestics and Their Employers.* Philadelphia: Temple University Press.

Rose, Damaris. 1993. "On Feminism, Method and Methods in Human Geography: An Idiosyncratic Overview." *The Canadian Geographer* 37, no. 1: 57–60.

Roth, Paul A. 1989. "Ethnography Without Tears." *Current Anthropology* 30, no. 5: 555–569.

Rutledge Shields, Vickie, and Brenda Dervin. 1993. "Sense-Making in Feminist Social Science Research: A Call to Enlarge the Methodological Options of Feminist Studies." *Women's Studies International Forum* 16, no. 1: 65–81.

Sandoval, Chela. 1991. "U.S. Third World Feminism: The Theory and Method of Oppositional Consciousness in the Postmodern World." *Genders* 10: 253–276.

Schenk-Sandbergen, L. C. 1992. "Gender in Field Research: Experiences in India." Occasional Paper, IDPAD, The Netherlands.

Scheper-Hughes, Nancy. 1992. *Death Without Weeping: The Violence of Everyday Life in Brazil.* Berkeley: University of California Press.

———. 1983. "The Problem of Bias in Androcentric and Feminist Anthropology." *Women's Studies* 10: 109–116.

Scheuneman, Janice Dowd. 1986. "The Female Perspective on Methodology and Statistics." *Educational Researcher* 15: 22–23.

Scholte, Bob. 1972. "Toward a Reflexive and Critical Anthropology." In *Reinventing Anthropology,* edited by Dell Hymes, 430–457. New York: Pantheon.

Schrijvers, Joke. 1993. "Motherhood Experienced and Conceptualised: Changing Images in Sri Lanka and the Netherlands." In *Gendered Fields: Women, Men, and Ethnography,* edited by Diane Bell, Pat Caplan, and Wazir Jahan Karim, 143–158. London: Routledge.

———. 1986. *Mothers for Life: Motherhood and Marginalization in the North Central Province of Sri Lanka.* Eburon Delft: Offset Kanters Alblasserdam.

———. 1979. "Viricentrism and Anthropology." In *The Politics of Anthropology: From Colonialism and Sexism Toward a View from Below,* edited by Gerrit Huizer and Bruce Mannheim, 97–115. The Hague: Mouton.

Scott, Ellen, and Bindi Shah. 1993. "Future Projects/Future Theorizing in Feminist Field Research Methods: Commentary on Panel Discussion." *Frontiers: A Journal of Women Studies* 8, no. 3: 90–103.

Seshaiah, S. 1979. "Selecting a 'Representative' Village: A Village in Japan." In *The Fieldworker and the Field: Problems and Challenges in Sociological Investigation,* edited by M. N. Srinivas, A. M. Shah, and E. A. Ramaswamy, 213–245. Delhi: Oxford University Press.

Shaffir, William, and Robert Stebbins, eds. 1991. *Experiencing Fieldwork: An Inside View of Qualitative Research.* Beverly Hills, Calif.: Sage.

Shostak, Marjorie. 1989. "'What the Wind Won't Take Away': The Genesis of Nisa—The Life and Words of a !Kung Woman." In *Interpreting Women's Lives: Feminist Theory and Personal Narratives,* edited by Personal Narratives Group, 228–240. Bloomington: Indiana University Press.

———. 1981. *Nisa: The Life and Words of a !Kung Woman.* Cambridge: Harvard University Press.

Smith, Dorothy E. 1987. *The Everyday World as Problematic: A Feminist Sociology.* Boston: Northeastern University Press.

———. 1974. "Women's Perspective as a Radical Critique of Sociology." *Sociological Inquiry* 44, no. 1: 7–13.

Smith, Sidonie, and Julia Watson, eds. 1992. *De/Colonizing the Subject: The Politics of Gender in Women's Autobiography.* Minneapolis: University of Minnesota Press.

Sommer, Doria. 1988. "'Not Just a Personal Story': Women's *Testimonios* and the Plural Self." In *Life/Lines: Theorizing Women's Autobiography,* edited by Bella Brodzki and Celeste Schenck, 107–130. Ithaca: Cornell University Press.

Spalter-Roth, Roberta, and Heidi Hartman. 1995 (forthcoming). "Small Happinesses: The Feminist Struggle to Integrate Social Research with Social Activism." In *Feminism and Social Change: Bridging Theory and Practice,* edited by Heidi Gottfried. Urbana: University of Illinois Press.

Spivak, Gayatri C. 1988. "Can the Subaltern Speak?" In *Marxism and the Interpretation of Culture,* edited by C. Nelson and L. Grossberg, 271–313. Urbana: University of Illinois Press.

Sprague, Joey, and Mary K. Zimmerman. 1993. "Overcoming Dualisms: A Feminist Agenda for Sociological Methodology." In *Theory on Gender/Feminism on Theory,* edited by Paula England, 255–289. New York: Aldine De Gruyter.

———. 1989. "Quality and Quantity: Reconstructing Feminist Methodology." *American Sociologist* 20: 71–86.

Srinivas, M. N. 1979. "The Fieldworker and the Field: A Village in Karnataka." In *The Fieldworker and the Field: Problems and Challenges in Sociological Investigation,* edited by M. N. Srinivas, A. M. Shah, and E. A. Ramaswamy, 19–28. Delhi: Oxford University Press.

Srinivas, M. N., A. M. Shah, and E. A. Ramaswamy. 1979. *The Fieldworker and the Field: Problems and Challenges in Sociological Investigation.* Delhi: Oxford University Press.

Stacey, Judith. 1994. "Imagining Feminist Ethnography: A Response to Elizabeth Wheatley." *Women's Studies International Forum* 17, no. 4: 417–419.

———. 1991. "Can There be a Feminist Ethnography?" In *Women's Words: The Feminist Practice of Oral History,* edited by S. B. Gluck and D. Patai, 111–119. New York: Routledge, Chapman and Hall.

———. 1990. *Brave New Families: Stories of Domestic Upheaval in Late Twentieth Century America.* New York: Basic Books.

Stanley, Liz, and Sue Wise. 1990. "Method, Methodology, and Epistemology in Feminist Research Processes." In *Feminist Praxis: Research, Theory, and Epistemology in Feminist Sociology,* edited by Liz Stanley, 20–60. London and New York: Routledge.

———. 1983a. "'Back into the Personal' or: Our Attempt to Construct 'Feminist Research.'" In *Theories of Women's Studies,* edited by Gloria Bowles and Renate Duelli Klein, 192–209. London: Routledge.

———. 1983b. *Breaking Out: Feminist Consciousness and Feminist Research.* London: Routledge.

———. 1979. "Feminist Research, Feminist Consciousness, and Experiences of Sexism." *Women's Studies International Quarterly* 2: 359–374.

Stoler, Ann Laura. 1991. "Carnal Knowledge and Imperial Power: Gender, Race, and Morality in Colonial Asia." In *Gender at the Crossroads of Knowledge: Feminist Anthropology in the Postmodern Era,* edited by Micaela di Leonardo, 51–55. Berkeley: University of California Press.

Strathern, Marilyn. 1987. "An Awkward Relationship: The Case of Feminism and Anthropology." *Signs* 12, no. 2: 276–291.

Swedenburg, Ted. 1989. "Occupational Hazards: Palestine Ethnography." *Cultural Anthropology* 4, no. 3: 265–272.

Tedlock, Barbara. 1991. "From Participant Observation to the Observation of Participation: The Emergence of Narrative Ethnography." *Journal of Anthropological Research* 47, no. 1: 69–94.

Tixier y Vigil, Yvonne, and Nan Elsasser. 1976. "The Effects of the Ethnicity of the Interviewer on Conversation: A Study of Chicana Women." In *Sociology of the Language of American Women,* edited by Betty L. DuBois and Isabel Crouch, 161–169. San Antonio, Tex.: Trinity University Press.

Townsend Gilkes, Cheryl. 1992. "A Case Study: Race-Ethnicity, Class, and African American Women: Exploring the Community Connection." In *Revolutions in Knowledge: Feminism in the Social Sciences,* edited by Sue Rosenberg Zalk and Janice Gordon-Kelter, 63–78. Boulder: Westview.

Trinh, T. Minh-Ha. 1989. *Woman, Native, Other.* Bloomington: Indiana University Press.

———. 1986. "Difference: 'A Special Third World Women Issue.'" *Discourse: Journal for Theoretical Studies in Media and Culture* 8: 11–37.

Tsing, Anna Lowenhaupt. 1993. *In the Realm of the Diamond Queen: Marginality in an Out-of-the-Way Place.* Princeton: Princeton University Press.

Tuana, Nancy. 1993. "With Many Voices: Feminism and Theoretical Pluralism." In *Theory on Gender/Feminism on Theory,* edited by Paula England, 281–299. New York: Aldine De Gruyter.

Tyler, Stephen. 1986. "Post-Modern Ethnography: From Document of the Occult to Occult Document." In *Writing Culture: The Poetics and Politics of Ethnography,* edited by James Clifford and George E. Marcus, 122–140. Berkeley: University of California Press.

Udayagiri, Mridula. 1995. "Challenging Modernization: Gender and Development, Postmodern Feminism and Activism." In *Feminism/Postmodernism/Development,* edited by Marianne Marchand and Jane Parpart, 159–178. London: Routledge.

Visweswaran, Kamala. 1994. *Fictions of Feminist Ethnography.* Minneapolis: University of Minnesota Press.

———. 1988. "Defining Feminist Ethnography." *Inscriptions* 3, no. 4: 27–41.

Wade, Peter. 1993. "Sexuality and Masculinity in Fieldwork Among Colombian Blacks." In *Gendered Fields: Women, Men, and Ethnography,* edited by Diane Bell, Pat Caplan, and Wazir Jahan Karim, 199–214. London: Routledge.

Warren, Carol A.B. 1988. *Gender Issues in Field Research.* Qualitative Research Methods Series 9. Beverly Hills, Calif.: Sage.

Warren, Carol A.B., and Paul K. Rasmussen. 1977. "Sex and Gender in Field Research," *Urban Life* 6, no. 3: 349–369.

Watson, Graham. 1987. "Make Me Reflexive—But Not Yet: Strategies for Managing Essential Reflexivity in Ethnographic Discourse." *Journal of Anthropological Research* 43, no. 1: 29–41.

Watson, Julia, and Sidonie Smith. 1992. "De/Colonialization and the Politics of Discourse in Women's Autobiographical Practices." In *De/Colonizing the Subject: The Politics of Gender in Women's Autobiography,* edited by Sidonie Smith and Julia Watson, xiii–xxxi. Minneapolis: University of Minnesota Press.

Wax, Rosalie H. 1986. "Gender and Age in Fieldwork and Fieldwork Education: 'Not Any Good Thing Is Done by One Man Alone.'" In *Self, Sex, and Gender in Cross-Cultural Fieldwork,* edited by Tony Larry Whitehead and Mary Ellen Conaway, 129–150. Urbana: University of Illinois Press.

Westcott, Marcia. 1979. "Feminist Criticism of the Social Sciences." *Harvard Educational Review* 49, no. 4: 422–430.

Wheatley, Elizabeth. 1994. "How Can We Engender Ethnography with a Feminist Imagination? A Response to Judith Stacey." *Women's Studies International Forum* 17, no. 4: 403–417.

Whitehead, Tony Larry, and Mary Ellen Conaway. 1986. "Introduction." In *Self, Sex, and Gender in Cross-Cultural Fieldwork,* 1–14. Urbana: University of Illinois Press.

Williams, Anne. 1990. "Reading Feminism into Fieldnotes." In *Feminist Praxis: Research, Theory, and Epistemology in Feminist Sociology,* edited by Liz Stanley, 253–261. London and New York: Routledge.

Williams, Brackette. 1995. "The Public I/Eye: Homeless Me Working You: A Homework Report." *Current Anthropology* 3, no. 1: 25–51.

Wilson, Ken. 1993. "Thinking about the Ethics of Fieldwork." In *Fieldwork in Developing Countries,* edited by Stephen Devereux and John Hoddinott, 179–199. Boulder: Lynne Rienner.

Wolf, Margery. 1992. *A Thrice Told Tale: Feminism, Postmodernism, and Ethnographic Responsibility.* Stanford: Stanford University Press.

———. 1990. "Chinanotes: Engendering Anthropology." In *Fieldnotes,* edited by Roger Sanjek, 343–355. Ithaca: Cornell University Press.

———. 1985. *Revolution Postponed: Women in Contemporary China.* Stanford: Stanford University Press.

———. 1968. *The House of Lim: The Study of a Chinese Farm Family.* Englewood Cliffs, N.J.: Prentice-Hall, Inc.

Yang, Jeff. 1994. "Coming into the Country: Asian American Writing's Wider World." *VLS—Voice Literary Supplement* 122: 23.

Zavella, Patricia. 1991. "Mujeres in Factories: Race and Class Perspectives on Women, Work, and Family." In *Gender at the Crossroads of Knowledge: Feminist Anthropology in the Postmodern Era,* edited by Micaela di Leonardo, 312–336. Berkeley: University of California Press.

2

Understanding the Gender System in Rural Turkey: Fieldwork Dilemmas of Conformity and Intervention

GÜNSELI BERIK

CONTEMPORARY APPRAISALS of feminist ethnographic methods have raised questions about the ethics of feminists' research on women less powerful than themselves (Patai, 1991; Stacey, 1991) and drawn attention to the associated fieldwork dilemmas (Wolf, 1993; Scott and Shah, 1993). Many argue that the nationality, class, race, and ethnicity differences between researcher and researched cannot be erased by research methods that attempt to generate intimacy and a sense of commonality of interests as women. Furthermore, given the power asymmetries, an ethical field relationship is argued to be impossible for feminist researchers to attain (Patai, 1991). In light of my own field experiences with women carpet weavers in rural Turkey, I would like to take issue with these claims and their pessimistic implications for fieldwork methodology.

For the benefit of future feminist field research, the more relevant issue is to explore the circumstances under which feminist researchers may approximate, if not attain, egalitarian and ethical field relations. I argue that the gender system in which one carries out fieldwork could play an important role in mitigating, even offsetting, the power asymmetries inherent in other differences between the researcher and the researched. In my case, since I was from the same national and ethnic background as the carpet weavers I studied, my urban, middle-class background and my residence in the United States were the major distinctions that would have defined an asymmetric field relationship for me.[1] Yet my conformity to gender norms in rural Turkey transformed me into a cultural insider and paved the way for nonhierarchical field relations with women. In an environment where kinship, specifically its inherent age and gender hierarchies, structured virtually all aspects of social life, I assumed a range of subordinate kinship identities on account of being a woman. Thus, gender became the primary factor shaping my field relations, to the point where class difference became insignificant.

Although being as much of an insider as possible helped me approximate egalitarian field relations, it also gave rise to my fundamental difficulties: I could not shape my fieldwork in a feminist manner, and I helped to perpetuate hierarchical gender structures. One dilemma centered around negotiating my identity in the field. In order to ensure the viability of my research project, I adhered to rules of conduct appropriate for rural women; I acquiesced to the assignment of subordinate identities to me and thereby represented myself as different from who I was. The second dilemma centered around the possibility of my assistance in empowering rural women. My doubts about the feasibility and efficacy of possible interventions resulted in my inability to intervene to improve the lives and working conditions of women. Here I recount my experiences surrounding these two dilemmas, which I call the "conformity" and "intervention" dilemmas, respectively.

This task is an uncommonly difficult one. First, I write as an outsider to the debates over feminist research methods and the problematic interview methodology. As someone who believes that information useful for feminists can be generated through fieldwork, however, I am not a disinterested outsider. As an economist, I was neither trained in fieldwork methods nor encouraged to use them. In my Ph.D. dissertation research I used them through hands-on practice and common sense. Economics as a discipline views fieldwork as an essentially worthless undertaking. In cross-sectional research such as mine, economists tend to work with large data sets, usually national census or survey data drawn from representative samples, rarely questioning the quality of the data they use. They regard the quality of fieldwork data and the economists who collect and use them with suspicion. They consider fieldwork extradisciplinary; methodological as well as conceptual trespassing into other disciplines (notably sociology and anthropology) generally devalues an economist's research.[2] Reading the contemporary critiques of feminist field research methods, therefore, I am troubled that not only economists but also feminist writers call into question the value of fieldwork.

My second difficulty is that I am scrutinizing the field research process for the first time, ten years after I completed the fieldwork. Since my discipline places no value on fieldwork or on self-reflection in its evaluation, neither in 1983 nor since have I recorded or even reflected very much on my field experiences. Certain dilemmas that I faced and decisions that I made are etched in my mind, however, and I will recount these here.

First, I introduce my research and my expectations as I embarked on the fieldwork and describe the difficulties that shaped my dilemmas concerning conformity and intervention. Second, I recount fieldwork experiences surrounding these dilemmas and tell how I approximated egalitarian field relations. In the conclusion, I comment on the issue of unequal exchange between researcher and researched.

Entering the Field: The Project

In my research I examined the factors that shaped women's productivity and earnings and the factors that shaped women's decisionmaking power in the household, including the changes in women's status and power with their participation in paid work.[3] I was therefore interested in understanding both the gender system in rural Turkey and the interactions among family form, agrarian structure, and weaving production form in determining the level of women's earnings.

My research methodology combined participant observation with open-ended and structured interviews of women weavers in villages in several different provinces in the western, central, and southern parts of the country. I ended up with ten case study villages and 133 structured interviews with weavers in ten months of fieldwork.

I embarked on my research without any formal training in field methods but with some experience in rural Turkey.[4] I approached the research with a feminist sense of purpose. For me this meant a twofold task: understanding and transforming the gender hierarchy. When I started my fieldwork, however, I did not have any illusions about the contribution of my research to the "transformative" project. As one of the few studies of rural women, and the first of its kind on women carpet weavers, its primary contribution had to be producing basic data on rural women's lives and working conditions. Secondarily, and only in the medium-to-long term, I hoped that my research would be useful in the formulation of public policy in improving the working and living conditions of women.

Therefore, my primary concern was obtaining data rather than doing activist research. In the research design stage of my research, my contacts at the International Labour Office (ILO) in Geneva, which funded the research, proposed that I pursue an action-oriented (participatory) research strategy that would involve weavers in researching their own situation, consciousness raising, and organizing. Evidently they were interested in producing tangible change through the research process. I was sympathetic, but I declined their request. The reason was not that I deemed consciousness raising paternalistic and therefore unethical (Patai, 1991) but that I did not think that this research method would be either feasible for a lone researcher to undertake or effective in achieving its goals. My dilemma was that if I were to engage in a more interventionist method, given patriarchal and political constraints, I would seriously risk not being able to complete the research. Therefore, any benefit to women would be limited by the short life of the project. Moreover, I did not think that it was feasible for a single researcher to complete the research with the proposed modifications within the agreed-upon time frame. As I recount below, my experiences confirmed to me that my decision was the right one.

Entering the Field: The Difficulties

As in any other field research, the basic challenge for me was being accepted by my hosts and the community. Yet there was a particular set of difficulties in this process for me stemming from the political context of research in the early 1980s, the constraints of the economics discipline on fieldwork methodology, and the fact that I was a woman researcher in rural Turkey.

The Political Milieu

The early 1980s was a particularly difficult period for fieldwork in Turkey. In the environment of the martial law that followed the 1980 military coup, the population was frequently subjected to questioning. On a number of bus trips to villages, I underwent identity checks at military roadblocks set up to apprehend "terrorists" and marriage certificate checks on the few occasions when I stayed with my husband in hotels on the way to a village.

In Turkey, rural inhabitants' contact with strangers and outsiders is limited to contact with the agricultural extension officer, the military police, the land registration officer, the primary school teacher, and perhaps the midwife or doctor. Generally suspicious of outsiders, rural people became even more sensitive about their relations with outsiders in the aftermath of the military coup. Although my introduction to a village was always through a local contact, it was not uncommon for some to suspect that I was either a member of the secret police or a tax officer trying to determine the taxable income base of carpet weaving. The latter identity was plausible because I was seeking detailed income data.

Under martial law, I needed permission from the regional martial law commander in order to embark on research, which in my case meant four separate petitions. Moreover, judging from the experience of other academics, neither the permission nor a response to the petition were guaranteed. I embarked on my research without such authorization. I only had an official letter from the Ministry of Education certifying my identity as a doctoral candidate in economics in a U.S. university. When the authenticity of my identity was questioned, I handed the letter over to my hosts to allay their fears. I was never sure, however, that some zealous local military commander or someone who wanted to use the newly affirmed power of the military would not create trouble for my research. In this environment, then, in order to conduct research, I had to counteract being assigned the identities of terrorist, disreputable woman, tax collector, or member of the secret police.

Research Design and Method

My attempt to reconcile the demands of economics with my conception of sensible fieldwork presented greater difficulties than I had imagined. I was after detailed, quantifiable data on a number of sensitive topics (such as components of annual household income and gender arrangements with respect to control over income), which was time-consuming to collect. Raising questions about some of these issues could be offensive to men and even to some women, because my questions were interpreted as contesting the gender system.

My task became more difficult when, after the pilot case studies in two villages, I decided against using the most efficient research instrument for collecting quantifiable data—the questionnaire—and opted for a more open manner. The questionnaire format imparted an official, halting feeling to an otherwise pleasant visit. Moreover, on the few occasions when men were present and inspected the questionnaire form, my questions about household income made them worry about my motivation. Thinking that my questions concerned taxes, they gave me inaccurate information.

Instead I relied on a casual conversation format in the context of a social visit where the subjects we talked about were loosely structured around carpet weaving. I used my notebook sparingly during interviews. In breaks during the interview or later in the day, I wrote down what I remembered of its contents to use in filling out the questionnaire. This approach resulted in a considerable amount of missing information, which the systematic study that I planned required. Thus, I had to visit several of the weaving households more than once, and some villages three times. This "inefficiency" in data collection was the price of getting more accurate information and having more congenial relations with the people whose lives I was trying to understand.

A second difficulty stemmed from my disciplinary concern for getting variation in my sample so as to make generalizable statements possible (albeit tentative or conditional ones). I wanted to see if the regional variations in gender arrangements and the extent of gender inequalities could be explained by variations in household forms and production structures in weaving and agriculture. Thus, my research design was more extensive in scope (in terms of the number of village case studies) than conventional anthropological research. This meant that there were communication difficulties stemming from regional peculiarities, including adjusting to local dialects and variations in units of measurement and terms related to weaving and other economic activities. In each village I had to go through the process of acceptance by the community and adjustment. And I did not have the time to win over the hearts and minds of the community that a researcher who planned to carry out in-depth fieldwork in a single locality had.

Negotiating the Gender System in Rural Turkey

As a woman doing fieldwork, I had to contend with the gender system, as have many other researchers in sex-segregated societies (Altorki and El-Solh, 1988). As a Turkish woman, I felt bound by the rules of conduct that guide the behavior of rural women. Pressures to blend in culturally and become as inconspicuous as possible determined my mode of communication and conduct. At issue was not only my respectability and safety as I moved about in rural Turkey, mostly in the women's world, but also my ability to reach women and interview them.

Conforming to Gender Norms in Rural Turkey

The strategy that helped to dispel suspicions about my identity, remove the obstacles to acceptance, and virtually guarantee the viability of my project was my conformity to a mixture of rural and urban gender norms. Only in retrospect could I identify the rules I followed as a strategy, however. They emerged spontaneously as rules of conduct during my first pilot study, and they were as much my choice as the community's way of negotiating my presence and movement.

Conformity to gender norms acceptable to the rural community meant, first, adherence to the rules of behavior that guide rural women. My movement was subtly restricted. On visits to weavers, for example, I would not take the route through the main street or the square where the coffeehouses were located—even if that was the shortest route—but the back alleys. I was deferential to older men and women. When greeting elders, for example, I would kiss their hand, whereas in the city a simple handshake would be acceptable. For me, adherence to these rules was not a major concession. I was conscious of them but not uncomfortable with them.

The source of my main field dilemma was the second aspect of conformity: my acquiescence to the extension and elaboration of both actual kinship relations and kinship idioms in the rural communities. I was acutely aware and uncomfortable that I was assigned, and accepted, a range of subordinate kinship identities on account of being a woman: I was accompanied by either my father or husband to the villages, thereby emphasizing my identities as a daughter and a wife. In many villages I would be addressed by men as "sister" or "uncle's wife," which transformed me into a fictive kinswoman. These are widely used idioms among peasants and working-class people in Turkey that function to extend the incest taboo to unrelated men and women. In general, I acquiesced to a subordinate role vis-à-vis men in the villages. Whether I was treated as an adult depended on the presence of my father or my husband: When they were around we would be in the company of adults, certainly the head of the household and usually also his wife. Otherwise I spent more time with young (unmarried) women.

My missing attribute as a married woman was that I was childless, and that was remarked upon frequently. In rural Turkey, being childless is probably the worst predicament that could befall a woman (or a couple), and there is intense social pressure on couples to have a child right after marriage. After finding out how many years we had been married (two years at the time), men and women would offer their sympathy and consolation. It was difficult for them to comprehend and believe that this was by choice. At my age of twenty-nine the choice was clearly anomalous. Whether by choice or not, however, childlessness was an attribute that disempowered me relative to married women with children.

Conforming to rural gender norms did not mean that I had to completely transform my urban identity. In none of the villages did I adapt my clothing to the local dress. I did not cover my hair, which conformed with the community's expectations of an educated, urban woman. On the other hand, I did not wear trousers, short skirts, or short-sleeved shirts either, which I would have done in the city. The fact that I did not wear lipstick or nail polish was commented upon approvingly on more than one occasion.

In the Company of Kinsmen

In rural Turkey, it is not socially acceptable for young women to travel on their own without being accompanied by an older woman or a male relative. As I embarked on my research, there was very little discussion in my family as to how I would establish myself in each case study village. Culturally, we knew that it would be difficult to establish my respectability and ensure my safety unless I was introduced or accompanied by a male relative at least on initial visits.[5] I felt comfortable that my father or husband would come along with me.

My husband, a Turkish graduate student in the United States, accompanied me on my initial field trips. My father did so after my husband returned to the United States, seven months into my fieldwork. In two instances, he left after becoming acquainted with my hosts for a few hours. On my visit to another village he stayed with me.

In six villages my husband was present for the entire duration of the initial visit (one to three weeks). He became a de facto cofieldworker. He would interview the men, usually in the coffeehouses, which I would not venture into. He incessantly absorbed essential information on topics about which men were more knowledgeable, thereby balancing my access to knowledge of men's and women's worlds. His perceived role and mine differed, however, depending on the gender system in the rural community: In the majority of the case study villages, where spatial segregation by gender was not acute and patriarchal restrictions were mild, the rural community accepted me as the researcher. My husband was perceived as either assisting me or asking questions out of idle curiosity while he waited for me.

In three case study villages, where there was a greater degree of segregation of men's and women's activities and lives and there were greater restrictions on women's physical mobility, however, no introduction would convince anyone that we were in the village to carry out *my* research. It was simply unthinkable that my husband would accompany me for my work (even though my traveling alone would have been equally unthinkable). Thus, my husband was assigned the identity of *the* fieldworker. We went along with this switch in identity when we realized that research was possible only under these assumptions. My husband's presence gave men "control" over the researcher, and the mundane nature of his questions perhaps allayed their fears as well. In reality, he became a "decoy" fieldworker, deflecting the men's attention while I interviewed the women. His presence gave me respectability while at the same time disempowering me as an urban woman and placing me firmly in the familiar subordinate category of wife. Had my husband not been present, I would have had difficulty in reaching the women in these villages: I would have been under suspicion, first, as an unaccompanied young woman, whose morals and association with village women would be suspect,[6] and second, as someone who was interested only in talking to women and whose inquiries could not be fully monitored by men.

In these villages such an identity shift and division of labor was forced upon us within a few hours after our arrival, and segregation was enforced for the duration of our stay (except in sleeping hours). For example, upon our arrival in a Konya village, the introduction and initial discussion in the office of the carpet cooperative made the four men present visibly uncomfortable. It was clear that my presence was unwanted in that small office. From their point of view, it must have been very difficult to justify my presence in an enclosed male space. Every time I tried to ask a question or engage in the conversation, the person I was trying to address would look away. The eye contact problem, in turn, made me self-conscious and extremely uncomfortable. In this setting the usual transformation of a young nonkin woman into a fictive kinswoman was not happening. Soon I was chaperoned into and left alone in a female space, the carpet workshop. Thus, our modus operandi in this village had been clearly defined. Except at meals in our host's house, when only the host and his wife and children were present, I was moved into a room with the women, and my husband remained with the men.

My adherence to rules of conduct that prescribed kinsmen-mediated field relations posed a personal dilemma. The company of my father or my husband was invaluable for my project. Yet their presence emphasized my identities as daughter and wife. Although these happened to be valued credentials for the rural community, I had no control over the subordinate meanings evoked by these identities in the rural community. It disturbed me that these meanings were often completely contrary to the nature of my actual (egalitarian) relations with both my father and my husband.

The fact that I was not engaged in concealment or deception about my identities helped to resolve this dilemma somewhat. It was also clear to me that my identity in the field was as much the outcome of the community's preferences as of my efforts. Above all, however, my justification for the subordinate identities I assumed in fieldwork was that this was the only way I could gain acceptance and achieve my objective of understanding the lives and working conditions of the weavers. This is a dilemma confronting women doing fieldwork in rural Turkey. I do not believe that an approach that challenged the sensibilities and norms of the community chosen for fieldwork would work in rural Turkey (or anywhere else, for that matter).

Class and Gender in the Field

Besides virtually guaranteeing the viability of my project, my conformity to gender norms in rural Turkey helped perpetuate the hierarchical gender structures and reduced the class difference between me and my research subjects. My identities as daughter, wife, and childless woman and adherence to standards of propriety for women in rural areas disempowered me vis-à-vis men and leveled my standing with the women. It is very likely that initially men were conscious and suspicious of the multiple privileged identities and power I represented as an urban, educated woman—through the example I set and the ideas I could communicate to women. The more I was transformed into an insider via my conformity with gender norms, however, the less of a threat I became to men. My position was not in any way superior to that of the women; at no time did I feel more powerful than or superior to the women, much less the men, in the villages.

Other variables besides conformity may also have contributed to the leveling of my status relative to women. The fact that I did not act superior to or look down upon the rural people, my being Turkish rather than a foreigner, a student rather than a faculty member, all helped reduce the social distance between me and the weavers.

Greater gender segregation also created a dynamic that reduced the significance of the class difference. In villages with greater patriarchal constraints, it was easier to interview weavers and there was greater potential for intimate conversations. Men would not come barging in on an interview, as they did in less segregated places, thereby affecting the natural flow of conversation among women and making a subsequent visit necessary. Moreover, segregation created a sense of mutuality of shared womanhood between myself and the women. The first evening in one of these villages, when our host's wife asked whether I would like to eat with my husband, and therefore with the men, or with the women, without any hesitation I said I preferred to be with the women. (Normally guests would eat with her husband, but she was not sure how to serve properly when the guest was a woman.) I instantly felt that my choice took away one barrier between me and these women. That night and later, when I was in the company of the same group of women, I felt that I became one of them and a part of their life, and that I acquired my knowledge of them in a context in which they could also ask questions about me. Despite my urban, educated background, our predicament as women was the same: We were confined to the same room. Our conversation was relaxed, informal, and uninhibited, and what we discussed ranged from children and my background to aspects of their lives (illnesses, daily routine in weaving workshops and at home).

To be sure, I was privileged in some basic ways: I (rather than a rural woman) was the one undertaking the research, I had greater access to a world beyond the village, and I was free to pack up and leave for my privileged world at any time. But these were not indicators of privilege that were central or even relevant to the research relationship. My class background was insignificant in shaping my field relations with weavers.[7] My gender, age, marital status, and conduct were much more central to their judgment of me. If I failed to meet their expectations of proper conduct, the women and men whom I visited could at any time frustrate my efforts to carry out my research. If that happened, my ability to leave would have represented defeat, not power.

As a result of this dynamic, I felt that frequently I was able to achieve genuinely close, nonhierarchical relations with women, in spite of the brief nature of my visits in villages by the standards of conventional anthropological research. The women I interviewed were curious about me, but few seemed impressed or intimidated by my background.

I do not think my fieldwork experience was unique. I believe that the primacy of gender and the insignificance of class in structuring field relations may be a more general outcome of conducting fieldwork within the gender system prevailing in rural Turkey and many other parts of the Middle East. Judging by the similarities between my research experience and that of Abu-Lughod (1986), I suspect that this gender system and its variants would similarly shape the field experiences of researchers with personal attributes similar to mine. Moreover, it may be worthwhile to explore whether conformity to the local gender norms helps researchers approximate egalitarian field relations with women in other parts of the world as well.

The Cost of Nonconformity

Had I not conformed to the gender norms acceptable to the rural community, I would most likely not have been able to interview the women, would not have had congenial relations with them, and would have ended up with inaccurate information about their lives. Worse still, I could have brought violence upon those women who associated with me. I was reminded that my semiconscious conformity and delicate negotiations with gender norms in rural Turkey were imperative by what turned out to be one of the most painful experiences in my fieldwork.

I was visiting a village in Nigde. Several months earlier, I had spent an afternoon there, accompanied by my husband, by the somewhat reluctant invitation of a local carpet dealer. This time I was alone. I went back to get a better feel for the gender arrangements in the village, which were in striking contrast to the conditions prevailing in the case study village nearby and elsewhere. In this village, for example, there was a bride price, a very low marriage age for women (thirteen to fourteen years), an unusually high fertility rate, and a strong son preference.

Although the women remembered and welcomed me, my connections had become obscured over the intervening months. I was a stranger in that my association with a man was not immediately identifiable. I was instantly aware of my vulnerability as a lone woman researcher trying to move about the women's world without the approval and mediation of men. What is more, I later realized that one of the women who welcomed me was in danger herself because of her association with me.

She was a thirty-year-old mother of three, whose husband worked as a petty street trader in urban areas for a major part of the year. She supported herself and her children by weaving carpets for the local dealer on a putting-out basis. At that time her husband was in the village. During my visit he came home, visibly angered that his wife was associating with a stranger (albeit a woman) whose visit had not been cleared by him. My visit was clearly a transgression into his territory. As an urban, educated woman I probably also represented a potential threat to his grip over his wife.

Trying to keep calm, I continued asking my questions in his presence. I was probing into his wife's physical mobility, her control over her weaving income, and other gender norms in the village. These questions enraged him even more. When I asked whether she did her shopping in the weekly market in a nearby town, especially in view of the fact that her husband was away for most of the year, her husband replied that she did not need to, because peddlers brought fruit, vegetables, and clothing to the village. He added, "If I hear that she has gone to the market in my absence, I will come back and break her legs." Even in villages where wife beating was common, it was beyond the bounds of propriety for a man to threaten to beat his wife in front of a woman stranger. The message was clear: I had no doubt that he would beat his wife, not only if she were to go to the market but also as soon as I left.

I tried to shift the conversation to topics that seemed to me to be more innocuous. Yet the air of hostility was too heavy for me to continue much longer. As I left, I realized that through the unmediated (by a man) and unapproved (by a man) way in which I had tried to establish contact with the women in this village, I had most likely become instrumental in the violence to be inflicted upon this woman. I had been careless about sufficiently transforming myself to an insider by conforming to gender norms. This was an infraction of rules that was not going to go unpunished. In the name of contributing to knowledge about gender hierarchies, I had most likely brought violence upon this woman. And I was powerless to prevent it from happening.

I never found out what happened to her. Shortly after I left her house, I left the village, and within a week I was back in the United States. Although this was an extreme example in its tone of hostility, there were other instances when I was subtly reminded that my research was at the mercy of men who might not grant their approval for their wives or daughters to associate with me. In order to do research I had to pass the invisible but very real male barrier. Men's tacit approval (I had to at least symbolically request their permission) was necessary for relating with women. My observance of appropriate gender norms was therefore of utmost importance.

To Intervene or Not to Intervene

The second dilemma I faced during fieldwork involved the divide between academia and activism, or the project of understanding and the project of transforming the living and working conditions of women. Concurrent with my decision not to pursue a participatory (action-oriented) research methodology, in the field I did not take up the opportunity to transcend the distinction between activism and research either. In the only instance when weavers asked me to intervene regarding their working conditions, after I determined that my intervention would be in vain, I decided not to intervene.

The Konya case study was by far my most intense field experience. It was shocking and emotionally draining to witness the objectification of women as a source of wealth in this village. The idiom governing kinship relations in the village challenged my middle-class notions of family relations: these *were* exchange relations. As an example of what caused my virtual culture shock in these villages, I can mention the fact that fathers referred to newborn girls as "factories," indicating their future earning status as weavers.[8] I was also disturbed by what I viewed as religious exploitation: the daily readings of the Koran under the supervision of an elderly woman who was contracted by the workshop owner. The prayers were in Arabic (but written in the Latin alphabet), which meant that weavers did not understand a word. The intention of the workshop owners was to blend work with religion to create a holy atmosphere for young women in order to appease their parents. Even a few weavers mentioned it as a positive attribute of the working conditions. I felt pity, outrage, nausea, and helplessness. Yet I had to be reserved, silent, and nonjudgmental in order to grasp how the women coped under these social arrangements.

The operation of workshops here, as elsewhere, was illegal. The workshop owners did not register the weavers with the Social Insurance Institute, and most likely the workshops were not even registered as business establishments. In one workshop several weavers asked me to file an official complaint on their behalf or to publicize the operation of the workshops. I was perceived both as a rare messenger out of the environment of confinement and as a privileged person who could be credible and powerful enough to do something about their complaints. Their grievances stemmed from their weariness of having to weave day in, day out, from dawn to dusk, and ranged from the lack of social insurance registration of the workers to seeking ways to make carpet weaving illegal. Clearly, these weavers perceived themselves as powerless to change their situation. As was typical in rural Turkish society, they wanted the change to be effected in a top-down way by the state.

Among the weavers' grievances, the lack of social insurance coverage was the only tangible plea upon which I could act. Such an intervention would have been personally gratifying and would have posed no risk for my project (provided I notified authorities after I completed the fieldwork). After much frustration and soul-searching, however, I did not file a complaint with the Social Insurance Institute. Although the bureaucracy overseeing the social insurance system was within my reach, I knew that my intervention was unlikely to result in any benefits for the weavers. The situation was more complicated than a matter of ensuring the employer's compliance with the law. The future income security of these weavers could not be ensured without changes on the legal and social front as well as enforcement. Specifically, unless the social structure within which kinsmen controlled and benefited from women's labor were changed, the law would remain unenforceable.

Although this course of action made sense, it did not put my conscience at ease. I felt that I had betrayed the weavers, despite the fact that I hadn't promised to act upon their complaints. These young women must have been disappointed. It was also ironic that although I was concerned about the well-being of these women, and in a village where I felt the great urgency of the plea to intervene, when presented with a request that was seemingly easy to fulfill, I chose not to intervene. Even though I did not expect to have an immediate and direct impact on weavers' working conditions when I embarked on my resarch, it was frustrating not to be able to respond to these pleas.

My research illustrates the constraints on the ability of a lone feminist researcher to bring about change. It also revealed the strong economic incentives for maintaining the gender hierarchies around which carpet weaving was structured. There existed a trade-off between increasing weaving income and improving the weavers' lives and working conditions. Weavers generated a considerable portion of the income that raised household wealth. Given the very labor-intensive production process, higher incomes from weaving were achieved at the expense of the well-being of weavers, who bore a heavy workload and were deprived of schooling. There was no guarantee that the weavers would either have a say in how those earnings were spent or receive any benefit from the earnings they generated. By demonstrating these trade-offs, my research provided a cautionary note against expectations of easy solutions and provided insights that could help activists and policymakers design policy and create forms of organization that could lead to change. This transformative project, in turn, requires organized and collaborative efforts that involve the participation of activists, researchers as well as the women being researched.

Conclusion

Recent evaluations of feminist field methods identify an inherently hierarchical relationship as the only possibility for feminist researchers who come to the field with a host of privileged attributes. There is scant recognition of the leveling effect that the researcher's gender may have in defining her field relations as she adapts to the rules of conduct appropriate for women in the research community. Sharing the same nationality with the research subjects may be the necessary condition for reducing the class hierarchy in field relations through conformity.

My experience is that my privileged background as a university-educated, urban, middle-class Turkish woman who lived in the United States created a hierarchical relation with the women weavers only in the abstract. In practice, the research dynamic in the midst of rural Turkish society removed the power implications of my privileged identity. As I negotiated my identity in the field, my gender became the primary factor shaping my field relations, and its leveling effect was not offset by my other attributes. In fact, the effect was reinforced by my student status and my egalitarian manner. As a result, I was for the most part able to establish what I thought were genuinely close relations with women. As a feminist researcher, I had the basic fieldwork dilemma that my actions helped reproduce the hierarchical gender structures in rural communities—through my conformity with rural gender norms and my decision not to engage in a more interventionist research methodology and process.

As for the nature of my exchange with the weavers, my field experience seems to support Patai's (1991) contention that the exchange between researcher and researched is always an asymmetric one. In a tangible and objective way, the research changed my life and not theirs: I completed my Ph.D. dissertation and subsequently got a job on the basis of my degree.[9] Although I kept in touch with several weavers in the first few years after my return to the United States, I did not keep the contacts up. Because I lived in the United States, there was no possibility of more contact through reciprocal visits either.

Although I adopted a noninterventionist stance, to the extent that I could help, I tried to be responsive to the weavers' requests for advice and information—albeit there were not many of these: questions on how to deal with bureaucracies (e.g., a couple's request for information on adoption procedures), requests for advice on birth control. But I do not view these or the token gifts I brought to my hosts or the photographs I sent back as payment to even out an exchange.

In fact, I do not think it is accurate to characterize my field relationship as either an "exchange" or an "unethical" one. I am not convinced that comparing the returns to the researcher with those to the researched is the appropriate standard for an ethical research relationship. Moreover, as a standard that is impossible to meet, its usefulness for feminist research is questionable. With this standard, feminists may as well forget about conducting fieldwork altogether. If, instead, one were to adopt comparison of expectations with actual returns as the yardstick, then many field relations might be characterized as ethical. Such a standard might be not only more practical and less paralyzing for future feminist fieldwork but also more appropriate.

In my case, I do not know what each weaver expected to gain by talking to me. Of course no weaver expected to get a Ph.D. degree and a job in the United States as a result—the returns that would have made the field relationship, strictly speaking, equal. Nor do I think that the women I interviewed expected any individual benefits of the kind I would have wished for them, for example improvements in their position within the household. Perhaps the weavers got more out of their association with me than I thought they did; perhaps my photographs of them or their children were an invaluable return for the basically mundane information about their lives that they gave me in the few hours they spent with me.

Critical appraisal of field research processes and self-reflection are important tasks for feminist researchers. Yet our quest for better, if not ideal, research approaches should not lead us to overlook the constraints and very difficult circumstances that shape most feminist fieldwork. Looking back, given the constraints I described, I do not think that I could have shaped my field relations in any other way, short of not conducting the research at all. The choice for me was either fieldwork with the dilemmas I have recounted or no fieldwork. My primary responsibility was to complete the research in the most ethical way possible and to produce economic data on gender hierarchies. And that I accomplished.

NOTES

I dedicate this chapter to the memory of my father, Münir Berik, who passed away while I was completing it. I thank Cihan Bilginsoy for sharing and recalling many of the experiences recounted in this chapter and Diane Wolf for the opportunity to write about my field experiences and for many useful comments and discussions.

1. When I was growing up, the urban middle class in Turkey consisted of salaried employees and professionals, most of whom worked for the government and enjoyed a modest lifestyle—such as living in a two-bedroom apartment, hiring the services of a cleaning woman once every week or two, and owning a few consumer durables but usually not an automobile.

2. See Bardhan (1989) on some of the issues concerning research methods utilized by economists and anthropologists.

3. See Berik (1986, 1987) for a summary of research findings and policy conclusions.

4. As a high school student, I had participated as an assistant in an archaeological excavation in Central Anatolia, with frequent contacts in the nearby village. During graduate school I also worked one summer as an interviewer in a village near Ankara for a university-sponsored research project on rural transformation.

5. See Abu-Lughod (1986) for a description of the meaning and consequences of being introduced to the research community by a male relative.

6. In one of these villages, the weavers reported that their fathers and husbands were always suspicious of their contact with urban women (teachers or nurse-midwives) for fear that they would "open up the eyes" of the young women.

7. It might have been more relevant if I had been situated in a well-defined hierarchical relation to the weavers such that I could wield power over them (such as, the daughter or wife of the landlord talking to the tenant, from whom the tenants could expect favors and benefits and toward whom they could harbor fears or reverence).

8. Other examples are the following: Whereas age at marriage in rural Turkey is somewhere between seventeen and twenty-one, here I encountered women who at twenty-five

or twenty-seven had just married, because until then their fathers had not arranged their marriages on account of the weaving income their daughters provided. All the young married women I interviewed were, in their words, "paying off the debt" that their fathers-in-law had incurred for their wedding. I encountered three sisters who had financed seven pilgrimage trips of their father to Mecca (when only one is a religious requirement, and only for those who can afford it). All three had very poor eyesight (wore thick glasses) due to years of continuous weaving. I encountered a young woman whose husband bought an automobile with his wife's weaving earnings and who, at the time of my visit, was on vacation on the coast with his male friends. See Berik (1989) for a detailed account of the operation of the workshops and their interlocking dynamic with the gender system in these villages.

9. Albeit, looking at the unequal exchange question from the perspective of the researcher, one may not find unequivocal or easy rewards. At least in my discipline, the career returns of fieldwork do not compensate for the hardships and anxieties entailed.

REFERENCES

Abu-Lughod, Lila. 1986. *Veiled Sentiments: Honor and Poetry in a Bedouin Society.* Berkeley: University of California Press.

Altorki, Soraya, and Camillia Fawzi El-Solh, eds. 1988. *Arab Women in the Field: Studying Your Own Society.* Syracuse, N.Y.: Syracuse University Press.

Bardhan, Pranab, ed. 1989. *Conversations Between Economists and Anthropologists: Methodological Issues in Measuring Economic Change in Rural India.* New Delhi and Oxford: Oxford University Press.

Berik, Günseli. 1986. "Women's Employment in Handwoven Carpet Production in Rural Turkey." Ph.D. dissertation, University of Massachusetts, Amherst.

———. 1987. *Women Carpet Weavers in Rural Turkey: Patterns of Employment, Earnings, and Status.* Women, Work, and Development Series, No. 15. Geneva: International Labour Office.

———. 1989. "Born Factories: Women's Labor in Carpet Workshops in Rural Turkey." Women and International Development Working Paper Series, No. 177. Michigan State University, East Lansing, Mich.

Patai, Daphne. 1991. "U.S. Academics and Third World Women: Is Ethical Research Possible?" In *Women's Words: The Feminist Practice of Oral History.* Edited by Sherna Berger Gluck and Daphne Patai, 137–153. New York: Routledge.

Scott, Ellen, and Bindi Shah. 1993. "Future Projects/Future Theorizing in Feminist Field Research Methods: Commentary on Panel Discussion." *Frontiers* 13, no. 3: 90–103.

Stacey, Judith. 1991. "Can There Be a Feminist Ethnography?" In *Women's Words: The Feminist Practice of Oral History.* Edited by Sherna Berger Gluck and Daphne Patai, 111–119. New York: Routledge.

Wolf, Diane L. 1993. "Introduction: Feminist Dilemmas in Fieldwork." *Frontiers* 13, no. 3: 1–7.

3

Skinfolk, Not Kinfolk: Comparative Reflections on the Identity of Participant-Observation in Two Field Situations

BRACKETTE F. WILLIAMS

The Power to Signify the Significance of Being a Stranger

Thinking back about the process of becoming a fieldworker, a participant-observer, within and across different field experiences, raises for me a range of questions about shifting aspects of identity and their combined and differential relations to what Jan Pouwer (1973) has called the "translation of the translator" in fieldwork signification. Thinking through the place of race, class, and gender as shifting aspects of identity during fieldwork raises further questions about the meaning of these concepts for and to the participant-observer, when such concepts are themselves continually being constructed and reconstructed by those who are translating the translator.

With regard to these questions, Pouwer's early (1973) discussion of "stranger's value" and its relation to issues of identity shifts in the process of constructing a fieldworker identity is well worth revisiting. He argues that anthropologists are especially conscious of "the pervading force" of signification because "they have stranger's value." That is to say, they focus on others' forms of behavior. The stranger's value of a social anthropologist, Pouwer considers to be "most apparent and forceful with respect to non-western societies," but for the well-trained anthropologist it also enables "the study of remote or even adjacent sectors of his own society" (1973: 2). During the latter studies, the anthropologist can expect to "face again . . . the rewarding frustration which is typical of his position in an exotic society, in that he is both involved and detached at the same time" (1973: 2). At the most advanced stages of fieldwork, Pouwer contends, it is not unusual for the anthropologist to become "almost a stranger to himself" as he experiences an "almost schizophrenic" relation to a prefield identity (1973: 2).

Yet, even as the anthropologist becomes a stranger to him- or herself in his or her own society, is the stranger that he or she becomes to himself or herself the same stranger he or she is to those who translate him or her? Pouwer differentiates between the anthropologist and most members of the so-called exotic society he or she studies and distinguishes the seemingly similar process of identity shifting in exotic places from that of the identity constructions and shifts wrought by relations between the anthropologists and local translators as anthropologists seek to determine the relative utility of stranger's value in their own society. Within one's own society such translations are made more difficult by issues of who has the power to affix any specific code, when, and under what circumstances. That is to say, the anthropologist in the so-called exotic society is "involved and detached" in ways that are impossible within his or her own society, precisely because he or she is never exterior to the ongoing relations between power and signification. It is the power relations represented in acts of signification that shape how, and to what extent, an identity can be affixed but not fixed.

In these situations, there are no clearly distinct "foreigner classifications" to neatly oppose to "native/insider classifications." As I have argued elsewhere (Williams, 1995), the continuous situatings of self and informants in the available system of categorical identities and their ongoing relations to conceptions of power and privilege make it necessary for researchers engaged in knowing their home turf through participant-observation research to engage in doing their homework as part of conducting fieldwork. In doing their homework, they must continually try to figure out the power implications of who they are (or, better put, how they are being construed and by whom) in relation to what they are doing, asking, and observing. They must do their homework at the same time that they conduct fieldwork, and as they assess the merit of "information" gathered for the analysis of the specific research questions they pose. There is no time or social space in which one's prior knowledge of the social order, its categorical distinctions and associated status assessments can be set aside, pragmatically or analytically, in a manner that allows one the kind of involved detachment suggested by Pouwer's notion of stranger's value as a defining feature of the anthropological enterprise. The construction of the power to signify stranger's value requires the anthropologist to continuously calculate the *political* identities of subjects that are embedded, in varied entwined forms, in the very aspects of his or her own and the subjects' social personae as personalities and as persons occupying particular social positions. Neither the constructions of subjects by the anthropologist or by his or her informants nor the subjective powers of signification stand outside the overall field of power relations and the manner in which these configure psycho-

logical profiles and social-role constructions during any given interaction between the anthropologist and the subjects of an investigation.

This difference, and the difference it makes, is evident even as we consider
Pouwer's initial concern with the cross-cultural translation of concepts, especially
as these concepts move across the vernacular of field language into the jargon of
anthropology. These concerns are typical, and by now highly familiar, within the
discipline. Whether translating a "foreign" language into another "foreign" language or translating a "dialect" of a nationally defined "standard" language into
that standard, the question of how best to render a conceptual world is serious
and highly problematic for all research and researchers (Geertz, 1983). However,
the problem is made all the more difficult when the translators (i.e., the infor-
mants/natives) translating the anthropologist take the act of linguistic translation
or language choice to be the first step in transforming or revealing the "true" identity of the anthropologist as an identity representation within a single field of
power relations. Rather than merely translating to render a conceptual world, informants' acts of translation may deem the anthropologist to be "uppity," an "educated fool," or one who "speaks deep" in order to mask connections to previous
vernacular cultural roots. While translating the anthropologist as linguistic or
cultural translator, informants listen to what is said at the same time that they ask
(sometimes openly, sometimes silently or after the fact), who does the anthropologist think himself or herself to be when he or she does not choose to speak the
local/indigenous language—a language that some racially or ethnically defined
"we" *know* to be the anthropologist's mother tongue? The translation is muddled,
not by the translator as linguist, but by the power code that designates his or her
relation to the task of translating the anthropologist's identity features that are
not specific to his or her identity as participant-observer.

A second concern was less familiar at the time Pouwer wrote. He focused attention on the "silenced informants who haunt [the anthropologist] in his quiet moment" (1973: 3), not merely because the anthropologist has failed to make sense
in translating the informant and his world of concepts but because the failure to
do so is thought to result from the interpenetration of the anthropologist's translation with those of the informant as translator. "Natives" translating the translator have placed him or her in a category, the occupants of which are not accorded
the right to engage in certain types of translations.

Recognizing that his racial characteristics placed him within a range of different types of colonizer roles, upon arriving at a field site in West New Guinea,
Pouwer is at pains to distance himself and his identity as an anthropological fieldworker and participant-observer from those colonial identities with which he suspected he might be confused. In a now-familiar move of the anthropological enterprise's initial rapport-building phase, he decides to give a speech to introduce
himself. During this speech he selects the most pervasively present colonial identities and attempts to indicate that these are not identities with which he wants to
be associated. However, without these recognizable identities, "participant-observation" as a trade had no identity.

I must have looked like a foreign no-man, for the position of anthropologist was an unknown to them as it is to large numbers of "civilized" people. I translated my speech from Dutch into Malayan, the lingua franca of West New Guinea. In his turn the District Officer, an East-Indonesian Ambonese, translated the speech into a simpler version of Moluccan Malayan. His Mimka interpreter then proceeded to translate both translations into the Mimka language. Finally, it was up to the chiefs and their followers to render the address, considerably watered down and distorted by three translations, into their classification of foreigners. They then provided the fourth translation in succession. Small wonder their response to my presence could best be described as . . . "Let us be polite, but not commit outselves. Wait and see." (1973: 6)

Moreover, as they waited to see, the language problem, as serious as it was, was not one of simple layers of distorted linguistic translation but rather was shaped by the problem of behavioral interpenetration of the subject classifications Pouwer sought to distinguish. Pouwer's language problem ultimately did little to define what his translators were waiting to see. As he went about building rapport and conducting research on various topics, his methodology and the actions it required placed him in positions in which he acted like members of the person categories from which, as anthropologist and participant-observer, he was at pains to distinguish himself. His actions over time and across social space resulted in the construction of role identities and shifts between these identities. Nevertheless, it was also in part because these translator constructions were contained within, and shaped by, certain racial features of his personal identity as a non-Mimka colonizer that these features both fixed and overrode boundaries between any social persona in the foreigner classification. Hence, as his translating observers reasoned:

"It is quite probable that the new Red-Man (*Mìra-Mìra Wè*) that is a white man turned into a Redskin by the sun, will replace our present District Officer. . . ." The translator translated. End of First Act.

"However, there are certain inconsistencies in the behaviour of the newcomer. Just like some Roman Catholic missionaries, he seems to be deeply interested in our sacred stories and our rituals. The District Officer is not really. So the prospective District Officer could equally be a priest. But then how to account for a married priest? There are two possible answers: either he is a married ex-priest, or he is a priest turned into a Protestant exactly because he wished to marry. . . ." The translator translated. End of Second Act.

"But whosoever he is, he always carries with him a pencil and sheets of paper. . . . He is Tuan Torati, that is, Mr. Paper, Mr. Letter. . . . His letters, although dangerous, can [be] beneficial . . . to safeguard the ownership and content of our traditional lore. . . ." The translator translated. End of Final Act. The fieldworker impersonates a solicitor, a glorified clerk. (1973: 7)

Thus, linguistic translation difficulties notwithstanding, the more problematic issue is both the absence and presence of a fixable identity relation between the anthropologist as stranger of value and the range of impersonations (stranger's-value enactments of other social personae) he *might* be taken for in order to render him most valuable or least dangerous. Note, however, that whereas the first two translations are selections from foreigner categories, the third translation, "Letter-Man," is a product of translator/anthropologist interactions and of the potential sociopolitical value to be wrung from those interactions. In the shifts from one foreigner category to another, it is his lack of sociopolitical fixity and its relations to his pattern of social interactions with the informants who translate the translator that ultimately shape shifting translations. By contrast, it is the potential use to which these translators might put the slippage between foreigner practicing the craft of stranger's value and valued stranger that defines the final act and creates within it a social persona that is neither foreign nor native but both.[1] Although Pouwer's translation of Letter-Man as "glorified clerk" places him firmly within foreigner classification, in fact, Letter-Man is a new category for culturally incorporated identity—a stranger of intracultural value.

Culturally incorporated identities such as honorary kin, blood brother, and Letter-Man that are end points of a rapport-building process contrast with identities that form the boundary conditions within which translators' translations begin. For example, Drexel Woodson, an African American anthropologist conducting fieldwork in northern Haiti, experienced a process of identity incorporation through the creation of a new cultural category consistent with local views of desired power relations between himself as participant-observer and the priestess and deities translating him. As a person of African descent, mongrelized blood quality notwithstanding, he was classified by local residents as *bon mounn: oun blan noua rouj ki gen brénn* (a good person: a red black foreigner with a brain). Despite this "skinfolk" connection, Woodson was unable to interview Nani, a *mambo* (i.e., a vódou priestess), about her work because both she and her husband were "strangers" to the local community. They were neither born nor raised in that locality, and although they had resided there for an extended period of time, they were concerned that their already delicate relations with other long-time residents might be further eroded by Nani's interactions with Woodson, a foreigner prying into controversial matters (see Woodson, 1990: 549–552, for a description of the couple's social position). It was only after Nani decided that because "anthropology and Vódou are kindred forms and ways of seeking knowledge, their practitioners should talk," that she allowed Woodson to interview her. During the interview her assessment of the legitimacy of anthropological practice was "seconded by several *loua,* especially Gran Boua, who considered [Woodson] a 'good person: a red black person with a brain.' . . . Boua also concluded that [he] was a reliable source of *kléren* and cigarettes." Therefore it was "useful" for Woodson "to attend ceremonies [and] write down [the *loua's*] prescriptions" (Woodson, 1990: 55).

Under these circumstances, the social persona that precedes the construction of the anthropologist as participant-observer is an ambivalent, betwixt and between, identity—neither foreigner in a totally unknown form nor native of a fully knowable type—resulting from historical linkages between "shared" race as potentially shared culture that made vague such designations as inside and outside.[2] It was, in part, this designation that Zora Neale Hurston sought to clarify with the distinction between "kinfolk" and "skinfolk," where one could imagine that all of one's skinfolk were not one's kinfolk (or lacked a good brain) and gave the skinfolk a bad name (Hurston, 1942). For better or for worse, however, in contemporary power grids, being skinfolk tends to establish boundary conditions for the construction of other social personae within which betwixt-and-between anthropologists can act and interact. It is being skinfolk that allows those in this neither-here-nor-there category to act in ways that, for better or worse, can be interpreted as good person with a brain or Miss Ann down home or an "educated fool" slumming downtown. Such constructions do not begin with subjects' action in a place but rather with the place of subjects' possible identity configurations in a national and international order of status reckoning. These positionings create a type of subject-object that must continually do the homework of self-constructing by asking: "What might the persons with whom I am interacting think me to be if I were not posing as an anthropologist?" Doing one's homework is locating, within the vectors of an answer to this question, the space left available and open to the construction of the stranger's value that is necessary to formulate and implement an identity for "participation-observer." Sometimes being Miss Ann is a "good enough" identity for this purpose, whereas at other times it just will not do.

As difficult, then, as the fixing of identity in the "exotic" world may be and as much as it shares with such a process in one's own society, at both the center and the margins of whatever is deemed the exotic and what is considered one's own, the relations between power and the ability to fix, distance, or both, aspects of one's participant-observer social persona are different insofar as the latter forces both the anthropologists and the "subjects" constantly to challenge and puzzle over where and when to draw the boundary between inside/indigenous and between outside/exotic.

This lesson Hortense Powdermaker quickly learned as she moved her anthropological research from the exotic terrain of Lesu in New Guinea to postemancipation Mississippi; from conducting fieldwork to ascertain the lifeways of an exotic people to doing her homework to understand interracial relations and processes of subordinate-group acculturation in the southern region of her "own society."[3] Like Pouwer and other anthropologists in exotic lands, in Lesu she was able to construct and manage the power of stranger's value as it was positioned and buttressed by the colonial order. The colonial order provided the context for interaction-based shifts in the relevance and prominence of her race, gender, and marital status as identity features.

In the United States, despite the fixity of her gender and racial features—blue eyes, brown hair, "white" complexion—and her middle-class status, when in the company of Negroes, Powdermaker was taken for a Negro by both Whites and Blacks. She retained that identity as she traveled from Tennessee to Mississippi in the company of an African American woman, in part because the African American woman owned and was driving the car in which they traveled. Once she was in Mississippi, the identity shifting that produced this categorical displacement of phenotypic and interactional features ceased. But as it did, Powdermaker gained from this fixity no starting position that was "outside" the social order she sought to study. She had been told by racially defined, though not locale-defined, natives who were also social science colleagues, that she could not expect to arrive in Mississippi, pitch her tent, and inform the natives that she was there to study them.

She decided instead to acquire an acceptable identity as "visiting teacher" and to enlist the support of the local establishment (read: White folk) in making contact with those who were under their jurisdiction, spatially, economically, and albeit in highly complex ways, culturally (read: Negroes as natives and anthropological subjects). In a fashion not unlike Pouwer, she also delivered an introductory speech as a first step in self-definition and rapport building.

The speech to define her social persona and to describe her fieldwork project was held at the local courthouse with the "leading citizens" in attendance. She listened as her sponsor, Mr. Green, attempted to translate her and to identify the value to be attributed to her as a stranger seeking to dwell and "work" among the citizens. In addition to selecting those features of her social background that made her appear as close to the identity "southern Belle" as possible, her sponsor also tried to convince the citizens of Sunflower County, Indianola, Mississippi, that they should be pleased that Powdermaker had selected their community over others open to her. Yet when he finished, Powdermaker reports: "the leading citizens of Indianola were completely unconvinced by Mr. Green's operation or by my few words." Instead, "They were suspicious of a Yankee and did not want their 'niggers' studied by anyone . . . the expressions on their faces, and the tone of their voices indicated both fear and hostility" (1966: 139).

Powdermaker's response was intended to reassure the good citizens that her work represented no danger to them and their position in the order of power relations. "The first question: 'Are you interested in changing the status quo?' My answer: 'I am here to study it,' which happened to be the truth" (1966: 139). Her truth was, as the leading citizens no doubt recognized, a truth the enactment of which had already altered the status quo, transforming them from her equal citizens to her secondary subjects, the controllers of Negroes in need of being studied in an "exotic" region of an otherwise nonexotic society. But insofar as there were no Negroes at the welcome table to be consulted about the desirability of being studied by a person to whom the leading citizens might give permission, it was also a truth that indeed served not only to maintain the status quo but also to assist in its reproduction. This reproductive potential notwithstanding, whether it was to Georgia or Alabama that she could have gone, the leading citizens made clear their preference that she, as southern belle or Yankee meddler, could go to blazes. It was not until she used the power of an "aristocratic" acquaintance in a nearby town, who put pressure on these leading citizens, that she was able to gain entrée in the form of their permission and rudimentary cooperation to undertake the study (Powdermaker, 1966).

Unlike constraints posed by Powdermaker's overdetermined racial/gender identity, Pouwer's overdetermined colonizer/gender identity was open to the play of identity shifts into which his informants could interject their translations and eventually produce a potentially new set of identity features adequate to provide him a place in their classification based on his own pattern of interaction. Powdermaker was, as many of us are, too much a part of the system of social classifications to construct the momentary liminality necessary to create an outsider status from which she could begin building rapport as a participant-observer. As the Pouwer, Powdermaker, and Woodson examples are intended to suggest, the range of possible identity features that serve as the constraints within which the identity of the anthropologist as participant-observer is constructed produce different vectors. Those vectors also differentially pull a reddened white man, a red black foreigner, and a blackened white female across the social spaces plotted by the stranger's value of a lesser-known discipline.

Even out there "among the exotics," when these identity processes are viewed up close and personal, we can quickly recognize that there are no profiles out of which to construct *generic identities* for participant-observers or informants (key or otherwise). Who are *you* and *what* are you to *me*? These questions are, and must be, continually asked by both the anthropologist as would-be generic participant-observer about himself or herself and by informants, in their varied and shifting local social personae, about themselves. Even when the answer is, "I am first and foremost an anthropologist, and you are first and foremost an informant," such statements are accompanied, however implicitly, by other identity representations copresent in the social order of power relations.

There are times in exotic situations when the power differential between the anthropologists and the local residents allows anthropologists to interact with the local residents as if the diverse and often contradictory features of their own identity constructions could be held constant or pragmatically compartmentalized. However, as anthropologists move within and across the social spaces that constitute the full range of their "own society," all the features, in fact, remain in play. The question is what role highly varied and social-context-sensitive features of identity construction play as anthropologists act out their own dynamic relations to power and privilege. The question becomes one of how, in any given interaction, these features help to shape activities through which "data" are gathered.

Sweet Home Alabama and the Care of a Good Woman

In 1979 I traveled to a rural area in Alabama to conduct fieldwork observations among elderly African Americans—my "skinfolk" of another generation and geographic space. My assignment was part of a three-field-site project designed to provide a social and cultural context for questionnaire data focusing on the relation between formal and informal care received by persons seventy years of age and older. The project assumed that a richer understanding of how such kin-based urban and rural networks formed and operated in relation to the services provided by formal, extra-home agencies could best be acquired by anthropologically trained participant-observers capable of generating an ethnographic context for the interpretation of the quantitative questionnaire data.[4]

I selected a county in Alabama that, given the project's objectives, seemed to have a good demographic profile. Two residents of the county whom I knew from my undergraduate days agreed to assist me to find lodging and make initial contacts. With the site selected, I hopped a plane to Tuscaloosa, picked up a rental car and map at the airport, and took what seemed an endless journey down a pitch-black road cut through a pine-tree-infested Alabama countryside. Finally, I turned right at the taillight reflectors on the mailbox that marked the driveway to my friends' house and for the first time really consciously asked myself: What are you doing in the *South?*

Unlike my numerous interstate trips through southern states en route from New York to my family's home in Arizona during my undergraduate years, my many years of graduate school incarceration in Baltimore, and despite frequent family trips to, and periods of childhood residence in Texas, a solitary drive down a country road in Alabama, knowing that I would remain there for ninety days, served to culturally constitute the South as a place. It was a place that, until this project, I, on the one hand, had no desire to even visit but that, on the other hand, was the historical and anthropological center of my textbook knowledge of Blackness and its cultural construction in the United States. Yet other than being symbols of my racially defined historical and cultural past, alive and well and living in an Alabamian present, who were these particular people to me and who was I to them? How might our joint and separate efforts to answer this question influence the project in which I was involved? How might it be influenced by the place from which I came—Baltimore, by way of Arizona—one place an acceptable "heard from" locale from which Black folk could "legitimately" hail, the other a cultural netherland of the Black world? How was it influenced by my age, race, gender, class, and educational background (features of a possible social identity), and somewhere down the list, my claim to the identity anthropologist as participant-observer? In the end, it was "Whose child are you?" and "Who let you come way off down here all by yourself?" that provided the context within which other aspects of my identity were defined, valued, and sorted out across interactions and the social spaces I encountered. With few exceptions, my interactions began with or were soon framed by these questions.

Although it was certainly necessary for me to gain the cooperation of the people I wished to study and their tolerance in order to undertake the project, it was neither necessary nor possible to gain permission in any formal sense. My friend and her husband, together and independently, introduced me to various persons associated with local government, churches, formal and self-help agencies, and businesses. Each of these introductions provided opportunities for brief descriptions of the project; some of the contacts later led to opportunities to give intro-ductory speeches before small gatherings in offices, churches, fields, nightclubs, parking lots, front porches, and backyards. None of these gatherings, however, could accurately be construed as permission-granting bodies. They simply were ways of "spreading the word."

The composition of these "audiences" varied by race and class. Some were gender-specific, whereas others included both genders and several generations. Following each presentation, some of the people with whom I spoke referred to the other members of the gathering as "those people" or used this expression for the types of persons they thought I was interested in interviewing. The "those people" classification was always in opposition to a largely implicit self-definition, which placed the speaker outside the category to which he or she applied the expression. As one might expect, the act of making such speeches, and the self-presentations involved, continued throughout the field period. Often gatherings included one or more persons who had been part of previous audiences. During these gather-ings persons would replay for me earlier renditions of my effort complete with either praise or criticism, depending on whether the "assistant" thought I did better or worse the second time around. At each presentation some listeners were more interested in how I said things than in what I said. Some found "proof" in my style of speaking that I probably had kin connections, albeit untraceable, to some community member with whom the speaker believed I shared a "likeness" or with whom I shared my surname. Overall, while I made an effort to present myself as an anthropologist engaged in a particular research effort, they sought as much to place me as to understand and evaluate my project's goals. Who was I to be do-ing what I was doing, and why was I doing it to them or other members of their community?

Characteristic of this process was my first introduction after leaving my friends' home to take up residence in a boarding hotel in the county seat. To the white operator of the hotel, I was a northerner, sent down there by some social agency to meddle into the affairs of "our local black folks," who, he was quick to inform me, were quite capable of managing their own affairs without benefit of some Washington bureaucrat. This aspect of a social identity followed me and re-mained fairly constant as I introduced myself to various White officials in the for-mal agencies that were part of the project, even when these agencies were federally funded. They too wanted to know whose child I was. Was I related to some of the people in the county? And if not, why would I agree to come way off down here by myself? The fact that I had come to carry out a research project was not seen as a motivation obviously distinct from one based on kin ties. Some translators, Black and White, knew of my friends, but because they, too, were recent trans-plants to the community, this connection served as much to raise questions as to settle unstated doubts. Throughout the field period, efforts were made by many to use me as a potential source of information and insight into the behavior of these relative "strangers."

For some of my White informants, as well as for many of the African Americans I later interviewed and with whom I interacted formally and informally, it was important that I was, by their reckoning, a young woman trying to make something of herself. For them, as for the older African Americans, it was not good that I was not married and that I had no children, but it was understandable, because schooling was both necessary and "all right" in its place. Still, a "life" too long delayed, I was told, was no life at all. During the early weeks of the field period, White informants I encountered were also quick to clue me in to the personality of the local Black population: They were a friendly lot but not too quick to take to strangers asking a lot of questions. African Americans, perhaps thinking that I knew more about the ways of southern White folk than most of the time I did, characterized them as just that, White folk, and indicated that they had not changed. They warned me not to let the "New South" rap fool me.

White folk were quick, and often correct, to point out some of the misconceptions of the project's assumptions and the ways these might lead me to misconstrue the subject population I sought to locate. Young people, they pointed out, had headed up North in "droves," leaving behind many of the old people, who, as in the "old days," were taken care of by the White folks for whom they had worked or still worked. What they, along with younger African Americans still present, were less quick to point out was that the "taking care of" to which both referred included holding power of attorney over these elderly persons' land and homesteads. For the White informants, this was not the business of a busybody outsider; for the younger African Americans, it was not thought the concern of a young person. These were old ways and old folks' business.

When during my stay, the county experienced a serious flood and a local White store owner refused to make a requested donation to aid the victims, the young people who wanted to boycott the store expected that I would join their picket line because of my age. Some of the older people who ventured an opinion as to what I should do, however, ignored my age in favor of simply assuming that I would not join in. Others told me that I should not join, either because "educated people [knew better]" or because, racial identity notwithstanding, "strangers" had no place in local affairs.

The matter of my "strangerhood" was by that time complicated by the fact that I had moved from the hotel to board with an elderly informant, and so some who cautioned me against involvement feared that she might suffer a reprisal as a result of my actions. With comments like "You know, folks take ya'll for sorta kin; you look a little bit more like her than I first noticed," they marked out features and factors to which they thought I ought to attend in order to avoid the charge of, and dangers visited upon "uppity" kin.

I shared this position as potential uppity kin with other young African Americans in the community. At another point in my stay, a protest march was organized in the adjacent county after a child was seriously injured on broken school yard equipment. By then I had moved "down the country" to live in a trailer with a young teacher. Young teachers (midtwenties to early thirties) in the adjacent county, angered by the disrepair of school equipment and the failure of authorities to address the problem despite the many complaints they say had been registered, wanted to participate in the march. But most feared that they would either lose their jobs, or worse, their elderly relatives, whose property titles were "held" by Whites granted power of attorney, might be expelled from their own property. Many, I was told, had experienced such expropriation during the 1960s protests that took place in the county. During the protest march, these fears were further encouraged by the White males, mostly young men, who rode alongside the protestors in pickup trucks, their SLR cameras with telephoto lenses trained on the crowd to identify the marchers. Rumors circulated that these White photographers would turn their pictures over to their parents, who retained the authority to expel the Black elderly from their own land or to see that teachers who participated were fired. This visible sign of the protestors' vulnerability was often paired with invisible signs of guilt for those who blamed themselves for "being away at school," leaving their grandparents without benefit of the assistance that might have prevented their error.

Before and after this event and other less dramatic ones, I spent hours with participants and nonparticipants, discussing what they thought ought to be the role of a "stranger" of skinfolk affiliation in matters of this type. Although their diverse responses had to be factored into my decision, no rationale which simply chose among the possibilities they provided could serve as adequate ground for my decision. For example, my concerns in this last instance were split between past consciousness and present commitments. Among the march organizers was an old college associate who, although I had not seen him since our college protest days, I could hardly fail to support as he struggled on his home turf. In general, as was the case with the informants who translated their own and my relations to the identity factors of race, age, and education, it was in terms of stranger/kin/friend ties that we asked and gave varied answers to the questions: "Who are you and what are you to me? Whose child are you and what are you doing way down here by yourself?"

In these interactions and the discussions that followed over the definition of what kind of stranger I might be taken to be and what that meant for interpretation of my actions, the representations of skinfolk identity and the context-specific issues these raised were not gendered per se. That is to say, for those translating me as one who should or should not participate, and defining what constituted participation, the gender aspect of my identity did not surface as an autonomous variable. Instead, it was always embedded in assessments of the identity features of a student or of a person alone in a strange place. Femaleness underscored and lent urgency to the phrase "way down here by yourself" (more often stated in the exaggerated, down home and comfy, "by yo' lonesome") and what it implied for my expected conduct. Just as education mediated, but did not erase, female features of what I ought to have been doing to get on with my life without undue delay, femaleness too far from kin/community space made gender the unstated context for each asking of pertinent identity questions.

An intellectual concern with the social welfare of skinfolk could and did mediate, but could not erase this displacement. Thus, the problem of my gender meant that I learned sometimes to hear this question as "what kind of mother lets a young girl run around playing what, what did you say, anthro . . . what?" and to reply accordingly. Older women said it outright; older men shook their heads, wondering what the world was coming to, or just wanted to know how long it was going to take me to finish up my work and get back to my family. I learned to hear their concern with making a quick job of my task as "you [female child that someone must value] have no business hanging around in strange places all alone; except insofar as your education requires." I hedged my commentaries in terms of the project's value to me as a learning experience for future, degree-related fieldwork. In response to my responses of that type, the question was often rephrased by young and old alike as "Couldn't you find any other trade to take up?" Or "Does your mother (sometimes your folks) know what you are *doing?*" (sometimes, where you are?) At other times, for those with the power to offer assistance, words gave way to a call for action: "Have you found enough old folks yet? Our pastor said to send you around on Sunday, he can get you a few."

The identity of anthropologist as participant-observer could neither be constructed nor situated outside the double-edged, multifaceted question: "Who are you and what are you to me? Whose child are you and what are you doing down here by yourself?" and the response it inspired. Each response provided a construction of kinfolk that had embedded within it sociopolitical representations of skinfolks. This construction could be applied to the specific conditions of particular interactions to provide culturally sensible interpretations of my identity as a person conducting research "down home." It also set the parameters within which I had to figure out the politics of racial and other status positionings as these applied to particular persons with widely ranging agenda, none of which were especially pertinent to my fieldwork objectives.

"Speaking Deep" and Hiding Out Behind God's Back in Guyana

Given my experiences of kinfolk and skinfolk in Alabama during 1979, it was with no little amusement that later that year, while conducting fieldwork in Guyana for the second time, I read in a letter from a friend the question: "What are you doing way down there [in Guyana] behind God's back?" A women of African American descent, my friend had escaped from the Bronx, leaving behind a West Indian husband, to seek her fortune and cultural roots while attending a nursing school in Birmingham, Alabama. Her letter alternated between wondering what had possessed me to go to Guyana and conveying tales of the strange ways and doings of

Alabamans. It seems she had always heard that Black folk in the South had some strange ways, but nothing had prepared her for how oddly they could actually behave. She wondered what kind of people were in Guyana and whether they were friendly to African Americans. She had heard the "like other West Indians and Africans, they do not think very highly of *us*" (my emphasis). Upon my return to Baltimore after my first summer field experience in Guyana, a faculty member commented to me that he was sure that I was not one who had thought that because I was of African American descent, fieldwork would be easier in a country with a large African descent. I recall my friend's letter and the faculty member's remark here because her comments better characterized my sense of a non-relation to Afro-Guyanese during that first field venture than did his remark.

Despite my textbook knowledge of a shared historical connection to Africa and to slave ancestors and cultural traditions, before, during, and after my first trip to Guyana that knowledge did not constitute grounds on which to think of Afro-Guyanese as belonging to the same African American (or for that matter Black) identity to which I belonged. Certainly they were historical skinfolk and, in Pan-African negritude, politically defined "brothers and sisters," but beyond that, they were not in any sense of personal connectedness "my people," nor did I expect the historical similarities or the ideology of Pan-Africanism to be of any constructive value to me. My experience of regional, class, and color fractures as well as of urban and rural differences among "my own people" suggested to me that the presence of large numbers of Black folk would mean a multitude of internal differences around which I would have to maneuver. During my stay there, this was the one given, but also hard-won, perception we came to share.

In 1976 when I went to Guyana for the first time, I expected it to be a one-time journey. Although I had come to accept the anthropological requirement that completion of the doctorate would necessitate fieldwork outside the United States and with people other than "my own," I had planned to go to Africa, or more specifically, to Liberia, the one place in Africa where I understood there were repatriated persons of African American descent that I could study as a practice run for my return to home base.

During the first month of my three-month stay in Guyana, I lived in a boardinghouse in Georgetown, the capital city, making daily trips to the University of Guyana library to read and returning to converse with the other members of the boardinghouse population or with other persons I met in Georgetown or at the university. I spent my time there primarily listening to and trying to learn Guyanese Creole and to become accustomed to English spoken with a British accent. After a month of being understood but understanding little, with the assistance of two Guyanese scholars, I located a community in the rural area of East Coast Demerara where I decided to spend the remainder of the summer observing children's games in order to learn what I could of how these games might be involved in cultural socialization across the ethnic segmentations that, according to pluralist theory, ordered Guyanese social life.

As a neophyte participant-observer, my mission was twofold. I was interested in learning how to select informants, to observe without being too obtrusive, to create follow-up interview schedules, and to determine what other types of qualitative and quantitative ethnographic data would be necessary to "make sense" of the children's games. I would have to master each of these techniques in order to understand the games as aspects of the local culture and of its relation to the national society. Equally important, I was interested in the specific research questions I had formulated about cultural socialization and ethnic segmentation in children's games. Moreover, I wanted to accomplish these tasks without offending anyone's political sensitivities.

After a week of daily trips from Georgetown to the community to get to know some of the families and to find a room to rent, I moved. Accompanied by one of the Guyanese scholars, a male of East Indian ancestry, I arrived at the home where I had rented a room. Soon after dropping my bags, I was greeted by one of the couples I had met on my earlier trips. They invited me to attend a wake, noting that it would provide a good opportunity for me to learn about the African (Afro-Guyanese) culture, to announce my presence, and to explain my reason for coming to Guyana. Although the idea of having my first encounter with strangers at a wake did not appeal to me, I decided they were right; after all, they were the natives and hence by definition right. So off we all went to the wake. Apart from the fact that I ultimately became more fascinated by what constituted a wake than by the range and types of children's games I observed, my first wake introduced me, in one blow, to problems of class, gender, and what I would later call "status geography." At the wake I was given an opportunity to make a brief speech. I explained that I had been in Guyana for a month, that I had come to study children's games in a rural community, and that my project was part of my graduate training in the discipline of anthropology. I informed the gathering that I had acquired the necessary papers from the proper government office but that I also required their forbearance in order to carry out the study in their community. No one said welcome, no one said no. Most people nodded and smiled, and in general, they murmured pleasantly when I finished speaking.[5]

Later I learned that, as I had suspected, few understood much of what I said because, as the Guyanese scholar explained, I had spoken "too deeply" (too much of an American accent; too standard a version of English). Given the difficulty I had understanding British accents (I understood one out of every ten or twelve words), I was surprised by the scholar's warning following his interpretation of my failed communication. Although we had both explained that I had no kin or "roots" in Guyana, he warned me that until that fact was fully accepted, some persons would be likely to think that I was simply putting on airs by speaking "deeply" and "pretending" not to understand Creolese (the term most frequently used for Guyanese English) and British-accented English. He was correct in his warning. Over the next two months many discussions, quizzes, "tricks" (things community members believed persons of Guyanese roots would know, even if they were "born American"), and other puzzling maneuvers were used by the Guyanese to discover who I really was and why I had really come (been drawn) to Guyana.

The room I rented was located in a section of the community nearest the seaside and the public highway. The section, I learned, was called "waterside." This section, and for the most part its residents, were considered to be of higher status and moral character than persons from the "backdam," the section farthest from the seaside and nearest to the community's farmland. In more general terms, the backdam was also the section of plantations where the slave quarters had been located, whereas the slave owner's and overseer's residences had been located in the front seaside section. The wake I attended was in the backdam section, and the persons who invited me were residents of that section.

Unaware of the symbolic and status significance of these spatial distinctions, I was still puzzling over how anyone could think that I was Guyanese, given that I could not speak properly and did not walk right. I even discovered that I poured water rather "poorly." However, part of my lesson in class distinctions and status geography was still ahead. It came at the end of the wake, when I returned to my rented room. The mistress of the house, a woman who considered herself a "Colored" woman, the Queen's subject, and only reluctantly a citizen of the new People's Cooperative Republic of Guyana, let me know in no uncertain terms that she was most disappointed and disapproving because I had spent time at a backdam wake and with "those people." She assured me that if I wanted to get along and be a respectable person, I would not be able to do so by attending wakes at the backdam.

Her evaluation of my lack of respectable conduct was certainly attributable, in part, to my gender: gallivanting around at all hours of the night and going in and out of just anyone's house were not proper conduct for a female. It was, however, no more a matter of gender than it was based on her assumptions about my class background, years of education, and U.S. American nationality. Yet even my class background, I would argue, was less important than the fact that although I was only a boarder, my conduct reflected on her household and its status among waterside residents. Her concern was to maintain, or perhaps reconstruct, the image of her (surname) family as an elite family within the community and her place in that status group. She had been born in the community but had been raised in the city, educated abroad, and had spent most of her life in Brazil working as a teacher before retiring to Guyana ten years earlier to assume control of her natal homestead. My interactions with persons from the backdam, regardless of whether they were more or less well-off economically than my landlord, posed status problems for her self-representation which my self-presentation as anthropologist and participant-observer could not override.

Over the next two months she softened her stance a bit as a concession to my "educational goals," but still thought that I should find some other way to acquire the information I needed. She was also displeased by the presence of the children who, as they learned by word of mouth that I was interested in watching children play, came daily to demonstrate games or to inform me of where I could go to watch groups of children playing. She complained about their lack of "manners," although they were always polite and as quiet as one could be while demonstrating games. But her complaints about the children and her attitudes toward them were less disruptive of my work than her attitude toward adults, because within a couple of weeks the children and I had found other places to play. Her attitude toward my adult visitors posed serious problems for my maintaining contact with the families I had met and from whom I was trying to learn Creolese and about other aspects of social life in the community. For many of them thought it more appropriate for them to visit me than for me to visit them, especially in the evening, as I, a female, would have to either be walked home or have to walk home alone. It was simply easier, they reasoned, for them to come for a visit and chat when their work was done and they had finished their evening meal.

Nonetheless, to avoid confrontations and the embarrassment of my landlord insulting them when adults came to visit me and we sat on the veranda, I increasingly spent time at their homes, most of which were in the backdam section. This solution only increased my problems with my landlord. She now chided me for starting gossip. People, she claimed (probably not inaccurately), were saying that I preferred the company of any "worthless" person to hers. Hence, staying away from "home" solved my problem of access, but it only underscored the fact that many of the persons with whom I interacted were not welcome to visit the place where I rented a room. Knowing the woman, they were accustomed to her conduct, but still their encounters with her created moments of tension that were part of the daily fabric about which I would later write (Williams, 1983).

Whereas the backdammers with whom I regularly interacted thought it morally worthwhile of me not to "take on her airs," other watersiders who shared some of her views, albeit in less dramatic form, were less positive in their evaluation of my conduct. This made it more difficult for me to gain easy access to their homes and to members of their kin networks. Moreover, interestingly enough, it was also with some members of this category that my identity as participant-observer was most recognized and accepted. Those who allowed me fairly easy and frequent access did so because they were concerned about my formal education. It disturbed them to think that my landlord's "old-fashioned" ways might get in the way of my completing my formal training. Some complained that she, of all people, being a teacher, should have been more sympathetic. From their standpoint, the guiding motive of my behavior—carrying out a project toward the completion of an advanced degree—had a class identity: it was proper conduct for a middle-class person or one aspiring to that status. From their standpoint and that of my landlord, the interaction pattern that constituted participant-observation also had a class identity. It was analogous to the indiscriminate behavior stereotypically attributed to lower-class persons and to those with no aspirations to better themselves, either morally or economically.

Under these rather typical conditions of class stratification, sympathy, even when empathetically constructed, can be an expensive commodity. My landlord had left Guyana at a time when the category "Colored" carried far more social weight than it did by the time she returned. Her family name was still much respected in the community, but her family members no longer lived there, and many no longer even resided in Guyana. They were not available to maintain and augment the social capital around which daily judgments of moral worth were made in the community. She was elderly and could not get around well enough to engage social networks in order to create new social capital. In light of these strictures, there were few good reasons why she should be willing to squander what in her view was much-needed status in order to accommodate the stranger's value of a less-than-valuable stranger.

Perhaps my landlord also suspected that my stranger's value formed the flesh of a Trojan horse. Since her return to the community, her "acting-big" ways had long annoyed many people in the community, and as I learned later, they used my presence to send her little "messages." Coming to visit was indeed for my benefit, but it was also to provoke her. The children did pass along my interest in their games, but it was their parents who saw to it that they were nicely attired and who sent them around for a visit, although they knew my landlord would be less than pleased. Children were also meaty little Trojan horses, spying items of interest and "disinterestedly" reporting the information back to their parents. This aspect of the children's behavior, as I was to learn during my second field trip, was among the characteristics of childhood that fit it into the social matrix of information gathering and status evaluations. I learned to guard against such indiscriminate dissemination of information from my own household by making fewer interesting items visible to children's eyes. It was also a challenge to determine what was interesting. But during that first field experience, in these and numerous other ways, my desire to interact without reference to status differences and their implications supplied opportunities for the reproduction or dissemination or both of the very differences that I was either ignorant of or sought to ignore as part of the definition of being an anthropologist engaged in participant-observation.

Although historical similarities and an ideologically defined politics of racial skinship provided implicit, albeit hard to reckon socially, connections between my identity as an African American and that of the Guyanese who claimed Afro-Guyanese identity, class stratification and status geography were the more salient factors in how we constructed the limit of participant-observation as a concept. The role of race in the signification of power difference came into play as Afro-Guyanese I had come to know translated my participant-observer conduct in terms of interracial distinctions and the presumed competitive positionings of these distinctions in the Guyanese social order.[6] It was at the point of these interracial problematics that the issue of our shared racial identity entered into how they constructed the limits of participant-observation and how I could respond to those limits. As a consequence, our shared "race," but fractured identity, served to further restrict the utility of the concept of participant-observation as I began interacting with persons of East Indian descent (Indo-Guyanese).

In Afro-Guyanese evaluations of the pattern of interaction I established, the class and status-geography elements that placed limits on the identity of participant-observation did not diminish, nor did the problems associated with being a female moving around alone. Instead, both backdam and waterside Afro-Guyanese reasoned that I would need to talk to "big people," even Indo-Guyanese, because big people were likely to be more educated than "small people" and hence more likely to be able to answer my questions. They also reasoned that I needed to move around in the backdam/waterside divisions of the community's Indo-Guyanese section in the same manner as in the Afro-Guyanese one. In short, conceptual ground won in these terms was held within the Afro-Guyanese population, and it was won more easily within the Indo-Guyanese population, because gossip and public speeches, given either by me or by others on my behalf, summarized for those translators the understandings that the Afro-Guyanese and I had struggled to achieve. These understandings became the context of interactions within and across the "racial" distinctions.

Specific tasks, such as interviewing an elderly person about the history of the community, about features of a ritual, or about other subjects, were most easily assimilated to this conceptual rendering of participant-observation. Engaging in general discussion about a "Guyanese culture" considered as patterns of interaction that transcended the particularities of the ethnic segments was viewed more skeptically. Nonetheless, the idea that I would need to interact with "all races of Guyanese" in order to get a sampling of "things Guyanese" met with little resistance and no noticeable disapproval from anyone other than my landlord. Within the context of our established understandings, initially Afro-Guyanese translators were much more tolerant of my habits of cross-racial interactions than they had been of my cross-class interactions and my spatial promiscuity.

Around the midpoint of the last month of my stay, this tolerance waned as I began to spend approximately equal time attending Indo-Guyanese and Afro-Guyanese events, visiting the Indo-Guyanese families I met as a result of these contacts, and in other ways dividing my time between the two major demographic components of the community. Few of the Afro-Guyanese shared my perception that I was devoting roughly equal time or attention to these activities. The Afro-Guyanese, especially those from the backdam, were less tolerant of my lack of a racial preference. Despite my protests to the contrary, I was directly and indirectly accused of harboring a preference for "things Indo-Guyanese."

I argued that if it appeared that I was spending more time on the Indo-Guyanese events, it was because my entrée into the area of the community had taken longer to achieve and that I was nearing the end of my field period and in general simply needed to spend more time working on what I understood least. This reasoning was sometimes interpreted to mean that Indo-Guyanese culture was more difficult to understand and hence more complex or better. Apart from that, my general protestations were never rejected outright. They were never clearly accepted either. Often they were met, sometimes explicitly, although generally in joking form, with a charge that I was being a traitor to "my race." I was not a traitor to Africans per se: instead I had sold out our "common ancestors" who were brought to the Americas "in chains."

Amidst the rattling of historical chains, little of stranger's value and its quest for a neutral position made cultural sense. Afro-Guyanese who had accepted, in the name of formal educational requirements, my need to ignore local status distinctions within the race found my failure to privilege racial boundaries more difficult to justify in the same terms. Those who had come to accept that my speaking deep was not a pretense of non-Guyanese kin affiliation, continued to accept that I was not Guyanese, but still found it useful at this point to remind me of Pan-African connections. Even those who had rejected these connections as ground on which I could evince interest in all Afro-Guyanese regardless of class and other status distinctions, now found them useful criteria in discussions of the limits I might place on time spent among Indo-Guyanese.

For some Afro-Guyanese, even as Pan-African skinfolk, it was, ideally, morally good to ignore racial distinctions in the name of shared "color"—people of Asian and African descent being treated as a major component of the non-White people of the world. However, like the act of ignoring class differences, for persons who expressed this option it was their differential connections to race and class distinctions that seemed ultimately to determine how they assessed the act's cost. Those connections also determined whether they viewed participant-observation as an autonomous set of actions or saw in the pattern of conduct it constituted aspects of locally recognized actions that had immediate status implications. For example, when I chose to attend an Indo-Guyanese event rather than an Afro-Guyanese event taking place at the same time, whether I was perceived as "taking my eye past" (i.e., insulting the dignity of) "the Africans" by preferring "things Indo-Guyanese," or was seen as simply doing my job in order to get an education, depended less on the act committed than on the feature of identity, class or race, that those assessing my actions attributed to me in relation to their assessment of what was at stake for them as my associates. Some Afro-Guyanese, who thought of themselves as "small" relative to the household sponsoring the event and who thought of me as a student, interpreted my choice as necessary for me to avoid incurring the jealousy of "big" people who might later try to obstruct my work. Others, big and small, who thought of me as a descendant of African slaves who should, therefore, sympathize with their racial struggle against the Indo-Guyanese, whom they viewed as greedy interlopers, interpreted my choice as a slight to, or denigration of, my race.

The Power to Signify Stranger's Value

In Alabama and in Guyana, whether the outcome of interpretations of my self-presentation as participant-observer allowed a forward step in the rapport-building process or resulted in three steps back to the mean, there was no generic kinship or fully generalizable skinship from which I, or any category of informant, could construct an interracial, cross-class, extraspatial identity for the concept of participant-observation. Each translator translating the translator has a general position in the social order of power relations and, as we well know, he or she has varying positions across events and the types of interactions they entail. The translating translators, like the anthropologist they translate, are composites of features that signify positions and that position each type of translator to signify the value of a stranger enacting stranger's value.

It is doubtful that anthropologists, even those in exotic lands, had the power to signify stranger's value so as to construct an identity for participant-observation that was autonomous of the range of role identities that constituted the social order of power relations into which they entered. As our age-old commentaries on the anthropologist as child might suggest, the question of who are you and what are you to me/whose child are you and what are you doing here, have always been a part of the rapport-building problematic. To ask oneself the question, to provide responses to one's "own" folk, race, or gender, is always to position oneself relative to the power to affix some role identity in a code of classifications. The shifting that occurs within and across field situations that are territorially or "historically" located within one's "own society" differs not in its absolute character, nor in its big and small consequences, but rather in the degree to which these shifts can be precipitated by the informant rather than orchestrated by the anthropologist. To do one's homework in order to facilitate fieldwork in "one's own" society is to learn how and where to locate the play between the precipitations of informants and the orchestrations of stranger's value.[7]

In essence, the construction of stranger's value, as Pouwer experienced it, comes not so much from being outside one's own society as from the existence of a major power disparity between a position or positions that locate the anthropologist as translator and those that locate persons who are qualified to become the translator's translator. Few if any in their "own society" are positioned to signify stranger's value, if that signification is intended to remove them from, or suspend them above, the social order of power relations, because few, if any, of those who would be informants qualify to fix a line between codes that classify insiders and outsiders. Moreover, even if they appear to fix the line between these codes of classification, they may lack the power to hold the line as the anthropologist creates a pattern of social interaction to give substance to participant-observation. He might, alas, appear as a priest gone Protestant in his quest for a wife, or as one who speaks deep to hide cultural connections to a homeland.

In the world of anthropological investigations, chiefs may intercede to translate speeches of intent and to set the stage for the game of "wait and see"; *loua,* greedy for cigarettes and a reliable source of *kléren,* may intercede on behalf of a red black foreigner, and an old "aristocratic" may put the squeeze on reluctant "commoners" in order to make possible the first acts of translation for a blackened White female. These openings provide opportunities for the translator to begin the work of providing his or her translators with clues as to what they ought to attend to and what he or she hopes they will ignore. If the anthropologist is successful in getting informants to ignore the requisite aspects of his or her identity features, then he or she can sometimes ignore those aspects of the social order of power relations that too severely constrain his or her construction or participant-observation to permit it an autonomous role identity. To select the requisite features to be ignored in fieldwork requires the anthropologist to continually situate himself or herself in the local order of status distinctions and to be aware of their symbolic, historical, and ongoing economic connections to his or her "own society" and its place in the social order of power relations. In short, to some extent good fieldwork in any society requires doing one's homework, however, within "one's own society," acts of self-identification—even near schizophrenic ones—and of doing homework cannot be compartmentalized in a manner that permits a distinctive identity for participant-observation. The identity for participant-observation retains the stripes of class, race, gender, and geographical hierarchy. Within the society of the "other," where the other lays claim to a shared transpatial identity such as skinfolk, doing fieldwork is not sufficient to allow an anthropologist to signify a stranger's value, apart from the homework required to situate himself or herself in a familiar order of power relations that make possible the premises of anthropology as a lesser-known discipline and as just another means by which to "make something" of herself or himself.

NOTES

1. Across these moves, many of his identity features of course remain "fixed" (i.e., some kind of reddened White man), while at the same time other features seemingly remain irrelevant to all constructions. That is to say, he seems not to have been taken for a female persona, within either the foreigner or the native classifications, and according to his discussion at least, his age does not seem especially relevant or problematic for fixing any particular identity position.

2. On this point and many others, I thank Drexel G. Woodson for his very helpful comments on this draft and for letters of advice I received during periods when I was in Alabama and Guyana and he was thinking through and experiencing his own constructions of relations between skinfolk and kinfolk in Haiti. I thank both him and Shirley McDowell for their editorial assistance. Of course all errors of interpretation here or faulty conclusions throughout the text are mine.

3. Powdermaker's study was the first long-term ethnographic study carried out in the United States by an anthropologist that did not focus on a Native American community.

4. Before selecting a field site where we were each to reside for three months, the three anthropologists (two African Americans, one Euro-American) that were selected for the project participated in the joint formulation of a set of questionnaires. The questionnaires were designed under the direction of a Maryland consulting firm contracted by the Administration on Aging and identified formal agencies and networks of persons who were informal caregivers for members of the subject population. All three fieldworkers were female, although I know of no significance that was associated with this fact in the organiza-

tion of the project and its methodology. Much of the content of the questionnaire, and most of the cultural assumptions that framed the content, had already been formulated based on a pilot study conducted by the project coordinator, a Jewish male anthropologist working in an Oregon African American community. It was expected that elderly African American subjects would reside in multigenerational households wherein their basic needs would be taken care of by a range of coresident family members, who would also assist them by mediating their relationships with formal caregiving agencies. This expected cultural pattern made African Americans an ideal population for the study. It was also expected that the pattern would be most pronounced in southern African American culture; hence two sites were selected in the urban and rural South (Atlanta and rural Alabama, respectively), and a third at a geographical point along the established migration route from the rural South to the urban North (downstate Illinois).

5. By midsummer I was still interested in children's games but had also developed an interest in wedding and wake rituals as sites of ethnic identification and contestation. I have never written up the material on children games. Some of my thoughts on the wedding and wake rituals can be found in Williams 1984, 1990a, and 1990b, and my more general theoretical conclusions about the role of these rituals in the representation and production of racial, ethnic, and national identities that resulted from a continuation of this interest into the second field period can be found in Williams 1991.

6. For an extended discussion of this issue, see Williams 1991.

7. For further discussion of Powdermaker's efforts to "bring anthropology home," see Williams and Woodson (1993).

REFERENCES

Geertz, Clifford. 1983. "Found in Translation: The Social History of the Moral Imagination." In *Local Knowledge: Further Essays in Interpretive Anthropology,* 36–54. New York: Basic Books.

Hurston, Zora Neale. 1942. *Dust Tracks on a Road.* Philadelphia: J. B. Lippincott.

Pouwer, Jan. 1973. "Signification and Fieldwork." In *Symbolic Anthropology/Meditation Recherches Anthropologue,* vol. 1, 1–13. The Hague and Paris: Mouton.

Powdermaker, Hortense. 1966. *Stranger and Friend: The Way of the Anthropologist.* New York: W. W. Norton & Co.

———. 1993 [1939]. *After Freedom: A Cultural Study in the Deep South.* Introduction by B. Williams and D. G. Woodson. Madison: University of Wisconsin Press.

Williams, Brackette F. 1979. "A Report on Informal Assistance to the Black Elderly in a Rural Alabama Community." Submitted to the Institute for the Study of Human Systems, as part of a project sponsored by the Administration on Aging (Grant No. AOA 90-8-1375). Washington, D.C.: ISHS.

———. 1983. "Cockalorums in Search of Cockaigne: Status Competition, Ritual, and Social Interaction in a Rural Guyanese Community." Ph.D. dissertation, Johns Hopkins University.

———. 1984. "Ef Me Naa Bin Come Me Naa Bin Know: An Analysis of the Role of The Afro-Guyanese Wake in Local Judicial Procedures, 1900–1980." *Caribbean Quarterly,* Mona, Jamaica (special edition in honor of Else Goveia): 26–41.

————. 1990a. "Dutchman Ghost and the History Mystery: Ritual, Colonizer, and Colonized Interpretations of the 1763 Berbice Slave Rebellion." *Journal of Historical Sociology* 3, no. 2: 133–165.

————. 1990b. "Traditionalism, Cultural Innovation, and the Problem of Cultural Inauthenticity." In *The Production of Nationalist Ideologies and the Construction of National Culture.* AES monograph, edited by Richard G. Fox. Washington, D.C.: American Anthropological Association.

————. 1991. *Stains on My Name, War in My Veins: Guyana and the Politics of Cultural Struggle.* Durham, N.C.: Duke University Press.

————. 1995. "The Public I/Eye: Homeless Me Working You: A Homework Report." *Current Anthropology* 3, no. 1: 25–51.

Williams, Brackette, and Drexel G. Woodson. 1993. "Hortense Powdermaker in the Deep South: The Conundrum of Race, Class, and Gender 'After Freedom.'" In *After Freedom: A Cultural Study in the Deep South,* by Hortense Powdermaker, ix–xi. Madison: University of Wisconsin Press.

Woodson, Drexel G. 1990. "Tout Mounn sé Mounn, men Tout Mounn pa Menm: Microlevel Sociocultural Aspects of Land Tenure in a Northern Haitian Locality." Ph.D. dissertation, University of Chicago.

4

Writing Ethnography:
Feminist Critical Practice

CAROL B. STACK

MY FIRST ANTHROPOLOGICAL RESEARCH began in the early 1960s when I chronicled the northbound movement of African Americans from rural Mississippi, Arkansas, and Louisiana to Chicago—research that eventually led to the writing of *All Our Kin* (Stack, 1972).[1] Twenty years later and back in the South, I watched daily the return of first-, second-, and third-generation urban dwellers following their own paths to rural southeastern homeplaces from midwestern and East Coast cities. I am currently completing a book about this dramatic return movement, *Call to Home: African Americans Reclaim the Rural South* (Stack, forthcoming). Using both memories and field notes for these two ethnographic studies, I try in this chapter to reconstruct the nature of my own comfort and conflict as an ethnographer. In the context of the politics and scholarship of the times, I explore the nuances of doing and writing ethnography as a white working-class woman. I do this by reconstructing the two projects, looking backward from the perspective of the present. Dramatizing both writer and subject in the historical context, I attempt to engage in writing culture as feminist critical practice.

The political energy of the 1960s was churning in "The Flats" (the fictive name of the African American community that is the site of *All Our Kin*) as well as in nearby neighborhoods and communities. "Black Power" leadership ignited relationships across community boundaries and new alliances emerged out of coalition politics. I was invited to participate in meetings with a group of welfare mothers from The Flats who had begun a welfare rights organization. Those of us

---

This article originally appeared in slightly modified form in *Frontiers: A Journal of Women Studies* 8, no. 3, 1993. Reprinted with permission of the publisher.

who were community workers and political activists believed that everything was in flux and anticipated that traditional boundaries could be transformed. Those were the times of Martin Luther King, John Kennedy, civil rights, Black Power, welfare rights, and Vietnam. Personal and political experimentation crisscrossed race, gender, and class divisions. Working within and through a divisive generation gap (especially in white communities), young people under thirty believed that anything was possible. We allowed ourselves to take risks, especially around political action. We were inspired as political activism crossed race and class lines. And we perceived the possibility of social change as a collaboration among people who understood basic social truths about equity and human dignity. This perception undergirded our belief that acting on such truths would set us free; we produced moral imperatives for our times.

In 1969, I was twenty-eight, a white, working-class, politically active, single mother—with a young son who was with me around the clock. The following thoughts are a fragmented compendium of my experiences then, as a young anthropologist in the field. Reflecting on the lessons I learned, over nearly three years living among residents in The Flats, especially from Ruby Banks, my closest ally in the community, is a complex task in light of present-day challenges to ethnography.

Ruby, who was also a single parent and the oldest daughter in a large extended family network, took on the challenge, and some of the fun, of teaching me to act appropriately as a woman, as a mother, and as a friend in her neighborhood. As friends become "kin" if they seriously take on kin responsibilities, Ruby and her kinfolk included me as a part of their family. This, of course, did not happen immediately but developed slowly as we came to depend upon one another to carry out the work of kinship, including the assumption of mutual responsibility for one another's children and other children in the kin group. This was more consequential than might be obvious, since many parents in The Flats were appalled at the widespread practice in the mainstream culture of allowing strangers to babysit. Their critique also included a distrust of public and private day-care centers run by outsiders to the community.

Ruby even carried notions of our kinship beyond The Flats. For example, when she was sick in the hospital, she claimed I was her sister, so the nurses would let me visit. Despite the disbelief of nurses and other hospital staff who looked at me and saw a white woman, Ruby's sense of what constituted kinlike exchanges among friends rendered her claim to the hospital bureaucrats honest with respect to her culturally constructed conception of fictive kinship. From experiences like these, I learned to stretch my previously acquired notions of the boundaries of kinship.

Ruby attempted to teach me how to manage my life as a single woman in The Flats. She warned me not to be alone with a man in the community. In her very careful instructions to me about interviewing men, she told me that if I got myself into an uncomfortable situation with a man and said no, I would be considered a racist. Given my graduate training, which included serious advice against developing sexual liaisons in the field (and startling examples of women anthropologists who had been murdered in the field for doing so), my emerging sense of feminist politics in 1968–1969, my strong desire to maintain my primary relationships with women in The Flats, and my goal of managing a research involvement that was not magnified by sexual/racial politics, I wholeheartedly agreed to follow Ruby's advice.

Despite an array of instructions on how to act appropriately in the community (which I often thought I would never grasp) and subtle tests of my knowledge and loyalty, there were long periods during my stay in the community when I was allowed to forget that I was white. Forgetting may have been a reflection of my own sense of comfort, which developed over time. Ironically, I felt this transition about midway into the study, when people in the community began calling me "white Caroline." They did this in part so I wouldn't be confused with Ruby's niece, whom they began to call "black Caroline." My new nickname offered a wry twist on my identity: my naming was both a sign of acceptance and an unfeigned marker. People teased and commended me for acting right, observing that I probably forgot my own whiteness from time to time. But my lapses were quickly roused when I heard my nickname, which was used more in public than in the privacy of family life. My presence was public; my presence was named. I was "white Caroline."

As I look back, I have no doubt that the meaning of my life was tied up with being in The Flats. Within a small group of associates we created a situation of trust—a safety zone in which we pushed boundaries and experimented, nourishing one another's curiosities, not just the anthropologist's. From time to time a group of us would venture outside The Flats into the nearby white hangouts, where people in The Flats felt they would not be safe without me. For example, we went to a couple of country-and-western bars a few miles from The Flats. These adventures and inventions, however, were mere tokens compared to the world Ruby and her close friends opened up to me.

From Ruby and countless other single parents in The Flats, I learned how rights and responsibilities for children were distributed within and across kin groups. As single parents, they were far less isolated from kin and informal supports than the few white single parents I knew in the middle-class world of academics in the late 1960s. During my stay in The Flats, I was learning what I later came to realize were feminist strategies for surviving as a single parent within networks of friends and extended kin. We took turns with the children. I learned about child keeping by practicing, which of course was a blessing to a single parent in the field. Over many months I learned women's strategies for negotiating kin, single motherhood, men, and the welfare system.

Near the completion of my fieldwork, I reread *Tally's Corner,* written by Elliot Liebow in 1967. Although I had read it earlier, I was startled by the fact that this well known ethnography was almost entirely about individual men—men at the doughnut shop, on the corner, on the streets. In my own work I learned about women's connections to one another and their social/familial networks, and through their eyes, about their connections to men. I asked different questions from Liebow's and became fascinated with the role of women's networks in family survival. Liebow left unexamined the question of where the women, children, and grandparents were. Where were the fathers, aunts, uncles, and cousins? I knew, and I wanted to write about the strength and resilience of women's ways of keeping families together.

When I stepped out of the field to write *All Our Kin,* in Langston Hughes's words from his short story, "Home," my "skin burned, I felt my color." I confronted my whiteness more absolutely as a writer than as a researcher. I felt more alone and color conscious as I began writing. I also felt what, looking back, I might call a "white woman's burden." Inside The Flats, folks devised ways to blunt, yet clarify, color differences in our everyday experiences. When I began writing the ethnography I became color/politically conscious. I felt a strong sense of social responsibility to those I had studied, and I was convinced that I could get the story right. I tried out every word I wrote on people I knew in The Flats. I listened to their responses, argued, and tried again. I wanted the story to ring true to their experiences. When I finally wrote the book, I wrote in deep seriousness on the very first page of the Introduction: "This introduction anticipates curiosity about how a young white woman could . . . conduct a study of black family life, and provides a basis for evaluating the reliability and quality of the data obtained" (Stack, 1972: xv).

This sample (and the tenor of the Introduction to *All Our Kin*) mirrors the rationalist assumptions of the times, implying a method for evaluating the reliability of the qualitative methods and the data presented in the book. The feminist criticism of fieldwork and the writing of ethnography in the 1990s is far less sanguine with respect to what constitutes good social science. The flat accent on reliability and objectivity of data is transformed through the filter of critical and feminist theory. Moreover, we are unconvinced that any attempt at clarifying our positionality does more than situate the perspective from which we believe we are "writing culture." The goal is to explore and experiment—to learn and write as much about our own understanding of how we locate our voice in our writing as possible. We acknowledge that how we position ourselves in our research and writing must be finely tuned with respect to the times, the region, the setting, and race/gender politics of the historical moment. With a sharp turn toward the fragmentation of voices and stories, the process of writing ethnography has turned inward toward subjectivity. We could argue that ethnography itself has been taken as illusion, the fiction of the writer herself. Indeed, the more extravagant postmodern theorists undertake a pulverization of the modern subject itself.

The 1980s were fragmented by a backlash against the legacy of legal and moral commitments that stirred the 1960s and 1970s. Some of the legal and institutional mandates that took root have already been uprooted. Dialectic within and across political agendas had dominated an epoch of contradictions. We have witnessed a fragile and ephemeral attempt at the institutionalization of liberation values (affirmative action, for example), alongside the emergence of the New Right morality. Nowhere in the country was the power struggle between, for example, forces such as Jesse Jackson and the New Right, fundamentalism and feminism, more graphic than in the South—or the "New South."

What emerged in the 1980s was a "politics of rebuttal": new racisms and ethnic antagonisms coexisting with dramatic shifts in power, both individual and global, and connecting the two. Individuals and political groups fashioned new identities, new roles, and multiple identities. Prochoice New Right feminists emerged, for example. Traditional coalitions were revisioned, and sometimes betrayed.

Set within the context of the American dream, the downward mobility, joblessness, estranged Vietnam veterans, homelessness, loss of hope, new racisms, distrust, and fear of new ideas produced new sets of contradictions. These changes took place in the context of deindustrialization in the North and South. At the same time, institutions were hammering out some progressive agendas that were indeed legacies of the 1960s and 1970s. Nostalgia for the past was exposed by disillusioned youth dressing in 1960s garb, and population movements emerged among adults. For example, the "small town boom" of middle-aged migrants reinforced a longing for the communities of memory.

In the 1980s I was nearly middle-aged, a professor, and my son was finishing high school. I was involved in ethnographic fieldwork among African Americans once again. This time I was studying people who were returning to rural southern homeplace communities. My research, which had been on the migration of African Americans from the Deep South to midwestern cities, was now on the return migration of people from the Northeast to the Southeast.

I spent nearly three years living in rural South Carolina, probing the meaning of home to those returning to the rigid race/caste system of the rural South. More often than not, my eighty-year-old widowed mother, rather than my teenaged son, accompanied me. My mother was genuinely welcomed by families in these rural communities. Together we learned how effective women community workers were in achieving their dreams to improve the lot of rural women. They succeeded in creating day care for working women, bringing Title XX funds to rural communities, and creating coalitions across counties working toward rural economic development. My mother and I also observed divisions between returnees and the old-timers and their struggle over an appropriate political pace and plan for social change. We observed together how identity politics shaped tensions between generations. But even more unmistakable on the political horizon were differences across gender lines.

Call to Home focuses on the return South of African American women and men bringing home urban knowledge, and on identity politics—how gender and ideology shape the commitments and political actions of women and men who return to their rural southern homeplaces. The book is about the collision between the multiple notions and aspirations that people bring home and the tightrope they walk in constructing workable identities in the South. Those who have returned have become artful in assuming personal and political identities appropriate to the situation at hand. I learned that on one level it was important for those who returned to be accepted back into the community as "home girls" or "home boys." However, many of the people who returned carried with them a political mission. They wanted to transform their home places, and no matter how hard they tried to be accepted within their communities, their more aggressive approach to social change labeled them as "outsiders." In church, at local political meetings, or in the creation of coalitions across race lines, people enacted multiple roles assuming the posture of home girl, outsider, or New Yorker, when appropriate. They also paid their respects to the rural elderly and struggled with differing identities depending on the situation, the moment, the nature of the coalition, the day, the audience, and their mood. Women and men talked about belonging and identity, about being and origins, about home, about place, about home place, and about locating their place and my place in the research setting.

Most of the people returning were in their forties, near my own age at the time, joining their grandparents and school-age children who had moved back home ahead of them. The parents of these return migrants were planning to return when they reached sixty-five or had put in the necessary years working in the North so that they could bring retirement benefits home.

Recollecting my sensibilities from my fieldwork in the 1980s, I relive, as I now write, the complicated and painful deliberations of people attempting to explain how they negotiated their identities—who they were, and who they came to be back home. After three years of intense political work attempting to bring day care to eight rural counties in the Carolinas, one politically active young grandmother, Doris Moody, talked to me about how she labors to negotiate her place back home. "We belong and we don't," she told me. I learned how Doris tempers her political stance to meet the political situation. She was careful to avoid moving too fast, acting the part of "home girl" when necessary. But she also shared her anxiety that if she and others accommodated to tradition too often, they would give in sooner or later to the ways things had always been done.

In informal settings, in homes, and as we traveled long distances across rural counties to meetings and workshops, I listened and participated in discussions about rural day care, public funds, political elections, the Farmer's Home Administration, school systems, and farm loss. In contrast to when I did my research in The Flats, where I was intimately drawn into women's kin networks, I felt more like a colleague or long-term visitor than an adopted family member. The formalities and civility of southern tradition created a place, but not a fictive home for me. On the other hand, I was deeply connected to women-centered political organizations in rural counties that were attempting to write a feminist agenda around the needs of rural women. In contrast to the male-dominated black nationalist politics of the 1960s, the leadership and organizing efforts of women were critical in these rural southern communities.

The women and men who returned home crosscut many walks of life and economic circumstances. Some were college-educated, experienced professionals; others had acquired organizing skills and knowledge of public sector programs and funding. Yet others returned disheartened; they had been houseless in the North, if not homeless. People often said that they returned changed—a different person from the person who had left the South. Likewise my status and sensibilities had changed since my early research in The Flats. Between 1975 and 1987, I was a professor at Duke University, a director of a Family Policy Center, and actively engaged in advocating reforms in state policy regarding families and children. I was nearly middle-aged and moderately middle class. My son was in high school, my father had died, and my mother was becoming elderly. Fortuitously, I returned to the field with a change in status somewhat similar to that of the middle-class people who returned South. I was close to their age and at the same life stage. As an outsider, I too was suspect, observed, and subject to unwritten rules, prescriptions, and restrictions.

In contrast to my fieldwork in the 1960s, this time I felt my color. The insider/outsiders who returned were themselves working out their own places in rural home communities. I, too, was negotiating a space and became increasingly absorbed in how my own history affects the way I do ethnography. I was displaced far from home. How could I locate myself in the space/geography, and what would people ask of me? Had I experienced anything similar to what they had experienced as they managed their lives as both outsiders and insiders? My memories brought to mind my experience as the only working-class Jewish person in the community in which I grew up and in all of the schools I attended from kindergarten through high school.

Sometimes when working with women's political networks organizing around the needs of rural women, I was associated with the few white radicals who had moved into these rural communities in the 1970s and had managed to maintain a power base as leaders in these alternative organizations. Because people perceived that I was not seeking a power base, I was invited to meetings near the hub of coalition building and decisionmaking. But this led to a difficult research dilemma. Often I was pulled by contending factions who wanted me to understand or take their side in difficult, ongoing debates. My best teachers in negotiating this tension were women community workers who skillfully moved back and forth between offense and conciliation.

The battleground over the construction of home place identities was located not only with respect to the white community but, all too painfully, among and across generations of African Americans in rural home places as well. Among the many examples from my fieldwork, one event illustrates the multiple oscillations in the management of identities among politically active women within the course of a single evening.

Elders in these rural communities are treated with respect. A banquet arranged by local community organizers in honor of Miss Hammer, an elderly community leader, was held at a local hotel on a summer evening when my mother was visiting me in the field. At this event the tension between deference and respect for elders, some of whom had risked their lives in early civil rights protests, and the politics of new leaders was brought into tension. The new leadership refused to perpetuate traditional brokerage systems between the local white and black power structures. They brought professionalized approaches and accountability to the management of local political organizations. They refused to immortalize the cachet of white pacemakers, those outsiders who retained power within local communities as organizers/leaders long after the civil rights movement.

At the banquet that evening, there was also a movement within the sponsoring organization to oust Mr. Jones, the remaining white chair of the organization. Mr. Jones was a long-term political associate of Miss Hammer's. They had started civil rights groups together. Although most of the anguish and debate took place in tense gatherings behind closed doors and in hotel rooms, the lines of argument and political coalitions divided the organization across generations, and between newcomers and old-timers. My mother and I, guests of the newcomers who initiated the debate, witnessed hurt feelings and deep emotions flowing over the new leadership in the local organization.

Following the banquet, my mother and Miss Hammer, age-mates and old acquaintances by that stage of my fieldwork (and the two oldest people present at the event), sat together to talk. People gathered around their memories. Everyone talked until all the dishes and favors and flowers were gone. My mother and Miss Hammer talked until the banquet room was turned into an empty hall except for the chairs gathered around them in a circle. The many voices of resistance heard that evening in private spaces merged, for the moment, into respectful home girl voices, in Miss Hammer's presence. There was no final resolution that evening; there was a respect for the elderly.

Willingness to engage in discussion with an anthropologist is an indication of fortitude as well as state of mind. Dolores Dodson, for example, investigated me ahead of time. She learned from a friend that I had written a book and borrowed a tattered copy, which she read before agreeing to meet me. Late one afternoon, I mastered her hand-drawn map, which I followed past several farms and two churches down endless dirt roads that led to her house. By the time I arrived, she had developed a critique of my work. We spent a couple of days comparing her experiences as a New Jersey social worker with my description of urban black families in midwestern cities. Amenable to building our relationship, Dolores was sure that she had something to teach me. One afternoon our conversation blossomed into a lively, overcrowded group discussion as friends and neighbors dropped in to visit. With everyone giving me her personal notions of how I should go about my study, Dolores, lending support to my project, declared, "You see here a white woman capable of learning."

During our conversation she gave the go-ahead to the women in the room, telling them about my current study and suggesting that they give me their notions of how I should go about it. Again supporting my project, my sponsor told the others, "It would be best, for the time being, if the white community was not aware of Carol's presence." In contrast to my experiences in The Flats, Dolores and her neighbors were asking me to be inconspicuous. The politics of race and power informed Dolores's belief that local whites viewed white outsiders who entered the black community as organizers stirring up trouble. However, these same women engaged the public sector at all levels—local, regional, and state—in their efforts to bring public funds to rural day-care centers. As they got to know me, they invited me to accompany them to public meetings and dropped their early misgivings about whether my presence would be known to the local white community. Although in this sense negotiating my own place became easier with the length of my stay, in another sense the public/private line was to remain problematic.

A couple of months after I had arrived in New Jericho, one of the local communities in my study, Howard, a county attorney, arranged to meet me over dinner for our second conversation. I waited until the last person left his office on Main Street. After a moment's pause, he made it clear that there was no public place where a white woman and a black man could eat together. "The word," he said, "would be all over town." It could destroy his reputation and his law practice. Hesitating, he suggested a take-out meal, which he volunteered to get, and sputtered softly, then out loud, that we weren't in New York City. "Can't even have a business meal together here." Home and the disposition of what constitutes public spaces deeply affected my research relationships with men in this study. In The Flats I was public and could be seen in public with men (but not in private). In these rural southern townships in the 1980s, long after local whites were aware of my presence, men could/would not be in the public spaces of whites with me. My conversations with men, for the most part, took place in the privacy of homes sequestered several miles away from the town squares.

When I was doing fieldwork in the 1980s, there was rarely a moment when the delicate balance of identity politics loosened its hold. However, when I returned to my post at the university and slowly began the process of writing ethnography, it was at the height of the postmodern moment. For all theoretical purposes, ironically, I suddenly felt freed of my whiteness. I was subject as well as author, and as such won license to write about my own subjective, authentic experience. I could/should/would write a fragmented story of return migration in multiple voices and reflect on the meaning of home through my own eyes. Mine was another voice. As a writer I could pay close attention to difference, ambiguity, shifting voices and roles. I too was seeing and being observed. Writing ethnography in these new times, I could shed the singularity of truth and improvise among shifting voices. Reflecting back to the late 1960s and early 1970s, my sense of social responsibility as an ethnographer was enveloped in a search for truth. A discourse of moralism and power, linked in part to the civil rights movement, to feminism, and to the anti–Vietnam War movement, informed a generation of activist anthropologists. As feminists we made claims and created alliances as our sisters' keepers. We created a discourse that focused on the unity of women's lives; this unity became a struggle for agency that homogenized women's lives. Given my own background growing up in a working-class family that struggled against poverty, I was personally alienated by race/class blinders in feminist theory and politics. However, interspersed among these prejudices, there were efforts among coalitions of women to counteract race/class bias in both theory and social policy. For example, working together with the Welfare Rights Organization in The Flats, we produced testimony against child-support legislation (IV-D) that pitted low-income welfare mothers against divorced lower- and middle-income mothers. The National Organization for Women, on the other hand, testified in favor of the bill, ignoring the best interests of very poor women. My political commitments have been toward the construction of feminist research and policy agendas that take seriously the relationships of race, class, and gender.

Agendas that tie research to social change can be at odds with current postmodern trends in the academy. In the latter part of the 1980s, the way was paved for ethnographers to go full circle and to rid ourselves of many notions, in particular, that we could tell another's truth. Gender itself became problematized, identities multiplied, and class and race became complicated and fluid constructions. We were engaged in a discourse of relativism and intersubjectivities in which we tried to deconstruct our own experiences and locate ourselves in our tale. In good spirit, we tangled with multiple voices and disentangled our own.

Critical theory and radical postmodern discourse have transformed ethnographic writing. Those of us still writing feminist ethnography face several dilemmas whose reconciliation is beyond the scope of this chapter. We are still in dialogue over the departure from grand theory, the crisis of legitimation, claims of representation, and the predicament of voice and story for the writing of ethnography.

Whereas I was very careful to avoid claims that The Flats represented African American culture in *All Our Kin,* I had been trained early on as an anthropologist to weave a coherent story, one in which the parts fit together and buttress the whole. I searched through my field notes for stories that fit together to explain rights and responsibilities with respect to children. In those days, as I am aware now, I paid less attention to the tensions and contradictions in people's experiences and looked less for the disjunctures and contradictions in the stories. I painstakingly transcribed and presented their narratives word for word in a search for accuracy, however, with little puzzlement over the discontinuities or over the construction of the narrative itself (Deleuze and Guattari 1983, 1987).

Critical theory and what we might call the humanity of understanding have taken us down a fascinating and important path away from a home base, and we will never return. As anthropologists we are inside and outside of the text, writing it and reading it, questioning its very construction, and searching for discontinuities and ambiguities in the narratives and the larger cultural texts. But in the end it is the ethnographer who lays her fingers on the keyboard to play the final note in the chorus of voices. Purged of an awesome and impossible claim that we write the "subject's" truth, I still believe it is possible that the ethnographies I write reflect a progressive and feminist social agenda. As feminist ethnographers, we take on a knotty paradox of social responsibility: We are accountable for the consequences of our writing, fully cognizant that the story we construct is our own.

NOTES

I am deeply grateful to reviewers for their critical stance and their suggested revisions for this chapter. I especially wish to thank Louise Lamphere for her wisdom and tenacity. I also received intellectual support and helpful criticism from Jean Lave, Allison Wiley, Carol Smith, Nancy Scheper-Hughes, Ann Ferguson, Amy Scharf, Carol Chetkovich, and Karen Greene.

1. "The Kindred of Viola Jackson" (Stack 1970) describes the migration of ninety-eight relatives moving from the rural South to midwestern cities.

REFERENCES

Deleuze, Gillis, and Felix Guattari. 1987. *A Thousand Plateaus.* Minneapolis: University of Minnesota Press.
———. 1983. *Anti-Oedipus.* Minneapolis: University of Minnesota Press.
Liebow, Elliot. 1967. *Tally's Corner.* Boston: Little, Brown.
Stack, Carol B. Forthcoming. *Call to Home: African Americans Reclaim the Rural South.* New York: Basic Books.
———. 1972. *All Our Kin: Strategies for Survival in a Black Community.* New York: Harper and Row.
———. 1970. "The Kindred of Viola Jackson: Residence and Family Organization of an Urban Black American Family." In *Afro-American Anthropology: Contemporary Perspectives,* edited by N. Whitten Jr. and J. Szwed. New York: The Free Press.

5

Relationality and Ethnographic Subjectivity: Key Informants and the Construction of Personhood in Fieldwork

SUAD JOSEPH

Relationality and Key Informants

As sources of information, as links to other informants, as agents of legitimation, as friends, and as anchors of human bonding in what, to some anthropologists, may feel like strange and alien places, key informants have enabled ethnographic work. The constructs of self of the ethnographers and their key informants intersect in multiple ways, affecting ethnographic methods, theories, and epistemologies. As feminist scholars[1] challenge the universalism of the individualist construct of self and theorize the historically/culturally specific constructs of self, the relationships between ethnographers and key informants must be rethought.

Until recently, researchers often assumed the universality of the Western construct of self as bounded, autonomous, and separate. Key informants were represented as autonomous others and independent sources of information. Relational constructs of the self, as alternatives to the individualized self, are not new in social and psychological theory. Many feminist ethnographers have become sensitized to diverse constructs of selfhood cross-culturally and to the impacts of their own culture, gender, race, or class in studying cross-culturally. Feminist fieldworkers, however, have only begun to problematize their own construct of self in relation to the constructs of self among the subjects of their research (E. Keller, 1985; Hurtado, 1989; Haraway, 1989; Kondo, 1990; Minh-ha, 1989). Relational theories of knowledge are being developed by theorists challenging the self/other binary (Gergen, 1990: 583; Rosaldo, 1989: 206). Earlier work, though, often identified relationality as dysfunctional and did not analyze the intersections of relationality and patriarchy (Minuchin et al., 1978). Feminist revisions of Western constructs of self, although linking relationality with patriarchy, often feminized the relational self (Chodorow, 1978; Gilligan, 1982; E. Keller, 1985; Joseph, 1993b).

The patriarchal relational construct of self, what I call patriarchal connectivity, that I found among men and women in Camp Trad, Borj Hammoud, an urban working-class neighborhood of Greater Beirut, Lebanon, is not unique. My findings resonate with aspects of Dorinne Kondo's descriptions of working-class persons in Tokyo (Kondo, 1990), Alan Roland's (1988) descriptions of India and Japan, as well as those by scholars of Western subcultures (Minh-ha, 1989; Anzaldua, 1987; Spivak, 1990). In these works, the subjectivities of the ethnographer and the subject are interwoven. These works, however, do not unravel the impact of the ethnographer's and key informant's patriarchal relational constructs of self on feminist fieldwork.

To raise questions for feminist research, I will focus primarily on my relationship with one key informant, Hanna Yusif,[2] a young Palestinian Lebanese, and his family, who lived next door to me in Camp Trad, Borj Hammoud, Lebanon, during the early 1970s when I began this fieldwork. Having been born in Lebanon, I was in the 1970s in many ways more like my Lebanese friends and family than my American friends in my sense of self. Growing up in an age and a gender-hierarchical family as the youngest and female, I had internalized many of the rules of what I call patriarchal connectivity. The conjunction of my sense of self with that of Hanna, similarly organized around patriarchal connectivity, had significant implications for my fieldwork. Below, I discuss the methodological, theoretical, and epistemological implications for feminist research of such patriarchal connective personhoods.

Patriarchal Connectivity and Personhood

Among the Camp Trad families, persons were viewed as always linked to others. With porous boundaries and shifting identities, men and women signaled maturity as a process of being parts of larger wholes. To capture this relational sense of personhood, I, like Catherine Keller[3] (1986), use the concept of connectivity (Joseph, 1993a). Camp Trad persons with significant relationships to each other expected to be able to read each other's minds, anticipate each other's needs, and shape their likes and dislikes in response to each other's. Communication in these connective relationships was often indirect, as intimates expected each other to know and anticipate each other's needs and thoughts. Persons often spoke to each other through third parties, taking communications once or twice removed as emanating from the source.

Connective relationships in Camp Trad were organized in the context of a patriarchal society. I use patriarchy to mean the domination of males over females, elders (males and females) over juniors (males and females), and the mobilization of kinship structures, morality, and idioms to institutionalize and legitimate these forms of power. The interweaving of patriarchy and connectivity (Joseph, 1993a) was crucial in Lebanon because of the centrality of kinship. So valorized were kin relationships that persons created idiomatic kinship with nonkin to harness the expectations, emotionalities, and obligations of kinship in public areas.

Connectivity, indirection, patriarchy, and idiomatic kinship intersected in Camp Trad to support the production of fluid selves trained in circuitous communication, gender and age domination, and the privileging of kin. Identities and personhood in Camp Trad were fluid and shifting not only because of the multiplicity of ethnic, religious, racial, class, kin, and gender groupings but also because of the psychosocial processes by which selves were produced. The dynamics I observed among the Camp Trad families were reproduced by others in Lebanon, although their enactment varied by class, education, and region.

Ethnographic Positionality

Camp Trad was close to the Lebanese village in which I was born and lived during the first years of my life. My parents had immigrated to a U.S. east coast town, raising their children in a tightly knit patriarchal Maronite Catholic family, relatively insulated from the culture and public institutions (except school and church) of the United States, guided by their Lebanese village morality. Connectivity, indirection, patriarchy, and idiomatic kinship were a part of my own sensibilities. Raised in a patriarchal connective family, I was trained to live by local Lebanese rules of feminine behavior. Modesty, indirection, deference to males and elders, equation of self and family, and merger of intimacy and identity were so much a part of my sensibilities that I often naturalized rather than theorized the similarities between myself and Camp Trad persons. I slipped into my extended family, developed idiomatic kin relations with neighbors in Camp Trad and friends in Beirut across age, gender, ethnic, religious, class, and national groups, and embraced the self for which I had been raised.

There were in retrospect, however, sharp edges in my reimmersion in my culture of origin. Although I knew little about feminism in the 1960s and early 1970s, I had on occasion rebelled against male dominance in my own family. Perhaps unintentionally I had shifted from my family's political perspectives, jolted by the student strikes of 1968, which were particularly radicalized at Columbia University, where I studied anthropology. Having left home while still single (something only males did in my family), I had begun, unawares, a journey of differentiating self from family.

Most of my Camp Trad neighbors, however, saw me as a *mughtaribi*,[4] a Lebanese who had emigrated and returned. Some of my neighbors knew my family, and one was a relative of my brother-in-law. Some of my neighbors, including the Yusifs, met my parents when they visited Lebanon in 1972. My Camp Trad neighbors saw me, as they saw themselves and each other, as a conglomerate of identities that allowed for possible alliances or fractures. To them, I was an American, an Arab, a Lebanese, a Christian, and a Maronite. I was a female of working-class origins, educated, and married. Most important to my Camp Trad neighbors, I was from a known local family, connected to a number of known local families. Each axis of identity provided a potential basis of connection or fracture with my Camp Trad neighbors.

Fieldwork processes that are standard for anthropologists intensified my reimmersion in the culture. I lived in the neighborhood that I studied, Camp Trad, Borj Hammoud, under basically the same set of circumstances as my neighbors. I spoke Arabic, their language, and only Arabic, the whole time I was in the neighborhood. I lived by their social rules (which were also my family rules), including rules of reciprocity, hospitality, generosity, respect, and modesty. The rules required an extensive and intensive exchange of visits that absorbed enormous amounts of time daily. The intensity of this relational embedment exposed me to neighborly social claims, as well as offered me the right to make local claims. Over time it became difficult to sustain a research attitude toward my neighbors, who increasingly became dear friends. Return visits to Camp Trad since 1971 have reinforced my feeling that my neighbors became a part of my life, etched in my personal life journey. Several have told me that I also affected the course of their lives. That I and my Camp Trad neighbors felt and made these statements to each other in 1994, twenty-three years after the start of my research, testifies to the depth of the encounter.

Camp Trad

I worked in Camp Trad, Borj Hammoud from 1971 to 1980[5], and again in 1993 and 1994. The initial fieldwork, carried out for my doctoral research, entailed over two years of continuous residence in the neighborhood. I carried out the fieldwork in the colloquial Arabic of Lebanon, using no translators and no research assistants.

I accompanied extensive participant-observation data gathering, the standard method of anthropologists, with extensive formal interviews with family members, averaging over ten hours of formal interviews for approximately one hundred families in a small four-street area of Camp Trad. A largely working-class municipality of Greater Beirut, Borj Hammoud housed about 200,000[6] Lebanese, Syrians, Palestinians, Jordanians, Egyptians, and people of European ancestry from almost every religious sect of the eastern Mediterranean[7]. About 40 percent of the residents of Borj Hammoud were Armenian (Orthodox, Catholic, and Protestant). Another 40 percent were Lebanese Shi'a. The rest were members of twenty different religious sects, including Maronites, Roman Catholics, Greek Orthodox, Greek Catholics, Arab Protestants, Syrian Orthodox, Syrian Catholics, Sunnis, Druze, and 'Alawites. Camp Trad was one of the most heterogeneous neighborhoods of Borj Hammoud.

Camp Trad's diversity was reinforced by Lebanon's system of representing its citizens in government and the distribution of public resources on the basis of the purported distribution of legally recognized religious sects. In addition, seventeen different sets of religious laws (personal status laws) were legally recognized. Such political uses of sectarian identities encouraged residents to manipulate the multiple identities available to them politically. Identities in Camp Trad were contradictory, plural, and shifting, like Gloria Anzaldua's (1987: 79) descriptions of the new mestiza's plural, contradictory, and shifting personality in the United States.

Hanna Yusif

Hanna Yusif lived across the hall from me with his parents and six siblings. Given that there were only two apartments on the floor, the Yusifs and I, like most immediate neighbors in Camp Trad, spent a lot of time with each other. I addressed Hanna's parents, Khalid and Amina, according to Arab custom, as Abu and Um Hanna, the father and mother of Hanna. I had idiomatic kinship relationships with all of Hanna's family—a sister relationship with Um Hanna and Abu Hanna, his Palestinian Roman Catholic mother and Lebanese Maronite Catholic father; a sister relationship with Hanna and with Farid, his next-oldest sibling; and a "tante" (aunt)[8] relationship to the five youngest.

Idiomatic kinship entailed expectations. Neighbors expected me to know what was going on in the Yusif household, as they expected the Yusifs to know about me. I was expected to privilege the Yusifs in the distribution of resources and they were expected to prioritize me in sharing their goods. My interventions in the Yusifs' familial issues and their, perhaps more modest, interventions in my affairs were expected and accepted. Our familial relationship gave us a sense of rights in each other. These rights were authorized by the patriarchal connectivity that supported our senses of personhood and moralized the relationships into which we grew. I had close relationships with several of the Yusifs, but my relationship with Hanna was recognized as special.

At eighteen in 1971, Hanna was in the eleventh grade and considering college, in a neighborhood in which the majority of youths did not reach the Brevet (equivalent to tenth grade) and few went to college. He took seriously himself, his familial role as eldest son, and his role as one of the more learned men in the neighborhood. With Abu Hanna, his father, often absent from home because of his work and late-night card playing and drinking, Hanna seemed, at times, a husband substitute for his mother and a father substitute for his younger siblings (Joseph, 1994).

In the neighborhood, Hanna was highly respected as a man of reason who worked for mutual respect among members of different religious, ethnic, and national groups. He belonged to the Syrian Social National Party and took it upon himself to try to organize neighborhood youths into politically progressive politics and worldviews. He was regarded also as a highly desirable match by many neighborhood unmarried women and their parents. He displayed a cultivated roguish masculinity, polished good manners, and a playful use of the abundant ritualized pleasantries available in the Arabic language. Hanna, at eighteen, was preparing for the authoritative position local patriarchy offered him.

Patriarchal Connectivity: Becoming a Sister

Hanna, like his parents and siblings, saw me as an extension of himself and his family. I reciprocated the involvement. Mostly I was the older sister and he the younger brother; although at times, as was characteristic of local patriarchy, the hierarchy reversed. Among the Arab families in Camp Trad, brother/sister relationships were charged with a love/power dynamic underwritten by patriarchal connectivity (Joseph, 1994). Brothers and sisters were expected to care for, nurture, support, and defend each other. A brother was supposed to look out for his sister's interests and to guide and control her activity. A sister was supposed to take her brother's wishes as her own, minister to him, and comport herself so as to maintain his and their family honor. This lifelong commitment to care for each other was reinforced by the fluidity of boundaries and the gender and age hierarchy characteristic of patriarchal connective relationships. Whereas the brother/sister expectations of my relationship with Hanna were muted by its idiomatic character, in many ways they paralleled the patterns I observed Hanna enact with his sister, those I observed in other brother/sister relationships in Lebanon, and mine with my own brothers.

Patriarchal connectivity shaped our mutual expectations. Hanna and I talked about politics, movies, the theater, national and neighborhood social events, and personal relationships. He confided in me and I shared many things with him. In a local culture in which young men could visit women in their apartments alone, but not often, he frequently came alone to my apartment during the daytime and early evening with no apparent violation of social rules. No doubt our age difference (ten years), my married status, the proximity of our apartments, my familial relationship with his family, my borderline role as a Lebanese American, and the visiting by other men for interviews also facilitated Hanna's visiting.

I often felt that Hanna expected me to agree with him, no matter what the issue was. I found myself sometimes, unawares, expecting the same of him. When I did not, or he did not, we often would talk at length to resolve, bridge, explain away, or diminish the differences. At other times, we glossed them over, pretending they did not exist, each seemingly aware that, in this culture, difference could easily lead to, or be perceived as, betrayal. Given the primacy of familial loyalty in patriarchal connective relations, we painstakingly assured each other directly and indirectly that the trust of each in the other was warranted.

Hanna rarely asked me for anything directly, nor did I of him. When either of us did, however, the other tried to fulfill the request. Brothers and sisters were expected to understand each other's wishes. If Hanna or I asserted a desire indirectly, the other tried to respond, although our misinterpretations of the other's desires at times led to disappointments. Each of us, at times, communicated to the other by talking to Um Hanna, knowing that she, in her culturally sanctioned maternal role of mediator, would convey the information.

Once Hanna and I were talking about the famous Lebanese singer, Fairouz. I had just attended one of her performances and described it enthusiastically to him. He praised her and noted that he had never seen her perform. Over the next few days, I had a similar conversation with the Kurakises, close mutual neighborhood friends of Hanna and me. They also expressed love of Fairouz and regret at never having seen her perform. I remember feeling bad that I had had the privilege of attending her performance and that family-like friends had not. It was difficult for me to accept that I could have something that my idiomatic kin did not, an operant aspect of connective relationships. And given the indirection of connective communication, their assertion of regret at not having seen her translated, for me, into a request that I do something about it. I knew that they could not afford the tickets to the expensive Piccadilly Theater themselves. Even though I was on a limited budget, I purchased orchestra tickets for Hanna and the Kurakises and myself. Although they were surprised at my gesture (my Camp Trad neighbors and family in Lebanon were frequently surprised that a Lebanese American could behave like a Lebanese), they did not persist with their culturally required initial protests. Their acceptance reaffirmed the growing bond of kinship between us.

The Kurakises invited me to a lavish Sunday dinner at their house. Without thinking about the implications, I mentioned to Hanna the delightful time I had had with the Kurakises. Within a few days, Um Hanna had invited me to share a meal at their apartment. I felt badly when I realized that Hanna might have read into my comment either an implied request for an invitation or an implied negative comparison to the Kurakises's hospitality. The constant attention to one another's needs and the possible meanings hidden in indirect communications intensified the investment and energy expended in maintaining the brother/sister relationship I had with Hanna.

Commingled with and structuring the expressions of love in brother/sister relations in the local culture were the expectations of gender and age domination—local patriarchy. The patriarchal family system offered me responsibilities and rights as a sister that I embraced almost unthinkingly. As the youngest female of an age- and gender-hierarchical patriarchal Arab family, I understood the rules of familial relationships. I expected to defer to men and elders and to have rights over juniors.

My relationship with Hanna entailed responsibilities and rights that I recognized and understood from my own upbringing. Since I was considerably older than Hanna, I expected to have, and did have, authority over him as an elder and an elder sister. No doubt my authority was augmented by my educational and class advantages. My marital status probably enhanced my position.

Hanna's gender, however, gave him authority. Having come into manhood during the years of my fieldwork, he increasingly asserted and tested his cultural role in relationship to his family, friends, and me. For example, he began disciplining his twelve-year-old sister Flaur when she behaved in ways he considered inappropriate to a young woman. She often rebelled or resisted his authority. Occasionally, he hit her. To protect herself, Flaur on a few occasions ran into my apartment. On a couple of occasions, when I heard fighting, I tried to stop him from hitting her. I had an older-sister relationship with Flaur and so I felt a responsibility to intervene on her behalf. Although Hanna was willing to talk about Flaur and often conceded points, he continued to discipline her. His brotherly authority over Flaur superseded my sisterly authority over him.

In my position of elder sister, I tried to protect Hanna at times. Once, after a fight with his father, he left home in anger. When Um Hanna told me about the incident I was appalled and asked Farid, his brother, to help me find him. I vividly remember the anxiety I felt driving with Farid on a winter night to Dbayye, a Palestinian camp north of Borj Hammoud, where Hanna's *khalta* (mother's sister) lived, hoping to find him there. The thought that his family relationship might rupture frightened me. That he would challenge his father's authority and that his father might reject him was alarming. As a daughter, I had avoided challenging my parents directly. My challenges were mostly indirect, quiet, slowly cumulative, and often without my own awareness that my behavior was moving me away from parts of my parents' culture. At that point, my family was my life. How could my idiomatic brother jeopardize relationship to his family? How could his father risk throwing his son out of the apartment? I had to do something. I had to make the family right again. I had to heal the wound. We did not find him that night, but Farid found him the next day. I felt relief when Hanna returned home. My actions were regarded as appropriate to my brother/sister relationship with Hanna.

The dynamics of patriarchal connective relationships allowed for shifts in roles. Hanna became my protector and played the part of an older brother in relation to my vulnerabilities as a woman in a culture that expected honorable women to be protected by male kin. When he needed guidance, he became my younger brother. The shifts in roles, supported by the range of identity options available in the culture, however, were constrained by the rules of patriarchy that privileged men and elders.

My relationships with Hanna and his family, though more involved and intense than most of my other relationships, nevertheless were not unique. I had similar relationships with a number of men and women and families from different religious, national, ethnic, and class backgrounds. To a number of persons, at different points, I was a daughter, a sister, an aunt, a niece, a cousin. Kinship idioms legitimated, moralized, and energized a host of relations into cross-sex and same-sex, cross-age and same-age kin relations. Imported with the kin idioms were the rules, rights, and responsibilities of familial relations. Neighbors came to have rights in me, I came to have rights in them. This culture was embedded in the constructs of self that I carried with me to the field and that I encountered among the neighbors who became idiomatic family to me.

As I prepared to depart in the spring of 1973, Hanna came alone to say good-bye. He had written a letter to me conveying his feelings. He read the letter as I sat next to him. When he finished reading, he looked up. Tears flowed from his eyes. I touched his shoulders and he fell sobbing into my arms, crying as I held him. I wept. My relationship with Hanna, his family, and others in Camp Trad and theirs with each other were normative for their patriarchal connective culture and the culture that I shared with them. At the time, I did not consider the implications of the character of these relationships for my data, methods, or theory.

Patriarchal Connectivity and Ethnographic Research

The patriarchal connective relationships I had with Hanna and a number of other Camp Trad neighbors to some extent affected what data I collected, from whom I collected them, how I collected them, and what I thought about the data I collected. Hanna, perhaps more than anyone else in the immediate Camp Trad neighborhood, understood my research and took an interest in it. Some examples of the impact of my patriarchal connective relationship with Hanna on my research may highlight some of the implications of the intersections of self and science.

In my original research, I had set out to demonstrate that persons identify with religious sects or ethnic groups because of material conditions. I analyzed the institutional pressures for sectarian identities. But perhaps because of my rejection of aspects of my own deeply religious upbringing, I found it difficult to accept that family-like friends could embrace rigid sectarian beliefs. My relationship with Hanna probably reinforced these blinders. Belonging to the secular Syrian Social Nationalist Party, he decried sectarian politics. He actively sought to bridge religious differences. He rarely went to church, was involved in few sectarian activities, and frequently was critical of clerical dogmatism. Identifying with Hanna may have reinforced my underestimation of the importance of religious faith to others.

Patriarchal connective dynamics also influenced what I regarded as data. Once I had developed idiomatic kinship relations with the Yusifs, the Kurakises, and others, they insisted on frequent visits, expecting me to become involved in their wider circle of friends. I thought of these visiting networks as part of my friendships, not necessarily as part of my research. It was clear to me, however, that I was being given access to data crucial to my analysis of the shifting nature of sectarian identification through these highly intersectarian networks. Although I had no training in network analysis, I developed a technique for assessing the role of neighborhood visiting networks as a counterweight to the institutional pressures for sectarian identification. It is likely that if my Camp Trad idiomatic kin had not expected frequent visiting, if I had not been trained in the cultural importance of reciprocity, and if I had not taken their need for me as a kind of family responsibility, I may not have collected the data on the basis of which I argued that the neighborhood street was a crucial counterpoint to formal sectarian institutions—an argument central to my earlier work.

Hanna and his family created some of my most significant networks. Suggesting interviews, Hanna set up meetings for me with people I might not otherwise have interviewed or who would not have seen me without his intercession. He created friendships for me. He brought his friends to my apartment and I received them as the friends of a brother. At the time, I did not think of these interactions in research terms, but the information was often important to my understanding of local events.

The culture of indirection also affected my research methods and data. My neighbors usually gave direct answers in formal interviews. When speaking informally about feelings, desires, beliefs, or sensitive subjects, however, they often shifted to indirection, implicating others present at the interview, including the researcher, in critical areas of expressing their feelings. Hints, vague suggestions, and meaningful gazes were offered as responses that I was supposed to interpret. Such communications had been the stuff of my early childhood. In Camp Trad, I spent hours talking with my neighbors in an attempt to interpret indirect communications, as I had as a child with my parents and siblings. In the process, I was implicated in the naming and shaping of the feelings, thoughts, and actions of these persons.

The culture of indirection played itself out in my relationship with Hanna as well. As a young male defining his masculinity, Hanna often communicated assertively. He also communicated indirectly with me, however. At times, he assumed meanings from my statements and conveyed them to Um Hanna, or conveyed information he wanted me to know to Um Hanna, or even to his sister, Flaur, who would then tell me. One example was his mistaken interpretation of what I told him about the meal at the Kurakises (see above) and Um Hanna's invitation to dinner.

Hanna often took statements I made to others that affected or reflected upon him to be intentional communications from me. I similarly found myself, at times, assuming that second- and third-hand statements were intended as communications from him. Completing the communication process required each of us to have relationships with as much of the full set of relationships of the other as possible. This not only reinforced our mutual immersion in connective patriarchical dynamics but also actively engaged us in eliciting, extracting, shaping, and creating each other and our local social world.

Hanna, like his family and several other idiomatic kin became, in part, significant for me. I became significant for Hanna and many other idiomatic kin. The Hanna who appears in various articles I have published about Camp Trad, I argue, had claimed a part of me in him, as I had claimed a part of him in me. His feelings, his thoughts, and the actions that I have described as his and as examples of certain local cultural patterns, I would still describe as his and as descriptive of local patterns. I now additionally argue, however, that they are not his alone as an autonomous, bounded, separate individual but rather they are his as part of a web of relationality that included me the ethnographer as his idiomatic sister.

Idiomatic kinship was patriarchal, making gender and age hierarchies significant in my relationship with Hanna. The love/power dynamics of brother/sister relationships empowered Hanna with the cultural authority and responsibility to protect me. He took it upon himself, as an idiomatic brother, to defend me and my work. He was especially helpful with the young men in the neighborhood who were inclined to be suspicious of my work. On a number of occasions, he reported having arguments about my research with neighbors in which he stood up for me. I was struck by the emotional quality of his reports. He seemed angry and indignant that his friends would suspect me. I was aware of an asserted masculinity when he described these encounters. It seems likely that since he identified with me, his own honor was at stake. He could not, as an idiomatic brother, allow attacks on my credibility without his own status suffering. Seeing me in part as an extension of himself, he saw an attack on me as an attack on him. His status transferred to me, as my behavior impacted his. Since the neighbors saw him as a man of peace, Hanna's support of my work embued my project with respectable qualities.

The confluence of my own and local patriarchal connective sensibilities with patriarchal notions in anthropology in the 1970s also led me to conflate persons with family and to assume that any older members of the family could speak adequately for other members. In the 1970s, households were the operative unit of analysis in anthropology, in Camp Trad local culture, and in my own mind. Like residents of Camp Trad and most anthropologists at the time, I assumed that elder men and women represented their families. My questionnaires were structured to be answered by the household head on behalf of the whole household. Although I made appointments expecting to meet with both male and female household heads, I interviewed whomever had waited for me, at times even older children. When men were present, I and the women of the household deferred to men—although, because of men's absences, much of my data came from women.

When I realized, upon my return to New York, that households and families could not be viewed monolithically, it was difficult for me to isolate from my household-based questionnaires the behavior of specific persons or genders. For example, the female household heads usually answered my questions about who had visited the household and whom they had visited during the week. I treated those visits as representative of visits of the family. I did not record separately the visits of the male household heads and the adult children. No doubt many visits that were made by other family members were not captured in the data, and the data that I gathered cannot be disaggregated. In the case of the Yusifs, Abu Hanna was rarely home. Hanna acted as male household head and helped his mother with the interviews. Feminist interventions in anthropology in the 1970s made me realize, after I returned to the United States, that these data were not about families but were often about women, and that neither women nor families were unitary.

Working in the local patriarchy placed me in hierarchical relationships. Occupying both dominant and subordinate positions with the same or different persons made me realize that patriarchal power was shifting and situational. Hanna's involvement in my work reflected the power dynamics of patriarchy. I experienced not only the love, but also the hierarchy of the brother/sister relationship in my research. Assuming that our political beliefs should conform with our close brother/sister relationship, he wanted me to embrace his political views. He tried to get me politically involved, asked me to read Syrian Social National Party literature, and invited me to SSNP cell meetings. He wanted me and my research to be something for him. As a result of Hanna, I developed a more sympathetic understanding of his party's appeal than I might have otherwise.

My authority as an elder sister also led me to have expectations of Hanna. I asked him and came to expect him to make connections for me and to protect me in the neighborhood in ways I did not expect of others. When we spoke, I expected to be listened to with the respect due an elder sister. When I gave advice, I expected him to consider it seriously. I tried to persuade him to share my beliefs and intervened in his defense. The line between familial persuasion and patriarchal compliance often dissolved.

Patriarchal connectivity has also affected the way I have written my analyses. I have felt concerned about how I represented my idiomatic kin and how they might react to my representation. The difficulties of communication during the war that started in Lebanon in 1975, just days after I completed my doctoral dissertation, has meant that my work, all of which appeared after the war broke out, has not been readily accessible to Camp Trad residents. To my knowledge, they have not read my work. The volatility of the situation, which took a historic toll in human lives in Lebanon, made it risky for me to bring publications with me on my trips during the war. Yet the awareness of the possibility of their reading them in the future has lingered with me. Hanna and his family were concerned about how I would present them and Lebanon. They were highly aware of the negative image of Arabs in the United States. Exposed to the social sciences, Hanna grasped more fully than many others in Camp Trad the uses of scientific research. How he and others I cared about would respond to my work made me cautious in my writing. I was aware that sustaining familial relationships, even idiomatic kin, meant conditioning my speech. In a patriarchal connective culture, family loyalty is necessary for survival.

Personhood and Challenges for Feminist Research

The impact of constructs of the self by ethnographers and key informants raises multiple methodological, theoretical, and epistemological challenges for feminist research. Feminist ethnographers must become aware of their own and their subjects' constructs of self—the assumptions that are a core part of their personhood. As I have argued, for example, relative boundedness or porousness on either side affects relationships with informants and data gathering. It is not clear, however, that constructs of self necessarily affect all areas of ethnographic research systematically. The challenge for feminist ethnographic work is to ascertain whether, how, and to what significance they do. There is not necessarily a single answer.

Feminist research should also assess how power structures that are built into constructs of self impact research. I focused on the effects of patriarchy, but class, ethnicity, race, religion, and other forms of discrimination were also operative. Multiple forms of domination, working in complementary and contradictory ways, affect the position(s) of the ethnographer in local hierarchies, the position(s) of key informants, and the shifts in those positionalities. Since the feminist ethnographer is part of the power dynamic and power shifts, definitive descriptions may be elusive. The challenge for feminist ethnography is to capture a moment of a necessarily fluid dynamic and ascertain the significance of that moment.

The most crucial question for understanding the implications of relational constructs of self is, arguably, agency (Joseph, 1993b). The universalist assumption of bounded, autonomous, separative selves allowed for the attribution of individualist agency. Anthropologists have assumed that the person is actor and cause. Agency among relational selves cannot be singular. Relational persons shape and are shaped by others. Feelings, thoughts, and actions of actors are theirs but not theirs alone from their point of view and from the point of view I am suggesting.

As I look back, for example, at what I recorded as the feelings of my Camp Trad neighbors, I realize that I must reassess their feelings, my feelings, and the outcome of our relationships. Specification of the ownership of action, however, is often difficult, if not impossible, in connective relationships. Data descriptions need to convey the embedding of action in webs of relationality. Such specification is difficult not only for the anthropologists but for local people. In Camp Trad, ascertaining who was responsible for specific ideas or actions was a constant point of negotiation. These intense negotiations over agency further reinforced the very relationality they were purportedly undoing by trying to ascertain responsibility and cause.

If the construction of knowledges is relational (Gergen, 1990; Rosaldo, 1989), then the presentation of data needs to reflect its relational foundation. Although it is clear to me that feminist ethnographers must complexify identification and attribution of agency to account for relationality, including that of the ethnographer, it is not entirely clear how one does this in connective relationships. The challenge for feminist ethnography, in navigating the waters of relationality and agency, is to attempt to sustain the notion of agency while accounting for the diversity of its enactments in culturally specific notions of personhood.

As a strategy for raising questions for feminist research, I have focused on the constructs of self of ethnographers and key informants. My idiomatic kin relationship with Hanna was one of many that affected what I considered data, how I obtained data, how I analyzed and wrote about the data, and the very character of the data. The operation of my own and local constructs of connectivity, indirection, patriarchy, and idiomatic kinship contributed to the production of relational knowledges. Ethnographers, feminist and nonfeminist, almost always establish close and intimate relationships with key informants. Feminist ethnography, however, must problematize, complexify, and analyze the construction of self in the construction of scientific knowledges.

NOTES

Acknowledgments: I wish to thank the graduate students and faculty of the Gender and Global Issues program, University of California–Davis (UCD), and the members of the GGI conference on "Feminist Dilemmas in Fieldwork" held at UCD in March 1992 for their helpful comments.

1. C. Keller (1986); Minh-ha (1989); Gergen (1990); Fox-Genovese (1991).

2. Names of all Camp Trad residents have been changed.

3. Keller (1986: 9, 114) opposes the concept of connective self to separative self. She uses "connectivity" to imply a liberatory notion in which a person works toward both relationality and autonomy. I use the term to mean a relationality whose forms can change under different political economies.

4. I use the past tense throughout the chapter, even for descriptions that remain current, to avoid slippage into ahistoricism.

5. My fieldwork was carried out in 1971–1973 under a NIMH predoctoral research grant. I undertook subsequent research in 1974, 1976, 1978, and 1980. Unless otherwise indicated, the argument and most of the data refer to the period in the early 1970s just prior to the outbreak of the civil war in 1975.

6. No formal census had been done in Lebanon since 1932. This and other population estimates were gathered from discussions with local officials.

7. During the Lebanese Civil War, starting in 1975, almost all the non-Lebanese and non-Christians were driven out from or fled Camp Trad.

8. The use of French terms is a legacy of French colonialism.

REFERENCES

Anzaldua, Gloria. 1987. *Borderlands. La Frontera. The New Mestiza.* San Francisco: Aunt Lute Book Company.

Chodorow, Nancy. 1978. *The Reproduction of Mothering.* Berkeley: University of California Press.

Fox-Genovese, Elizabeth. 1991. *Feminism Without Illusions: A Critique of Individualism.* Chapel Hill: University of North Carolina Press.

Gergen, Kenneth J. 1990. "Social Understanding and the Inscription of the Self." In *Cultural Psychology: Essays on Comparative Human Development,* edited by James Stigler et al. Cambridge: Cambridge University Press.

Gilligan, Carol. 1982. *In a Different Voice: Psychological Theory and Women's Development.* Cambridge, Mass.: Harvard University Press.

Haraway, Donna. 1989. *Primate Visions: Gender, Race, and Nature in the World of Modern Science.* New York: Routledge.

Hurtado, Aida. 1989. "Relating to Privilege: Seduction and Rejection in the Subordination of White Women and Women of Color." *Signs* 4, no. 4: 833–855.

Joseph, Suad. 1993a. "Connectivity and Patriarchy Among Urban Working Class Arab Families in Lebanon." *Ethos* 21, no. 4: 452–484.

———. 1993b. "Gender and Relationality Among Arab Families in Lebanon." *Feminist Studies* 19, no. 3: 465–486.

———. 1994. "Brother/Sister Relationships: Connectivity, Love, and Power in the Reproduction of Arab Patriarchy." *American Ethnologist* 21, no. 1: 50–73.

Keller, Catherine. 1986. *From a Broken Web: Separation, Sexism, and Self.* Boston: Beacon Press.

Keller, Evelyn Fox. 1985. *Reflections on Gender and Science.* New Haven: Yale University Press.

Kondo, Dorinne K. 1990. *Crafting Selves: Power, Gender, and Discourses of Identity in a Japanese Workplace.* Chicago: University of Chicago Press.

Minh-ha, Trinh T. 1989. *Woman, Native, Other: Writing Postcoloniality and Feminism.* Bloomington: Indiana University Press.

Minuchin, Salvador, Bernice L. Rosman, and Lester Baker. 1978. *Psychosomatic Families: Anorexia Nervosa in Context.* Cambridge, Mass.: Harvard University Press.

Roland, Alan. 1988. *In Search of Self in India and Japan: Toward a Cross-Cultural Psychology.* Princeton: Princeton University Press.

Rosaldo, Renato. 1989. *Culture and Truth: The Remaking of Social Analysis.* Boston: Beacon Press.

Spivak, Gayatri Chakravorty. 1990. *The Post-Colonial Critic: Interviews, Strategies, Dialogues.* New York: Routledge.

6

Between Bosses and Workers: The Dilemma of a Keen Observer and a Vocal Feminist

PING-CHUN HSIUNG

IN THIS CHAPTER I analyze the challenges and opportunities I encountered when I conducted fieldwork in Taiwan's satellite factories in the summer of 1989 and the beginning of 1990. Methodologically, this chapter centers around the issues of negotiating entry, maintaining access, and resolving conflicts and tensions. My discussion derives from, and seeks to contribute to, the recent feminist debate appraising the power relations between researchers and informants. My analysis also must be seen in the context of earlier accounts of fieldwork in Asia, with special emphasis on those focusing on the Chinese communities in Asian countries. I first situate my own fieldwork experiences at the point where my personal trajectory as a Chinese woman intersects with my previous knowledge of the research topic. My dilemmas in fieldwork arise from a number of contradictions: between my roles as a participant and as an observer, between my status as an insider (as an indigenous woman) and as an outsider (a feminist), and between my vocal feminism and my role as a keen observer. My discussion of the dilemmas inherent in feminist fieldwork takes all these contradictions into account.

My experience as a participant-observer in a setting where the power structure is openly constructed and contested along class and gender lines provides invaluable insights for my analysis of patriarchal capitalist control in Taiwanese society. At the same time, however, my critical attitude toward capitalist practices puts me in direct conflict with the very phenomena I set out to study. From the beginning, therefore, I found myself in constant negotiation with the system itself and with the agents of that system—the bosses—on whom I depended for gaining entry, and sustaining access, to the satellite factories.

My indigenous status gave me many advantages. Knowing the language, the ecological environment, and the cultural norms and practices in Taiwan put me on par with my Chinese colleagues. Unlike foreigners, I did not need to rely on a translator or research assistant.[1] As a native speaker, I was able to overhear simultaneous conversation on the shop floor and to engage in daily spontaneous dialogue with others on a variety of topics. From the first days of my fieldwork, familiarity with the ecological environment allowed me to get on a motorcycle (the most common transportation in Taiwan) in order to explore small factories in the midst of the rice fields and in dark alleys. My familiarity with Chinese culture and Taiwanese society provided the broader context I needed to interpret interactional relationships experienced at the micro level. On the negative side, however, my insider status as an indigenous woman rendered me subject to patriarchal control in the field.

At the same time, I entered the field as a researcher influenced by Western feminist scholarship, as an outsider who viewed existing class and gender inequalities with a critical eye. Together with what I learned as an insider, this outsider perspective enabled me to use my fieldwork experience to deconstruct the formation and mechanism of the power dynamics in the satellite factories. I have also come to challenge the dichotomous portrayal of the power relations between female ethnographers and female subjects, recently articulated in many discussions of feminist methodology (Patai, 1991; Stacey, 1991; Acker et al., 1991). I argue that in the fieldwork setting, the power relationship is more complex. In my view, it is simplistic to assume that the only power relation is that which exists between the researcher and the researched—the powerful and the powerless, respectively. To overemphasize a binary power relationship is to overlook the patriarchal context in which both the (female) feminist ethnographer and her female informants are caught and situated. It also fails to take into account the potential power possessed by individual agents of the patriarchal system. In order to contextualize feminist fieldwork, I propose that we think in terms of a multidimensional power relationship, of which the patriarchal/capitalist system, individual agents of the system, female informants, and female feminist researchers are the key constituents.

My own fieldwork involved me as an indigenous feminist researcher in a specific setting. I think it is nonetheless valuable to compare my experience with the reports of female researchers who entered Asian societies they observed as foreigners. A number of these foreign researchers of an earlier era provided valuable records of obstacles they encountered. Thus Mary Sheridan and Janet Salaff (Kung, Arrigo, and Salaff, 1984) and Linda Arrigo (1984) discovered, to their dismay, that the formal interview, a standard method of data collection in the West, fails to provide the same high-quality data when used in Asia. Lydia Kung (Kung, Arrigo, and Salaff, 1984) and Mary Sheridan (1984) also found it frustrating that although certain personal information that is usually not revealed openly in Western society is public knowledge in Chinese communities, other information is virtually inaccessible to outsiders. Moreover, several of these scholars were fully aware of, and readily acknowledged, their outsider status. Sheridan and Salaff (1984: 3), for example, discussed the ways in which their background, as Western-trained social scientists who "matured in the individual-centered humanism of Western civilization," affected their research. Although feminist scholars have only recently begun to reflect on, and analyze, their experiences in the field, these earlier accounts can provide useful information as we try to develop more comprehensive research methods. Less useful are fieldwork accounts that overly emphasize the positive aspects of the research procedure.[2] Thus Kung tells us that she "obtained an introduction to the management, explained my research project, and received permission to carry out informal interviews in the plant during working hours" (Kung, Arrigo, and Salaff, 1984: 98), but does not inform us how entry was negotiated, on what terms it was granted, how continuing access was sustained, and how potential tension was resolved.

By employing ethnographic data, my approach departs from mainstream sociology, where the deductive approach is practiced as a dominant mode of investigation. Being aware of the strength and limitations of quantitative as well as qualitative approaches, I was deeply concerned about the indiscriminate employment of statistical models by some of my colleagues. My concern echos what Chen Yiyun calls a Westernization of sociology in China, where the widespread use of computers has led many researchers to develop an addiction to positivism. According to Chen, Chinese researchers often adopt concepts and questionnaires originally designed for sociological enquiry in the West, without properly considering the very different social, cultural, and political context in which they were developed. And "certain foreign colleagues are even more ingenious: if they can get hold of a floppy disk of data, they can stuff China's numbers into a theoretical framework, and thus complete a 'sinological' treatise" (Chen, 1994: 70).

By discussing the embedded contradiction between the roles of a keen observer and a vocal feminist, I hope to shed light on some critical methodological issues that feminists need to address. At the same time, a pressing task is to question the applicability to Sinology of statistical models developed by Western social scientists. When sociology as a discipline was first introduced to China in the 1930s, it was pursued as knowledge deeply grounded in social realities. Leading scholars of the time, such as Fei Xiaotong, relied primarily on fieldwork data to disentangle the unique social fabric of Chinese society.[3] Before sociology becomes filled with shallow words and detached from the social reality of Chinese society, it is essential that we root sociology once again in the knowledge of the soil and its people. In this context, I am convinced that comprehensive and systematic fieldwork accounts are essential if we are to develop the research methods and the feminist scholarship appropriate to indigenous societies.

Entering Where Others and I Left Off

In the last years of my graduate study, I became interested in the work, marriage, and family experiences of Taiwan's first cohort of factory girls. Studies have documented that once married, most of them are forced to resign (Kung, 1983; Lu, 1986). A few reports indicated the existence of a large number of married women in the small factories (Niehoff, 1987; Stites, 1982, 1985). My hunch then was that Taiwan's first cohort of factory girls might have moved to factories in their neighborhoods or worked at home for these small factories on a piecework basis. My hunch was supported by what I had witnessed as a teacher in a junior high school in a fishing village in the central part of Taiwan in the mid-1970s. On my regular visits to my students' families, I saw that toys, plastic flowers, and Christmas ornaments were made by my female students, their aunts, and their mothers. "These are for the Americans," I was told.

Although factories with fewer than thirty workers composed up to 89 percent of Taiwan's manufacturing industry throughout the 1970s and 1980s, scholars have until recently failed to recognize the uniqueness and significance of these small factories in Taiwan's economic development. Studies of Taiwan's economic development have focused on large corporations in the Export Processing Zones. The failure to recognize the importance of the small factories in Taiwan's economic development evidences an intellectual bias in which the path and pattern of Western industrialization are held as norms in studying the economic development of the Third World. Such negligence could be partially logistical, in that it is much easier to gather data on large factories in the Export Processing Zones than to do research on the numerous small factories scattered in local communities.[4] Before I went into the field, the existing literature told me nothing about the operational mechanisms and labor politics of Taiwan's satellite factory system.[5] Knowledge of the effects of Taiwan's economic development on women has been based mainly on studies of young single women working in large factories (Arrigo, 1980; Diamond, 1979; Kung, 1976, 1983).[6] Except in a few cases, the experiences and lives of married women who work outside of the Export Processing Zones have been left out, despite the fact that, since the 1970s, the rate of increase in their participation in the labor force has been higher than that for single women (Gallin, 1984a, 1984b; Hu, 1982, 1984).[7]

Because so little was known at the time, I wanted to take an inside look at what was going on in the factories. Participant-observation seemed to be the best approach for my groundbreaking task since it would give me the depth and insight I was looking for. Before my departure, I was warned about the tensions between management and workers and how these tensions might create difficulties for me if I intended to cover both sides of the story. Covering both could become disastrous, I was told. It was suggested that I study either the management's or the workers' side of the story. I thought I would focus on the workers if I had to choose between the two.

In the summer of 1989, I set out to explore Taiwan's "economic miracle," a miracle created by small-scale and family-centered satellite factories and constructed by women through their paid and unpaid labor. I ended up spending three months in the factories. I worked in six factories and visited about thirty others during my first field trip. In December 1989 and January 1990, I revisited the factories and talked to the people I had met on my first trip.

In the field, I was seen, treated, and approached as an insider and outsider simultaneously. From the standpoint of people in the factory, my outsider status came from what I do (studying in the United States), whereas my insider status came from who I am (an indigenous woman). On a personal level, it was easy to get on a friendly footing with workers in the factory due to our shared experiences. During a break, an owner's mother, a widow in her midseventies, told me what types of odd jobs she had done to raise her children. When she described how hard it was to make straw hats at night under oil lights, I understood what she said, because when I was a child, my family once lived in a remote mountain village where there was no electricity or running water. I told her that I did my homework by candlelight and that my sister and I used to carry water from a mountain spring an hour away from our home. In one conversation, several male factory owners and I ended up talking about the games we used to play in the rice fields after school.

My coworkers' curiosity about my life and experiences in the United States allowed them to relate to me as both an insider and an outsider. The fact that I had been making extra efforts to get rice from Chinese grocery stores in Monterey Park, California, brought comments such as: "We never realized it could be an issue," and "I could never live without rice." My coworkers were surprised but delighted to learn that, rather than beefsteak, my favorite dish was bitter melon, a very popular vegetable in Taiwan but available only in a few Chinese grocery stores in the United States. During a conversation, I told a woman coworker in her early sixties that, being away from home, I once dreamed of a bitter melon dish, "but because I was too excited, I woke up before I had a chance to taste it in my dream." The few times I was invited to her home after that, she made sure that there was bitter melon on the table. When she and I went to their garden patch in the middle of the rice field to pick some herbs and dig out some sweet potatoes for a special soup I had not had since my family left that mountain village, I felt as if I had come home at last.

To me, working in the factory was like experiencing a life I had just luckily escaped by a small margin. Throughout these years, it has been clear to me that my continuing advancement in higher education has less to do with my school performance than with my father, who treasures his daughters as much as his sons, and my mother, who believes that there is no way that her daughters are inferior to anyone's sons. By the time I got into the university, many of my girlfriends from elementary school were married. As I moved on to various stages of my life, I have never stopped wondering what would have happened if the girl sitting next to me in fifth grade had been given the same opportunity as her brothers or I got, and what has happened to the female students I taught in the fishing village. When my coworkers told me stories about their work experiences and family lives, I felt as though it was my students or childhood girlfriends who were telling me what had happened to them since I left.

Between Bosses and Workers:
A Multidimensional Power Relationship

Once I was in the field, it soon became clear to me that covering both sides of the story was the only way to go. With factory sizes that ranged from three to thirty workers, it was virtually impossible to get access to workers without the consent of their bosses. Interacting with the bosses not only served my data collection purposes by giving me access to the workers, but hearing them talk about the operational struggles of their firms also gave me additional insight into the structural constraints experienced by Third World reporters. Even if it would not have been logistically problematic, I soon realized that an exclusive focus on the factory workers would have left me with an incomplete understanding.

My entry was granted by male factory owners partly because of the national (Third World) identity they perceived us to share. Almost all the factory owners complained about the problems that they have experienced due to the fluctuations of the global market. They readily pointed out the ways in which increasing competition, unstable demand, and changing foreign exchange rates affect their daily operations at the factory level. Beating the odds brought them a pride that has been missing among many Chinese people ever since the Opium War in the mid-nineteenth century. One owner believed that if he granted me entry, the major role of satellite factory entrepreneurs in constructing Taiwan's economic miracle, and the hard work their success entailed, might finally be recognized by the Taiwanese state and by the international community. Another owner saw himself as someone who was helping a compatriot to become internationally successful on her own terms. The connections and ties that I was able to establish with these factory owners should not be overly romanticized, however. My goodwill in establishing reciprocal relationships with them in the field put me in a vulnerable position that was subject to engulfment and potential exploitation. Throughout my fieldwork, I constantly struggled to gain as much autonomy as I could under the circumstances.

When I first met Mr. Li, the owner of a factory that assembled wooden jewelry boxes, I told him I would like to understand the production and operational mechanisms of Taiwan's satellite factory system. He was very enthusiastic about my project and promised to help me out by introducing me to all the satellite factories that did subcontracting work for him. In exchange, I offered to help in his factory. During the first two days, he took me with him whenever he went on routine visits to his satellite factories; I ended up visiting seven factories over those two days. Between the visits, I spent most of my time working on the shop floor with other workers. It didn't take very long for Mr. Li to realize that it wouldn't hurt to have an extra pair of hands around, even with my not-so-impressive productivity. As time went by, Mr. Li took me out less and less. My role as a worker (participant) gradually took over my identity as a researcher (observer). I didn't really mind this shift. Even though the work was physically taxing, it gave me a firsthand experience of factory work. I also gained opportunities to interact with other workers and learn what was happening on the shop floor. I would arrive at the factory in the morning and work all day long. Usually I didn't stay for the evening work but left around five or six o'clock in the afternoon.[8] Starting in the second week, Mr. Li occasionally had the manager ask me if I could stay for the evening work when there were shipment deadlines to meet. On those occasions, I ended up working in the factory until ten or eleven o'clock at night, and then went home to write my fieldnotes until three or four o'clock in the morning. By the end of the second week, I felt that the overtime was taking its toll on me, physically and with regard to my research.

The prospect of possible exploitation didn't really dawn on me until my first request to move on to another satellite factory was rejected by Mr. Li, who said, "There isn't anything interesting there. You can learn everything here, at Ta-you." It was only after I told him firmly that I had to complete my observations in at least one satellite factory of each type in the chain of jewelry box production that Mr. Li reluctantly introduced me to one of his satellite factories.[9] In his introduction, he referred to me as a woman who "just came back from the States and wants to understand how things work in your factory. . . . No, you don't have to pay her. She works for free. She takes notes every now and then. . . . It will just be a matter of five to ten minutes. . . . All you need to do is to buy her a lunch box" (e.g., buy me lunch). Similar concern over my free labor took a different form in another factory. After working in Wei-der for a week, I was told that the owner had said he would not talk to me unless I agreed to work in his factory for more than a month.

My free labor was an issue not only among factory owners. Different groups of workers also competed for my labor. One woman worker in her early sixties told me during a lunch break that I should not help a group of "outsiders," the subcontracting workers.[10] An insider herself, she explained:

> We are paid daily. The outsiders are paid piece-rate. When you help them to assemble the drawers, you aren't helping us in the factory. The work they are doing is not part of our job any longer. It has been subcontracted out. Besides, those women are young. They earn much more than I do.

Apparently, given the labor-intensive and physically taxing work, even an extra pair of inexperienced hands could save the workers some sweat.

Competition over my labor demonstrates only one aspect of the power struggle I experienced in doing fieldwork in Taiwan's satellite factory system. My efforts to cover the perspectives of both factory bosses and workers ran up against my political concerns over the workers' welfare. Such embedded contradictions intensified the pressures I felt about the hierarchical power relationship between the factory bosses and myself, a female feminist researcher originally from Taiwan.

I still remember vividly the grinding uneasiness I felt when a factory owner insisted on taking me to a factory right after telling me that the driver, who often had me accompany him on his daily delivery trips, was in the hospital after a severe car accident. The owner ignored my concern for the driver and my desire to visit him in the hospital right away. "Don't worry. He won't die," he said. On another occasion, comments I made that encouraged the restless workers to organize and confront the owner were reported to the owner. Although I was not thrown out of the factory, a possibility that had caused as much anxiety to me as to the workers at the scene, the owner made it known that such involvement on my part was inappropriate.[11]

These incidents illustrate the multidimensional axes of tension and of power relations in the factories: bosses are pitted against the researcher and the workers, whereas the workers confront the researcher as well as one another. The terms of my access to the shop floor and to the workers were largely determined by the imbalance in the power relationships between the factory owners and myself. Furthermore, my trip in the winter of 1989–1990 was rendered less than satisfactory by the dominating presence of their husbands when I visited the women workers in their homes. Initially, I had planned to conduct in-depth interviews with the married female workers whom I had met the preceding summer. As it turned out, when I arrived at the women's homes, I was often greeted by their husbands, who proceeded to dominate the conversation, even though many of the women had been very articulate when I had talked with them in the factories.

The Dilemma of a Keen Observer and a Vocal Feminist

On the shop floor, as men and women routinely interacted with one another, I encountered multidimensional power relationships structured around the patriarchal system and involving the Chinese women workers and myself. Consequently, I was forced to juggle two modes of self-presentation every day. In order to hear what the factory owners would normally say to the workers, and to see how wives could quietly disarm their bossy husbands, I complied with the observer principle of doing nothing to disturb the setting. On occasion, however, I found myself openly expressing my feminist beliefs and political position simply for the sake of my own sanity. The superior power position attributed to female feminist researchers in recent discussions of feminist methodology does not speak to my own fieldwork experiences. I thus find myself calling into question the dichotomous conceptualization of the power relationship said to pertain between female feminist researchers and their informants. Looking back, I am also struck by the fact that I constantly had to renegotiate the terms of my fieldwork with the agents—mostly men—of the very system I had set out to study. This process of negotiation gave me firsthand experience of patriarchal and capitalist control in Taiwanese society.

Doing fieldwork in overwhelmingly gender-defined and structured social settings presented me with a real challenge. On the shop floor, I did my best to be a keen observer, so that the setting would not be turned into an instance of "savage social therapy," which Marie-Françoise Chanfrault-Duchet and Patai describe as occurring in interview situations (Patai, 1991: 148). In order to capture and understand how workers in general, and female workers in particular, are perceived by their bosses, I had to subdue my feminist inclinations and the political beliefs that had brought me to the field in the first place. Instead of jumping to a quick conclusion, I calmly asked a male factory owner to explain why he believed that female home workers were "petty minded." With women workers, I was especially careful not to be self-righteous or to make others uncomfortable. At lunch, I followed my female coworkers to set up a folding table in the corner after all the men had taken the main dining table in the center of the kitchen. I didn't think I should say anything when a fight between the children of my coworkers A-chu and A-shia inspired comments such as: "Your kid and my kid always get into fights. This is simply because they are both boys. If one of them were a little girl, I bet they would not have fought."

In retrospect, I see that my compliance with the role of uninvolved observer served two functions. By giving priority to the voices and actions of the people in the setting, it allowed incidents to unfold and events to take their full course. It also prevented me from imposing my feminist ideology on others. My efforts to be an impartial observer ran into difficulties, however. In my fieldwork, I was surrounded by and subjected to various forms of everyday sexism—daily norms and practices that were overtly oppressive toward women or covertly perpetuated gender inequality. Posters for pornographic movies decked the electric poles, the walls of apartment buildings, and bulletin boards, side by side with advertisements for aphrodisiacs and surgical cures for impotence. Seminaked women danced erotically in flower carts at weddings, during festivals, and even in funerals.[12] On my visits to factories I was sometimes greeted with whistles and such remarks as "what a pretty woman," from male workers on the shop floor. Conversations there usually started with such questions as "Are you married?" "How many kids do you have?" and "How many years have you been married?" (in exactly that order). Although such personal questions are not out of place in the Chinese context, information about my personal background enabled others to judge me in accordance with indigenous norms and practices.[13]

Comments such as, "She is lucky to be married. Most men don't want to marry women with too much education," were exchanged among the male managers.

My female coworkers, on the other hand, believed that I should get a permanent, keep my skin pale, and wear skirts more often. On several occasions the women expressed their sincere concern over my childless status. Their comments ranged from simple curiosity, "Isn't it strange not having kids?" to female propriety, "It isn't very nice not giving his family descendants," to an opinionated moralism, "He is the only son of his parents, isn't he? Then you have to have at least one son for his family." The comments not only indicated the cultural norms to which every Chinese woman is expected to conform, but they reminded me of my ambiguous insider/outsider status and occasionally generated alienated feelings and discomfort on my part.

On the shop floor, I was overwhelmed by the pervasiveness of social control over women. Remarks such as "you women always complain," "you (women) don't know what you're talking about," were made daily in conversations to trivialize or ridicule women. I didn't anticipate that staying with my parents rather than my in-laws while I worked on the project would cause raised eyebrows.[14] One of my coworkers asked me specifically if I had "gone back" to my in-laws right after I arrived in Taiwan. When I told her in a matter-of-fact way that I had gone straight from the airport to my parents' home, I saw envy and amazement in her eyes. It was only later that I learned that this woman's in-laws had granted her only three visits to her parents since her marriage fourteen years earlier. Nonetheless, she said that she could not comprehend how my parents could have allowed this. In her opinion, my parents had failed to teach me how to be a proper daughter-in-law.

From all this, it is evident that my outsider status did give me a certain immunity when I inadvertently violated some of the patriarchal norms and practices. On the other hand, it did not give me the power or privilege to escape from the most overt form of patriarchal control, namely, sexual harassment. My gender took precedence over my academic credentials, for example, when a man who was supposed to help me get entry to a factory turned a factory tour into an incident of sexual harassment. He began by asking me what an American man would say to initiate a date. My indifferent response to his inquiry did not stop him from posing questions about how to talk to attractive women in English. When I refused his invitation for a date, he verbally insulted me: "What other fun can you have on Saturday afternoon when your husband is not around?" This incident demonstrates how easily individual women are perceived as, and turned into, sexual objects. Indeed, jokes or remarks that refer to Chinese women purely as sexual objects are part of everyday reality. A woman who showed up at work sleepy was teased as having had "too much of a good time last night." A manager offering a job to a deliveryman was heard to say: "Why don't you come and work for me? I'll make you a supervisor and get a pretty woman to be your assistant." In response, the driver said: "No, it won't work. That would deplete my vitality."

The pervasive degradation of women in the satellite factory system made it impossible for me, a female Chinese feminist, to confine myself totally to the observer role. At a banquet celebrating the newborn baby of a female worker, a man introduced as a lawyer joined our table. My coworkers made remarks such as "Mr. Wong is a big-time lawyer," "Mr. Li (owner of the factory) and our factory really rely on him," and "He makes big money." Mr. Wong looked extremely narcissistic in his three-piece suit, especially in contrast to me and my coworkers, who wore the usual yellowish T-shirts. What happened next was one of the few instances where my action interrupted the course of an event that could have gone in other directions.

> After several drinks, he moved next to me and started telling pornographic jokes.[15] While others around the table (maybe a total of five to six men and two women) were simply smiling and nodding, I found the jokes and scene offensive. I told Mr. Wong that he should stop making jokes which were degrading to women. "They are just jokes," Mr. Wong replied, "Don't be so serious." "I don't find jokes that are degrading to women funny," I said. Mr. Wong was a little bit uncomfortable being confronted, but offered to tell a "really good one" anyway. Before I had a chance to say anything, he started the joke by saying, "We are all adults. You, Dr. Hsiung, I assume you are no longer adolescent." At that point, I took my glass and rose from my seat. "I'm moving to the other table," I protested. "Don't take things so seriously. It's just a joke," Mr. Wong defended himself. "I'll leave if you continue," I said. I stood there and didn't want to put up with it any more. After a few awkward seconds, he said, "All right! All right! I'll leave." He bowed stiffly and left our table. He looked embarrassed.

On another occasion, I made comments about the unequal relationship between men and women when, on our way to a factory, my male coworker was jokingly trying to talk another factory owner into taking a mistress. After my comments, they looked a bit uneasy and changed the subject.

The incidents I have described illustrate the extent to which I was part of everyday gender politics while doing my fieldwork. My observer role demanded that I either pretend not to hear the sexist jokes or, adopting the customary code of silence, simply smile and say nothing, as Chinese women are expected to do. Whenever I was provoked to define and defend myself, I inevitably interrupted the action and so had an effect on the course of events.

Discussion and Conclusion

Recent discussion of feminist methodology and epistemology raises questions concerning the unequal power relations between the researcher and the researched. The debate focuses on the intrusion and intervention of the researcher into the lives of informants, the appropriation of the informants' private emotions/stories by the reseacher, and the dominant position of the researcher in presentation and representation of the researched (Patai, 1991; Stacey, 1991; Acker et al., 1991). My examination of the multiple axes of power relations in the field and the contradiction between my roles as a keen observer and a vocal feminist illustrates that the power relations are much more complex. The process of getting entry, sustaining access, and resolving tension involves negotiation between the patriarchal/capitalist system, the agents of the system, and the female feminist researcher. The conceptualization of a binary power relationship between female ethnographers and their informants does not leave sufficient room to explore how power structures are constructed and contested through everyday interaction between men and women.

The issues I raised in this chapter center around the logical contradictions that arise when an indigenous feminist does fieldwork in an active way, as a participant-observer. Nevertheless, they bear a strong resemblance to the difficulties mentioned in recent accounts of fieldwork by several First World feminists. For example, although I myself did not require the prior approval of government officials before entering the field, the sense of powerlessness I felt while doing my fieldwork corresponds closely with that experienced by Margery Wolf during her 1980 field trip in the People's Republic of China (1985). In her chapter, "Speaking Bitterness," Wolf discusses at length her experience of lost autonomy and her lack of independent access to Chinese women during her field trip in the People's Republic of China. I can very much relate to the pressures that made Diane Wolf create a false identity that conformed to the norms of the Javanese communities she studied but conceal what was really going on in her personal life (1992). As for Dorinne Kondo, although I did not go through the painstaking process that transformed her from a Japanese American into a "culturally competent" Japanese woman (1990), I was made fully aware of the gender ascriptions that I had unwittingly violated.

All in all, these recent accounts suggest that, although doing fieldwork in Asian societies poses different challenges to indigenous and First World feminists, the conflict between acute observation and feminist involvement represents an embedded contradiction that all feminist researchers need to confront.

NOTES

An earlier version of this chapter was presented at the American Sociological Association annual meeting in Miami in 1993. I appreciate Rita Gallin's supportive ears at the conference. Natalie Beausoleil, Francesca Bray, Shelley Feldman, Bonnie Fox, Charles Harris, Roxana Ng, Aysan Sev'er, and Diane Wolf have read various drafts of this chapter. I especially thank Diane Wolf for her useful comments and Francesca Bray, Shelley Feldman, and Roxana Ng for their encouragement and suggestions. I thank Liza McCoy and Joan Campbell for editorial assistance. In particular, I appreciate Joan Campbell's meticulous work.

1. The assistance of indigenous translators and research assistants is freely acknowledged in many accounts by First World researchers who have done fieldwork in Asia. Such helpers engage in a variety of tasks: doing simple translation, introducing the researcher to the local community, identifying potential informants, and even acting as the interpreter of local norms and practices. Nonetheless, few researchers have systematically analyzed how

using an indigenous translator or assistant affected their research project. Bernard Gallin's account on the roles of his translator is a rare exception (B. Gallin, 1966, appendix I).

2. Particularly in the earlier era, fieldwork accounts tended to focus on the steps taken by researchers or factors presented in the field that eventually helped the success of their field-work. A typical example is Kung's account of her fieldwork project on young female factory workers in Taiwan. Kung states that her presence should not have disturbed the setting "be-cause other anthropologists have lived in the area" (Kung, Arrigo, and Salaff, 1984: 97). According to Kung, her talks with female factory workers while they were working did not present any problems because the conversation "relieves the monotony" of factory jobs. She also came to the conclusion that her high educational background "probably height-ened their (the female workers') curiosity and increased their willingness to talk" (Kung, Arrigo, and Salaff, 1984: 99).

3. For a discussion of this early period of development, see Gary G. Hamilton and Wang Zheng, "Introduction: Fei Xiaoton and the Beginnings of a Chinese Sociology," in *From the Soil, the Foundations of Chinese Society* (Fei, 1992).

4. The first systematic attempts to examine Taiwan's small factories have been carried out independently by Cheng (1992), Hsiung (1991), and Shieh (1992).

5. I use this term to conceptualize Taiwan's small-scale, family-centered, and export-ori-ented factories. These factories are connected through subcontracting arrangements (Hsiung, 1991).

6. For example, Arrigo studied an electric factory with several hundred female workers (Arrigo, 1980). Kung did fieldwork at "one of Taiwan's largest factories," which employed some 4,000 female workers (Kung, Arrigo, and Salaff, 1984: 98). Diamond studied a textile plant employing about four hundred workers. Around 80 percent of them were young women (Diamond, 1979).

7. In 1984, about 43 percent of the labor force in manufacturing industries was made up of women. From 1967 to 1988, the growth of female labor force participation among young single women was 22 percent, whereas it was 65 percent for married women (Hsiung, 1991: 197).

8. The typical working schedule of the peak season in the satellite factory is:
Monday, 8:00 AM–12:00 NOON, 1:00–5:00 PM
    5:30 PM–9:00 PM
Tuesday, 8:00 AM–12:00 NOON, 1:00–5:00 PM
    5:30 PM–9:00 PM
Wednesday, 8:00 AM–12:00 NOON, 1:00 PM–6:00 PM
Thursday, 8:00 AM–12:00 NOON, 1:00–5:00 PM
    5:30 PM–9:00 PM
Friday, 8:00 AM–12:00 NOON, 1:00–5:00 PM
    5:30 PM–9:00 PM
Saturday, 8:00 AM–12:00 NOON, 1:00 PM–6:00 PM
Sunday, 8:00 AM–12:00 NOON, 1:00 PM–6:00 PM (every other week)

9. I eventually worked in six factories: one box body factory, one hardware factory, one glasses factory, one painting factory, and two assembly factories.

10. "Insiders" and "outsiders" are terms used in Taiwan's satellite factory system to dif-ferentiate two groups of workers. The former are workers hired by a factory on daily wages. They work in the factory on a monthly basis and are usually its main labor force. The "out-siders," on the other hand, are subcontracted workers. With four to ten members, each out-

sider group specializes in one specific semiskilled task, such as screwing the door to the boxes, pasting down the flannel, or assembling the drawer. A factory owner subcontracts a particular task to each outsider group. These outsiders are therefore constantly on the move from one factory to another.

11. Due to the lack of institutional support, labor politics in Taiwan's satellite factory system have been clandestine rather than confrontational. Only one such incident happened during the period of my fieldwork. In my dissertation I provide a detailed account of this incident. I also discuss the implications of such occurrences for our overall understanding of labor politics in the satellite factory system (Hsiung, 1991).

12. Although the commercialization of the female body is not new, the collective consumption of the female body by the hiring of seminaked women dancers at weddings and religious festivals is a recent phenomenon (Chang, 1993).

13. Such personal questions are not out of place in the Chinese context. Hill Gates describes the differences between the Chinese and American ways of personal interaction, "Where we (the Americans) make small talk about the weather or current events, for example, they (the Chinese) inquire if a new acquaintance has brothers and sisters, or ask the amount of her salary" (Gates, 1987: 5–6). The main function of more personalized small talk is to expand or enhance personal networks. Inquiries about personal matters such as birthplace, school graduated from, or work experiences are made to initiate/search for any possible connection.

14. The patrilineal and patrilocal norms call for a woman, upon marriage, to move into the household of her parents-in-law. The norms are incorporated into legal codes that give a Chinese husband the right to divorce his wife if she refuses to comply with the practice of patrilocal residence.

15. Telling pornographic jokes is common at banquets in Taiwan. Men compete for attention and entertain other diners, both men and women, with exotic and often offensive jokes. These jokes usually boast of masculinity by demeaning women. Recently, the implications of pornographic jokes for gender stratification and, especially, for gender politics in the workplace have been heatedly debated in Taiwan. Some argue that such pornographic joking is a form of sexual harassment (Wu, 1993; Xiaohongmao Shuishenbao, 1993); others stress the similarity between "joking relationships" and "patriarchal relationships." Pornographic joking, in this interpretation, is simply another, indirect, way for men to assert their power over women (Huang, 1993). But others encourage Chinese women to counter pornographic jokes with jokes that are equally demeaning to men (Lin, 1993; Xinliangxing, 1993).

REFERENCES

Acker, J., K. Barry, and J. Esseveld. 1991. "Objectivity and Truth: Problems in Doing Feminist Research." In *Beyond Methodology: Feminist Scholarship as Lived Research,* edited by M. M. Fonow and J. A. Cook. Bloomington and Indianapolis: Indiana University Press.

Arrigo, L. G. 1980. "The Industrial Work Force of Young Women in Taiwan." *Bulletin of Concerned Asian Scholars* 12: 25–34.

Chang, S. C. 1993. "The Gender Question in Folk Religion of Taiwan: Public Display of Naked Female Body in 'Electronic-Flower-Cart.'" Paper presented at the Conference of Gender Issues in Contemporary Chinese Societies, Miami Beach, Florida.

Chen, Yiyun. 1994. "Out of the Traditional Halls of Academe: Exploring New Avenues for Research on Women." In *Engendering China: Women, Culture, and the State,* edited by Christina K. Gilmartin et al., 69–79. Cambridge: Harvard University Press.

Cheng, J. C. 1992. *The Economic Structure and Social Characteristics of Taiwan's Small and Medium Size Factories.* Taipei: Langjin Publishing Co.

Diamond, N. 1979. "Women and Industry in Taiwan." *Modern China* 1, no. 1: 3–45.

Fei, Hsiao-t'ung. 1992. *From the Soil, the Foundations of Chinese Society: A Translation of Fei Xiaotong's* Xiangtu Zhongguo. Berkeley: University of California Press.

Gallin, B. 1966. *Hsin Hsing, Taiwan: A Chinese Village in Change.* Berkeley: University of California Press.

Gallin, R. C. 1984a. *The Impact of Development on Women's Work and Status: A Case Study from Taiwan.* East Lansing: Michigan State University, Women in International Development Publication Series, Working Paper no. 9.

———. 1984b. *Rural Industrialization and Chinese Women: A Case Study from Taiwan.* East Lansing: Michigan State University, Women in International Development Publication Series, Working Paper no. 47.

Gates, H. 1987. *Chinese Working-Class Lives: Getting by in Taiwan.* Ithaca: Cornell University Press.

Hsiung, P. C. 1991. "Class, Gender, and the Satellite Factory System in Taiwan." Ph.D. dissertation, University of California, Los Angeles.

Hu, T. L. 1982. *Xifu Rumen* [When a daughter-in-law enters her husband's family]. Taipei: Shibao Press.

———. 1984. *My Mother-in-Law's Village: Rural Industrialization and Change in Taiwan.* Taipei: Institute of Ethnology, Academia Sinica, Monograph Series B, no. 13.

Huang, Liying. 1993. "Youmo hu? Exi hu?: Nuren yu Huangse Xiaohua" [Is it humorous? is it disgusting?: Women and the pornographic jokes]. *Awakening,* 1 June, 24–27.

Kung, L. 1976. "Factory Work and Women in Taiwan: Changes in Self-Image and Status." *Signs* 2, no. 1: 35–58.

———. 1983. *Factory Women in Taiwan.* Ann Arbor: University of Michigan Research Press.

Kung, L., L. G. Arrigo, and J. W. Salaff. 1984. "Doing Fieldwork." In *Lives: Chinese Working Women,* edited by M. Sheridan and J. W. Salaff. Bloomington: Indiana University Press.

Lin, Fongmei. 1993. "Zhengqu Fayanquan: Nuxing yu Huangse Xiaohua" [Raising voices: Women and the pornographic joke]. *Xinliangxing, Libao* [Gender edition: Independent news], 1 August.

Lu, Ron Hai. 1986. *Tamen Weishemo Buneng Jiehun* [Why can't they get married]? Taipei: Weili Attorney Office.

Niehoff, J. D. 1987. "The Villager as Industrialist: Ideologies of Household Manufacturing in Rural Taiwan." *Modern China* 13, no. 3.

Patai, D. 1991. "U.S. Academics and the Third World Woman: Is Ethical Research Possible?" In *Women's Words: The Feminist Practice of Oral History,* edited by Sherna Berger Gluck and Daphne Patai, 137–153. New York: Routledge.

Sheridan, M. 1984. "The Life History Method." In *Lives: Chinese Working Women,* edited by M. Sheridan and J. W. Salaff. Bloomington: Indiana University Press.

Sheridan, M., and J. W. Salaff. 1984. Introduction. In *Lives: Chinese Working Women,* edited by M. Sheridan and J. W. Salaff. Bloomington: Indiana University Press.

Shieh, G. S. 1992. *"Boss" Island: Subcontracting Networks and Micro-Entrepreneurialship in Taiwan's Development.* New York: Peter Lang.

Stacey, J. 1991. "Can There Be a Feminist Ethnography?" In *Women's Words: The Feminist Practice of Oral History,* edited by Sherna Berger Gluck and Daphne Patai, 111–119. New York: Routledge.

Stites, R. 1982. "Small-Scale Industry in Yingge, Taiwan." *Modern China* 8, no. 2.

———. 1985. "Industrial Work as an Entrepreneurial Strategy." *Modern China* 11, no. 2.

Wolf, D. L. 1992. *Factory Daughters: Gender, Household Dynamics, and Rural Industrialization in Java.* Berkeley: University of California Press.

Wolf, M. 1985. *Revolution Postponed: Women in Contemporary China.* Stanford: Stanford University Press.

Wu, Zhongjie. 1993. "Shuo Huangse Xiaohua Zaocheng Xingsaorao" [Pornographic joking is sexual harassment]. *Xinliangxing, Libao* [Gender edition: Independent news], 1 August.

Xiaohongmao Shuishenbao. 1993. "Huangse Xiaohua bu Haoxiao" (The pornographic joke is not funny). *Xinliangxing, Libao* [Gender edition: Independent news], 1 August.

Xinliangxing. 1993. "Jiang Jiang Huangse Xiaohua ye Bucou?" [Let's all make pornographic jokes]. *Xinliangxing, Libao* [Gender edition: Independent news], 1 August.

7

Feminist Insider Dilemmas: Constructing Ethnic Identity with Chicana Informants

PATRICIA ZAVELLA

WHAT HAPPENS WHEN the ethnographic "others" are from the same society and are members of the same race or ethnicity, gender, and class background as the ethnographer? This chapter articulates the dilemmas I faced as a member of the group I was studying—Chicana working mothers—particularly regarding the terms of ethnic identification. My purpose here is twofold: I will discuss how my status as a simultaneous cultural "insider" and Chicana feminist researcher reflected a conundrum. My sense of Chicana feminist identity, constructed through participation in the Chicano movement, ironically hindered my understanding of the nuances of the ethnic identity of the women I studied and regarded as historical actors. My status as insider also caused the dilemma of how to present the ethnographic "others" to my peers, Chicano/Latino scholars who privileged the term Chicano. (As a product of the movement, I will use Chicano and Mexican American interchangeably here, except when referring to Mexican Americans from New Mexico.) These dilemmas eventually provided insight into the power relations involved when women of Mexican origin identify themselves ethnically. My discussion will contextualize the meaning of ethnic identity for working-class Mexican American women workers in two field research settings with different historical contexts.

There is a debate among ethnographers about conducting fieldwork with subjects who are of the same gender or race or ethnicity as the researcher. Chicano

This article was originally published in *Frontiers: A Journal of Women Studies* 13, no. 3: 1993. Reprinted with permission of the publisher.

scholars assert that insiders are more likely to be cognizant and accepting of complexity and internal variation, are better able to understand the nuances of language use, will avoid being duped by informants who create cultural performances for their own purposes, and are less apt to be distrusted by those they study. Some assert that ethnic insiders often have an easier time gaining access to a community similar to their own, and that they are more sensitive to framing questions in ways that respect community sensibilities (Romano, 1968; Paredes, 1977; Aguilar, 1988).

Others, however, note that being a member of a subordinated group under study carries particular problems and creates personal and ethical dilemmas for social scientists on the basis of their race, ethnicity, gender, political sympathies, or even personal foibles. Maxine Baca Zinn found that being an insider woman conducting ethnographic research with Mexican Americans meant continually negotiating her status, since members of the community being studied often made assumptions about her intents, skills, and personal characteristics. She reminds us that insider researchers have the unique constraint of always being accountable to the community being studied. Along with the cooperation engendered by one's insider status comes the responsibility to construct analyses that are sympathetic to ethnic interests and that will somehow share whatever knowledge is generated with them: "These problems should serve to remind us of our political responsibility and compel us to carry out our research with ethical and intellectual integrity" (Zinn, 1979: 218).

Women anthropologists and feminist fieldworkers have also long been concerned about relationships with informants and have grappled with the dilemmas of being insiders, particularly when they have important similarities with the population being studied (Fonow and Cook, 1991; Golde, 1986; Klein, 1983; Reinharz, 1992; Roberts, 1981; Thorne, 1979; Wax, 1979; Weston, 1991). Some have argued that ethnographic methods are ideally suited to research by women because of the contextual, involved, experiential approach to knowledge that includes the sharing of experiences with one's subjects, and which contrasts with the features of positivist approaches.[1] Ann Oakley, for example, in a widely cited article, argues that "in most cases, the goal of finding out about people through interviewing is best achieved when the relationship of interviewer and interviewee is non-hierarchical and when the interviewer is prepared to invest his or her own personal identity in the relationship"; and later asserts that "a feminist interviewing women is by definition both 'inside' the culture and participating in that which she is observing" (1982: 41, 57). Susan Krieger (1987) discusses how being an insider in a lesbian community enabled her to see how interviews were reflections of community norms, and her personal interpretations are sources of sociological insight.

Increasingly, feminist and other fieldworkers realize that we need to be sensitive to differences between our subjects and ourselves as well, and aware of the possible power relations involved in doing research by, about, and for women, and that feminist studies must include a diversity of women's experiences based on race, class, and sexual preferences, among others. Lynn Weber Cannon and her colleagues (1988) critique the white, middle-class bias of much qualitative feminist research and suggest that feminists take extraordinary measures to recruit women of color so as to include a variety of perspectives. Catherine Kohler Riessman (1987) points out that white women must be careful about analyzing interviews with women of color using their own narrative forms, lest they miss important nuances in meaning.

Women fieldworkers do not agree, however, on what constitutes feminist ethnography, nor do they agree on the role of the feminist insider as researcher. Judith Stacey (1988: 21), for example, suggests that feminist ethnography draws upon "such traditionally female strengths as empathy and human concern, and allows for an egalitarian, reciprocal relationship between knower and known." She questions whether there can be a truly feminist ethnography, arguing that the personal and ethical dilemmas inevitably pose insurmountable problems. In contrast to the goals of mutuality, nonexploitation, and empathy that she hoped for with feminist field research, Stacey argues that ironically this approach places informants at greater risk in the power relations inherent to any field research. By being involved in closer friendships, Stacey claims, informants are subject to betrayal and abandonment by the researcher, and thus feminist ethnography "masks a deeper, more dangerous form of exploitation." Stacey's naïveté, which she claims is overstated, is nonetheless disturbing. Although she confirms that conflicting interests and emotions are inherent to field research, there is not enough context in her discussion of her own "inauthenticity, dissimilitude and potential, perhaps inevitable betrayal" to assess how she tried to deal with the dilemmas she faced. A discussion of how she negotiated with those involved, or whether she reciprocated the trust and openness that her informants shared, could have convinced us that a feminist dilemma, not her expectations and behavior, was at issue.

There are two implicit assumptions in Stacey's formulation (and that of others who think of feminist methodology in this way) that remain despite her critique of feminist ethnography: that all women share some authentic feminine selfhood—with characteristics like being more cooperative, empathetic, attentive to daily life, or relational than men—so that women can thus bond with one another across time and space; and that feminist ethnography can somehow transcend the inequalities between women researchers and their subjects. Clearly these assumptions are problematic, particularly when Western ethnographers are doing research in the Third World or in working-class and poor communities in the United States. Micaela di Leonardo (1991a: 235) labels this perspective, which assumes that all women share common experiences or interests, as "cultural feminism," and argues that these assumptions form a women's culture as "invented tradition." Without "marking" the social location of the ethnographer and informants (their status based on class, race or ethnicity, sexual preference, or other relevant attributes) and with little presentation of the negotiations of differences between feminist fieldworkers and their informants, we cannot judge whether and how the ethnographer indeed has more power and privilege than those being researched. This lack of context leaves us with the impression that researchers and subjects are more similar than they really are and leaves unchallenged the questionable assumptions embedded in "feminist ethnography" as previously formulated.

Similarly, Marilyn Strathern (1987: 290) asserts that there is a "particularly awkward dissonance between feminist practice and the practice of social anthropology," and she implies that feminist anthropology is virtually impossible, since the two fields "mock" one another on the basis of fundamental differences in how the ethnographic "other" is construed. According to Strathern, ideally anthropologists interpret the experiences of traditionally non-Western, preindustrial, or peasant cultures by respecting their own emic view of the world, and more recently by creating space for other voices; yet the ultimate purpose serves the discipline. On the other hand, feminists, Strathern argues, construe the ethnographic "other" as men and patriarchal institutions, and therefore there can be no shared experience between them and feminists. Within her framework, feminists and their informants "have no interests in common to be served" by collaborating on producing an ethnographic text. Those of us who consider ourselves feminist ethnographers wonder where we and our women informants fit into her schema.[2]

Stacey and Strathern are correct in noting the inevitable ambivalence involved in doing ethnographic work. Their particular feminist positions, however, beg the question when the ethnographers are conducting research in real field sites. Feminist ethnographers must move beyond posing simple dichotomous methodological approaches to discussing how we as individual "marked" researchers—contextualized in our own milieu of research goals, ethics, sensitivities, and academic affinities—have grappled with the contradictions of feminist research. In other words, rather than assume some type of panfemale solidarity (with inevitable betrayal) or a lack of shared experience between researchers and subjects, we should realize that we are almost always simultaneously insiders and outsiders and discuss what this means for our particular research projects.

I will argue that my Chicana feminist perspective itself was problematic. In the framework of larger historical forces and political struggles, identifying myself as a Chicana feminist meant contesting and simultaneously drawing from Chicano nationalist ideology and white feminism—being an insider and outsider within both movements and ideologies. It was only in retrospect, when I came to understand how Mexican American women informants from New Mexico constructed their ethnic identity in very different ways, that I realized I needed to deconstruct and problematize my own sense of Chicana feminism so that I could "see" the nuances of ethnic identity among my informants.

My experience was a form of what Micaela di Leonardo (1991b) suggests is a general feminist fieldwork conundrum: we simultaneously seek out women's experiences and critically analyze male domination in societies whose customs anthropology has defended under the stance of cultural relativism. Thus feminists now face the dilemma of seeing those customs as patriarchal, and rather than defend their existence, want to advocate change for women's benefit. There is growing acceptance in the field that feminist and other researchers, then, must self-consciously reflect upon their status within the field site, on how they are situated within social and power relations, and place their own work within the changing tides of academic discourse as well. José Limón (1989: 484) reminds us that "however 'liberating' a narrative discourse that we propose to write, it is one always intimate with power, and many of our 'informants,' 'subjects,' 'consultants,' 'teachers,' 'friends' know it.... We must always decenter our own narrative self-assurance lest it be saturated with dominating power." Such self-reflexive analysis of our own experience will push us to provide "provisional" analyses that are always incomplete, but which make clear whose viewpoint is being represented (Rosaldo, 1989).

Constructing Chicana Identity

As part of my own process of becoming a Chicana feminist beginning in the early 1970s, I became conscious of the critical importance of ethnic identity. I and others of my generation who were involved in Chicano movement activities deliberately rejected the hyphenated term Mexican-American, which to us connoted assimilation. We adopted the highly politicized term "Chicano," which designated pride in our rich pre-Columbian heritage and the importance of celebrating our mestizo racial and cultural mixtures, and rejected the influence of the Spanish colonizers. The term "Chicano" also signaled the history of racism of North American society toward people of Mexican descent; it claimed the right to self-determination and control over institutions within the Chicano community, and called for spiritual and organizational unity of the Chicano people. An integral part of reclaiming our Mexican heritage was speaking Spanish and celebrating cultural values of communalism, the family, and brotherhood (*el pueblo, la familia y carnalismo*). Chicano movement ideology also had separatist leanings, suggested the importance of recognizing *Aztlan*—the mythical northern part of pre-Columbian society—as a symbolic celebration of our spiritual unity, and explicitly rejected white culture. The Marxists among us argued that Chicanos and Mexican immigrants were the same people, that is, we were a primarily working-class community *sin fronteras* (without borders) who held common interests as a racialized class. These activists pushed for political strategies and organizations that would encourage the development of class consciousness between Chicanos and Mexicanos (that is, Mexican immigrants), regardless of the U.S.-Mexican border (I. García, 1989; Gómez-Quiñones, 1990; Hammerback et al., 1985).

At the time, Chicana activists proudly embraced movement ideology, yet our identity as feminists was submerged. "Feminism" was seen as a white, middle-class term and itself a reason for dismissing women's views (Cortera, 1977; Gonzalez, 1977; Hernandez, 1980; Nieto-Gómez, 1974). Chicanos often tried to silence feminists by branding us "cultural betrayers," "white-identified," "man haters," and "lesbians." Despite these travails, many of us maintained our critiques of the Chicano movement, with its male-oriented organizational concerns, the outright sexism of some leaders, the lack of recognition of women, and the unquestioning acceptance of the patriarchy inherent in the ideology of *la familia*. I further embraced the feminist principles that household decision-making and the division of labor should be shared equally between partners, that women should feel good about their participation in the labor force, and that labor organizing should include women. Thus was my construction of Chicana feminism when I entered the field.

As I have discussed previously (1987), I started my field research in 1977–1978 with the assumption that my identity would provide an entrée to women cannery workers. I assumed that being a woman from a working-class background myself would provide ready access to this community of informants. Although women were generous with their time and insights, I found that indeed there were important differences between us. In retrospect, my expectations were naïve, for these were predominantly middle-aged, seasonal cannery workers who were being displaced from cannery employment in the Santa Clara Valley.[3] These women (and men) were acutely conscious of my privileges as an educated woman and assumed I had resources that as a poverty-stricken graduate student I did not have. More important, the very research questions I posed alerted them to significant political differences between us. I asked about how women made decisions, how they organized the household division of labor, how they felt about being working mothers, and about racism and sexism on the job. Implicit in my questions were Chicana feminist notions. As I came to understand, these women struggled to live independent lives—working in strenuous jobs, participating in the decisions as to how their wages were spent, taking pride in enduring the demanding labor process, and finding meaning in constructing a work culture with other women workers. Like many North American women, my informants supported feminist notions like "equal pay for equal work" and affirmative action.

These women also had very "traditional" notions about family, however, having originally sought seasonal employment because it allowed them to fulfill their familial obligations, and they identified themselves as "homemakers" for most of the year. With a few notable exceptions, these were women who "happened to work," and whose seasonal employment did not challenge the traditional notions that their husbands should be the breadwinners and heads of the family and that they should do most of the domestic work, although some did contest these notions somewhat. My feminist questions, then, pointed out the contradictions of their constructions of their selves and led to some awkward moments when women preferred silence to full discussions of problems in their families or with their husbands. It was at these times that my outsider status seemed glaring.

Furthermore, those who were politically involved in the attempts to reform the Teamsters Union from within were also aware of possible political differences between us. Thus my experience of "establishing rapport" often meant discussing my political sensibilities and commitments in great detail, and I worried about "contaminating the field" with my own biases.

Although my cannery worker informants identified themselves ethnically in varied terms, ranging from "Mexicana," "Mexican American," or "Chicana" to "Spanish," as a self-identified Chicana, I was not particularly concerned with variation in ethnic identification at the time I wrote the book, merely noting it in passing. I was more concerned with their political consciousness and activities and wrote a critique about how race and gender were incorporated into strategies for organizing cannery workers (Zavella, 1988). I did not explicitly analyze the connection between ethnic identity and politics, however, and I now see that that would have been an interesting relationship to pursue.

Reflecting back, I recall that most were of the second generation (their parents were born in Mexico, but they themselves were born in the United States). Among the second generation, those who identified themselves as Spanish or Mexican American were often the most conservative. Usually those cannery workers who were the most militant and most deeply involved in the Teamster reform movement explicitly called themselves "Chicanos" or "Mexicanos." Moreover, the ideological polarities that often erupted in organizational conflicts were present among the cannery worker activists with whom I did participant observation, and ethnic identification was central to ideological posturing. Some of the nationalist Chicanos advocated political strategies that focused on Chicano demands, whereas the more moderate or leftist Chicanos and Mexicanos pushed for multiethnic reformist strategies centered on bread-and-butter issues and downplayed ethnic differences among workers.

In sum, my cannery research experience challenged my Chicana feminist perspective, but more in terms of the gender politics within "the movement" and how class consciousness was framed in daily life. It was only in retrospect that I came to see the importance of ethnic identification with different political strategies. My shortsightedness was in tune with the field at the time.

Recognizing Heterogeneity

Writing in 1981, anthropologist José Limón pointed out that "Chicano" was a problematic term because it was rooted in folklore performances that were usually private (among fellow Mexican Americans), where it held both pejorative and positive connotations: To assimilated middle-class Mexican Americans, "Chicano" connotes the proletarian Mexican immigrant experience and later the militancy and celebration of the indigenous ancestry of the movement. When used by working-class Mexican Americans through customary nicknaming practices or in situations that are culturally ambiguous, "Chicano" can convey affection or intimacy or legitimize one's status as an authentic Mexican American. Thus, Limón argues, through the construction of a Chicano *public* ethnic identity (in discourse where English was used or in Anglo-dominated contexts), academics and activists drew upon its highly charged symbolic power that already held intraethnic tensions and "added political meanings to the term which did not meet with the approval of the larger community" (1981: 214).[4] Despite his cautions, the term "Chicano"—with its nationalist and gender-contested connotations that were added by the movement—is still the predominant term in the field of Chicano Studies.

It has only been within the past few years that we are seeing theoretical analyses that explicitly look for fine-tuned differences among Chicanos and distinguish Chicanos from Mexicanos and other Latinos. Researchers have found variation in how Chicanos identify themselves, with regional differences being very important (García, 1981; Hurtado and Arce, 1987; Miller, 1976). New Mexico, where there is a long-standing "ethnic sensitivity," has always posed a unique case in how Mexican Americans identify themselves. According to this analysis, Mexican Americans in New Mexico identified with their Spanish heritage and sought to dissociate themselves from racist sentiments directed at Mexican immigrants (Gonzalez, 1969). Thus people preferred the terms "Spanish" or "Spanish Americans," and women especially rejected the term "Chicano."[5]

The term "Spanish" (or the synonymous "Spanish American") became hegemonic in New Mexican society after World War I, and clearly demarcated native-born Mexican Americans from those who had migrated from Mexico,[6] yet challenged racism and discrimination against the Mexican American working class in education, politics, and the economy (Gonzales, 1986). This hegemony can be seen in the casual use of "Spanish" throughout the state today; it is a term that has become part of daily experience for Mexican Americans generally, and for our informants in particular. It wasn't until the 1980s that recent Mexican immigrants became a large presence in economically undeveloped northern New Mexican cities. Mexican migrants became integrated into a society where the major social categories of Anglo, Indian, and Spanish were already clearly established.

Constructing Hispana Ethnicity

In a second research project conducted during 1982–1983, a time of national recession, Louise Lamphere, Felipe Gonzales, Peter B. Evans, and I (1993) studied the effects of industrialization in the Sun Belt on working-class families, comparing Mexican Americans and whites.[7] We found that women's work in apparel factories and electronics production facilities sometimes brought important changes in family life as women became coproviders, mainstay providers, or, in the case of single parents, sole economic providers for their families. We argue that these working-class families are changing as women deal with the contradictions of full-time work and family commitments. Our women informants were more committed to full-time work than their mothers were, while their spouses were doing more housework and child care than we expected. Without the economic resources of highly paid professional women, these women constructed varied strategies to help mediate the contradictions of daily life—dividing up economic upkeep, finding day care for their children, negotiating a division of household chores and child care with husbands, roommates, or kin, and seeking emotional support and social exchange from relatives or friends. Mexican American and white women had similar experiences rooted in a common class status and family circumstances, yet within each group there was nuanced variation.

We were interested in ethnic differences and explicitly questioned our informants about their own sense of ethnicity and ethnic identity. As we began the analysis, in which ethnic differences were not as pronounced as we expected, we began to grapple directly with our informants' particular ethnic identity. We came to use the term "Mexican American" advisedly. The majority of our Mexican American informants identified themselves as Spanish or Spanish American, a custom at odds with my sense of ethnic identification.

Upon moving to Albuquerque before getting involved in this project, I became aware of the New Mexican prejudice toward Californians in general, and Californian Mexican Americans in particular, as being arrogant and assimilated, and I began to downplay my California connections. I had lived in Albuquerque for almost a year before embarking on research, so I had become accustomed to hearing the term "Spanish" in daily conversation and to hearing colleagues— aware of the ethnic sensitivity—referring to the local Mexican Americans with hyphenated terms like Chicano-Mexicano-Spanish community. When I found "Spanish" rather than "Chicano" or "Mexican American" on institutional forms where I was supposed to designate my ethnic identity, I even became accustomed (with only slight hesitation) to checking the "Spanish" box, even though that seemed to deny my Chicana identity. As a feminist, I was aware of the possible offense of using this term and restricted it to contexts within higher education, where it was more acceptable.

As I began interviewing women, then, in the course of chatting informally before starting the interview, I let them know how aspects of our identities coincided: I was a working mother with a young child myself who struggled to find day care and juggle work and family, my partner had been reared in Albuquerque, and we lived in the predominantly Mexican American South Valley. Further, my great-grandparents had lived and farmed in the northern New Mexican village of Tierra Amarilla and were part of the migration northward to southern Colorado, considered by scholars and laypeople to be part of the northern New Mexico culture region. In short, my own experience seemed to parallel those of our informants. Although I only got a chance to discuss our common heritage on a few occasions, having kinship ties in "the north" on the face of it made me a *manita*—figuratively a cultural compatriot. (New Mexicans use the terms "Hispano" or "manito" [literally, little brother] interchangeably, and use "Mexicano" when speaking in Spanish.) I hoped that my brief disclosures about my own ethnic heritage would allow my informants to express their own sense of ethnicity openly.

We asked questions about ethnic identity toward the end of the second interview, presumably when rapport was established and informants were comfortable with the interview format. Our strategy was to evoke their own terms by first asking them to designate a term for the Spanish-surnamed or Spanish-speaking people in Albuquerque, ask if that was the term they used for themselves, and then to ask for clarification about the meaning of whatever term they had selected. We also asked how whatever group they had identified (usually "Spanish") differed from Mexicans, and what they thought of the term "Chicano." As in previous research on ethnic identification in New Mexico, about two-thirds of our informants found that responding to questions about ethnic identity was a very sensitive issue. People made comments like, "I was afraid that you'd ask that." One man explained: "I'd play it by ear. Some people get offended real easy, because if other people's Chicano, they get real upset—others, uh, Spanish American." One could argue that these respondents were aware that ethnic identification expresses power relations, where being labeled or "naming" oneself can be a reflection of opposing or acquiescing to the subordination of the ethnic group (Gutiérrez, 1986). Or one could argue that since ethnic identification is so influenced by context, our informants were not aware of the norms within the interview situation and thus felt that choosing a term meant taking some risk.[8]

Yet when we asked further questions, they had difficulty articulating their meaning of "Spanish American," in part because their lives were so ethnically bounded. My first interview immediately signaled me that these informants were different from other Mexican Americans, and that they did not characterize their ethnicity in ways that were familiar. Geri Sandoval (all names are pseudonyms), a taciturn woman from the northern village of Mora, seemed reluctant to even discuss ethnicity. When I probed, however, she said that her family still owned a farm with a private *campo santo* (cemetery) that had been in her family for generations, that she was related to "everyone" in the general area, that her grandparents had been active members of the Catholic but renegade religious group *los penetentes*, and that they regularly celebrated Easter with traditional ethnic foods. She readily identified herself as Spanish American, but when asked how Mexicans and Spanish Americans differ, she said, "I don't know," and her tone of voice indicated she did not want to discuss it further. I let the matter drop.

In another interview, when asked about her ethnic identity, Delores Baca asked for clarification and then responded, "I don't know, I'm just me. I've never had that question asked of me." It turned out that this woman had the largest and most dense ethnic network of any informant, and she had participated in ethnic activities. Like Geri Sandoval, Delores Baca's grandparents had owned a small farm in a northern village but had sold it and settled the family on property in Bernalillo, near Albuquerque. Thus her parents lived across the street, and her eight siblings and several other extended kin all lived within walking distance, some with their own families. Delores had rich social exchange with her relatives—her mother provided daily day care while she worked, and her relatives often borrowed and lent money and clothes or did car repairs—and they saw one another frequently. Her wedding had been "traditional," with three attempts at mock kidnapping and finally a collective "ransom" so the festivities could continue, and a *marcha,* in which the godparents led the bridesmaids and attendants in a ritualized dance. When asked to describe her ethnic heritage and special traditions in her family, Delores didn't know how to respond. After some probes she described an elaborate festival in honor of San Lorenzo, of which her parents had been sponsors, and told me she had particpated in *matachines*—ritualized, costumed dances. When pressed about what ethnic term she would use, Delores responded, "I'd say I'm Spanish-Mexican, Mexican-Spanish, whatever. I'd tell them where I work, what I do, I guess." Despite being totally immersed in ethnic culture, Delores did not immediately see herself as having any special ethnic heritage or identity, and distanced herself from it by coupling ethnicity with occupational identity.

One of the final interviews, with Christina Espinosa, who was the child of a "mixed marriage," drove home these informants' points about the sensitivity of ethnic identity and added meaning that was new to me. On the basis of her looks, Christina's ethnicity was ambiguous, since she had fair skin but dark brown hair, and she had a Spanish surname from a former marriage (I initially thought she was white). It wasn't until the second interview, when we took information on extended kin, that I realized that Christina's German American father had left when she was young and that she was close to her Mexican American mother and maternal kin. When asked directly, Christina refused to provide a term for her own ethnic identity:

P Z : For the Spanish-surnamed population in Albuquerque, what word would you use to call them?
C E : I'd just call people by name. I don't like putting tags on people.
P Z : So if someone asked you what you are, what would you say?
C E : An Albuquerquian; I was born in Albuquerque, that's all I know. I don't know what my mom and dad did, that's their problem. You ask them what I am, that's not my problem. . . . I have a hard time 'cause I really don't see no difference. To me people are the same.
P Z : How are Spanish people here different from Mexicans?
C E : I don't really know. I don't really think they are. See I have a hard time when people say, you know, "Well look at that Mexican." I go, "How do you know they're not Spanish?" Because I really don't see no difference. To me they're the same. But now you can't tell them that 'cause they get angry. And I don't know why.

What was this, I wondered? Christina's kin network had a texture that seemed Mexican American, yet she refused to identify with any group and to characterize herself ethnically. Christina believed that Spanish and Mexicans, like all people, were "the same." Her defensive tone of voice and body language, however, indicated that this was difficult for her to discuss, for she had a "hard time" when people noticed Mexicans, who looked like the Spanish, who perhaps looked like her. Clearly she was trying to distance herself from claiming any ethnic identity.

Similarly, other informants emphasized the more neutral term "*New* Mexican." One woman, who had lived in the northern city of Española through high school and who was close to her husband's extended kin from the same area, could only explain: "I am what I am and I'm Spanish."[9] In general, our research reinforced previous findings that women had more aversion to the use of Chicano than men did.

Part of our dilemma was to figure out how to convey the seemingly contradictory evidence: our informants did not necessarily characterize their ethnic identity in ways with which we were familiar—they did not convey explicit pride in their ethnic heritage, and their use of the term "Spanish" seemed on the face of it to identify them with the colonizer part of their heritage. Yet our informants did not disclaim their ethnic heritage. They were mainly third generation, born in the United States, and their parents had migrated to Albuquerque from predominantly Spanish villages in northern New Mexico. Though they spoke English as their first language, they did not seem assimilated. They believed that maintaining the Spanish language was important and wished their children could learn it, but since they did not consider themselves fluent (often speaking to grandparents and elders in broken Spanish), this value could not be fully realized. They did not reject their ethnic heritage, but they also did not have strong views about its content.

Ethnic and gender subordination can be found in many forms in contemporary Albuquerque. Spanish Americans make up only about a third of the population. The city of Albuquerque historically was segregated by class and race/ethnicity so that predominantly Anglos lived in the Northeast Heights while the Spanish lived primarily in Old Town, and in the north and south valleys, with some pockets of Anglos in the two valleys. (There has been some recent residential dispersal, however, so that the southeast and north valley and central areas have integrated neighborhoods that include blacks and Navajos as well.) The electronics and garment work sites we studied have predominantly Spanish female work forces, although because of recruiting practices, only small numbers are Mexican immigrants. These women struggled daily on the shop floor to make their piece rates, cooperated with other workers, or engaged in collective struggle—including staging a strike for union recognition in one factory. Our informants, then, were located in working-class occupations where the majority of their coworkers were Spanish; their daily experiences and social worlds revolved around family and kin and at work and church activities where others were predominantly Spanish. Their lives were so immersed in ethnic social worlds that they had little information about others, so they did not know how their lives were ethnically distinct.

So when our informants used the terms "Spanish" or "Spanish American" in the early 1980s, the meaning included a sense of ethnic and class segmentation.

We eventually realized that despite their apparent diffidence, they had a definite awareness of their membership in a distinct social category and their constructions of meaning were complex. We discuss the varied meanings of "Spanish" in detail elsewhere (Lamphere et al., 1993).

To some, "Spanish" meant an ethnic category that was distinct from "Mexican." One woman said, "Spanish American is born here in America. . . . Mexicans to me are different than what we are, 'cause our language is different." Another meaning was to differentiate Mexican Americans from other ethnic or racial groups, sometimes using racial features like skin color or notions of "Spanish blood." A third meaning centered on aspects of the Mexican American cultural heritage, where a family still owned land in the north, networks of relatives still lived in rural areas, or there was participation in regional cultural activities such as the *penitentes* religious rites or the *matachines*. In short, these informants were a particular segment of the Mexican American working class, who were ethnically distinct with important regional differences from other Chicanos, but who did not explicitly claim ethnic identity unless asked, as in our interviews. Although they did not explicitly express ethnic pride, their struggles to retain their way of life were inherently political, but did not include politicized terms like Chicano.

In contrast to the situation among our informants, more recent research on ethnic identity among Mexican Americans in other areas shows that generation as well as region are important.[10] Collectively, this research highlights the regional variation of our New Mexico sample. Through their rejection of the term "Chicano" and the straightforward (as opposed to strident) ways they described their lives, these informants pushed me to a new understanding of Mexican American ethnicity and the importance of contextualizing our informants' own terms of identity.

The Politics of Ethnic Identity in Academia

A second dilemma arose when I attempted to present our research findings to fellow Chicano or Latino colleagues in the late 1980s. On two occasions, I made presentations on our research findings in ways that respected our informants' construction of identity and tried to contextualize their meanings. Yet I was attacked and my integrity questioned when I used the term "Spanish." Puerto Rican scholars in particular strongly objected to the use of "Spanish." One colleague claimed—to general agreement—that he had never even heard of anyone using the term "Spanish American" "*in the community*," so he could not understand how I could use it. They grilled me about my motivations and purposes, questioned my relationships with informants, and demanded to know how I would use the data. Embedded in their questions was the assumption that I was using the term "Spanish" as a euphemistic way of identifying Mexican Americans, and they implied that I was identifying with the white power structure and would use the data in ways that would harm my informants. It was only after other Hispana colleagues who were from northern New Mexico rescued me, asserting that indeed "Spanish American" was widely used even by scholars, that they relented. To someone who saw herself as a feminist activist scholar, this felt ironic and unfair. Clearly I had violated the Chicano/Latino academic cultural norms of ethnic identification.

I found myself in an ambivalent position: I was very sympathetic to their insistence that we scholars not buy into the racism and insensitivity involved in labeling a group by terms they would not claim, or in avoiding the mestizo racial content of the terms themselves, which "Spanish" seemed to imply. Chicano/Latino scholars are well aware of the pressures to be token spokespeople for "our people," and the importance of resisting any type of pejorative labeling and of perpetrating misconceptions about our communities. Yet I felt very uncomfortable about their assumption that by using "Spanish" I was somehow a "mainstream" scholar who would be insensitive to these issues.

In response to the critique, I cautioned my coauthors, and we self-consciously decided to use the term "Hispanic" instead, even though we felt uncomfortable with the Euro-centered sensibility it implied. "Hispanic" was a term agreed upon by an advisory committee formed from representatives of various Chicano and Latino political organizations, in response to efforts to sensitize the Census Bureau's accounting of people of "Spanish origin" in the 1970s census.[11] Yet because the Census Bureau then lumped together groups with very disparate histories, sociodemographic characteristics, political interests, and treatment upon immigration to the United States—notably Cubans, Puerto Ricans, and Mexicans (Portes and Bach, 1985)—many activists and scholars (including us) found "Hispanic" problematic.[12] The preferred term by the late 1980s was "Latino," which carried connotations of community self-sufficiency and empowerment and leftist political leanings. Yet "Hispanic" was the term selected by our informants after "Spanish," and seemed to be the next-best approximation of their own sense of ethnic identity.

The last piece of evidence concerning this dilemma came more recently. In 1991 the National Association for Chicano Studies passed a student-initiated resolution that condemned the use of "Hispanic" (National Association for Chicano Studies, 1991). (In the politics of the association, students have a political voice through a plenary session on student issues, so a student-initiated resolution carries a lot of weight.) We realized that we would be violating the Chicano/Latino academic norms once again if we continued using "Hispanic."

In retrospect, it is clear there were two contesting principles at work—the feminist notion that we should respect our women informants' constructions of their identity, and at the same time respecting Chicano/Latino academic norms regarding the public presentation of ourselves. A Chicana feminist approach to ethnography clearly would combine the two, fully aware that academic norms must include women's interests as well.

As a way of reconciling these competing dilemmas, and after much discussion, we eventually decided to use the terms "Mexican American" and "Hispana" (for women) interchangeably. "Hispano" (the generic male term) is a term indigenous to northern New Mexico and approximates the use of "Spanish," in that working-class people use it in daily life. But "Hispano" is also becoming politicized similarly to "Chicano." In a number of contexts in New Mexico, scholars and activists have begun using "Hispano" to signify Mexican American political interests (Sierra, 1992).[13] We hope that by using "Mexican American" and "Hispano" interchangeably we can respect both sides in this dilemma, yet we realize that no one term will please everyone. It seemed as if the "danger" that Judith Stacey identifies in doing ethnographic research concerned my own integrity more than violating our informants' sense of self. They, after all, were shielded from political critique by anonymity and by having their lives placed in context. I (and my colleagues) were subject to verbal jostling without the benefit of presenting our personal concerns and agendas.

I should note that we also had a similar dilemma about how to label our white informants, since most of them did not identify with the term "Anglo," which is widely used in New Mexico. When asked about ethnic identity, working-class white informants used terms that specified their own mixed and varied ancestry: "I'm a little bit of everything—German, Scottish, Irish, Italian, Danish, Slavic." Or they used terms like "Heinz 57, 31 flavors," which conveys a sense of culture that is processed. One woman evoked racial features and responded, "freckled and fair-skinned."[14] After more discussion and soul-searching, we decided to use "white" and "Anglo" interchangeably as well. We have yet to receive criticisms from white academics or activists for using this term. The term "white," however, is clearly problematic for people of European descent as well.

More telling, and a dilemma I came to see only recently, is that my Chicano/Latino colleagues and I were operating with a rigid construction of ethnic identity. Although Chicano activists generally agreed on the necessity of using "Chicano," this in turn muted the internal political and theoretical differences among Chicana (and Chicano) scholars. Thus I realized that I needed to deconstruct the "Chicana" part of Chicana feminism with which I identified and reflect upon how Chicana feminism itself was framed.

Chicana feminists have long contested the male-centered intellectual and political traditions of the Chicano movement and the white middle-class focus of the second-wave feminist movement. Yet Chicana feminists have simultaneously used concepts from Chicano Studies for analyzing the intersection of class and race oppression and have drawn from feminist studies concepts of patriarchy and male dominance in analyzing the Chicana experience (Cortera, 1980; A. García, 1989). Chicana feminists also identify with our long history of labor and political activism, although again many activists did not use the term "feminist." Chicana studies was the product of a "mixed union," which has been problematic, and created the need for Chicana feminist institutions, organizations, and perspectives (Zavella, 1989).[15]

In 1988 Beatriz Pesquera and Denise Segura did a survey of 101 Chicana faculty, students, and staff who belong to Mujeres Activas en Letras y Cambio Social (Activist Women in Letters and Social Change), an organization of Chicana/Latina activist academics; 83 percent of their respondents identified themselves as feminists. Pesquera and Segura argued that there have been internal differences since the late 1960s, but that these have become more noticeable in more recent years. They identified three types of Chicana feminists in their sample: Cultural nationalists emphasize the concerns of the Chicano movement, but want recognition of women's concerns and rights as well. Liberal Chicana feminists are oriented toward reform and hope to enhance the well-being of the Chicano community with a special emphasis on improving the status of women. Insurgent Chicana feminists, immersed in radical traditions, emphasize that Chicana inequality is the product of interrelated forms of stratification based on race-ethnicity, class, and gender—and for some, heterosexism. These women favor personal and institutional change, and compared to the other groups, are more actively involved in political activities (Pesquera and Segura, Forthcoming; Segura and Pesquera, 1993).

Pesquera and Segura's analysis helped me realize that my own thinking had undergone changes. The whole field of Chicana/o Studies has become more self-reflexive and sophisticated in its analyses of the experiences of Chicanos, male and female. Insider research, then, is more complicated than we had anticipated in the early flush of nationalist fervor, and we are beginning to realize how we are insiders and outsiders within several constituencies, each with its own norms and responsibilities.

Reconfiguring Chicana Feminist Ethnography

To be sure, I will continue to honor some of the norms of Chicano academic discourse, some of which are critical and in some ways parallel the concerns of feminist scholars—such as the importance of activist scholarship. I believe that Chicano scholars, like feminists and others who aim to reconstruct the canon and the structure of the academy, should continue their self-critical reflections on ethical and research dilemmas. In contesting the dominant discourses about women, in this case giving voice to Chicanas, Mexican Americans, and Spanish women workers, we must not be seduced into thinking that our work is without its own contradictions.

In the service of Chicana—or Hispana—informants, I had unconsciously privileged the Chicano side of my identity and not listened to women carefully. After returning to our interview data and culling from our own experiences of living in Albuquerque and observing working-class Mexican Americans, we came to see that our Hispana informants were telling us something new about ethnic identification. That is, within the constraints of their lives, "Spanish" meant accommodation, resistance, and struggle to these informants. They helped me to realize that I should deconstruct my own Chicana feminist viewpoint. The critiques of our Chicano/Latino colleagues notwithstanding, we must respect our informants' own constructions of identity, however politically unpalatable they may appear to us.

In conclusion, I want to return to the notion of Chicana feminist ethnography. The dilemmas I raise here really have meaning only within the constraints of my own life. I have no delusions that our research was collaborative in some type of panfemale sense that was based on special bonding or that broke down status differences between us and our subjects. Although women were remarkably cooperative within the interview setting, in sometimes subtle ways they pointed out the differences between us, and showed me how I had stakes in understanding their lives in ways they did not. In the cannery research project, my informants' political ethnic senses seemed more familiar, more like mine. In the New Mexico project, our informants' sense of ethnicity and identity was so different that we were forced into rethinking in order to recognize its implicit political nature.

In both projects, as in most academic work, the self-defined interests of the research subjects were elsewhere. The researchers defined the problem to study; we asked questions about work, family, and ethnic identity that they found sensitive and even uncomfortable; and our analysis will probably have little direct effect on their daily lives. And however self-consciously provisional an account we provide, our analysis is aimed at a primarily academic community and will provide real benefits to us. In paying careful attention to our informants' sense of their selves, I came in time to see my own Chicana feminist blinders. As we are becoming all too aware, when one claims or has attributed a categorical difference based on ethnicity, the power relations involved are readily apparent. My status as Chicana feminist researcher, then, created two audiences that I should be sensitive and accountable to. Increasingly, I share our Spanish informants' sense of struggle and unease in grappling with this "name game," realizing that I too construct an ethnic identity depending on the context.

Feminist dilemmas begin at home, and we cannot take a cultural feminist stance in our approach to fieldwork. As we go through the process of talking with people like ourselves who are called "other," we should try to understand our own feminism and political struggles. Chicana feminist ethnography, then, would present more nuanced, fully contextualized, pluralistic self identities of women, both as informants and researchers.

NOTES

Thanks to Felipe Gonzales and Louise Lamphere for the many extended discussions that helped me to clarify my ideas. For their very helpful critiques of this chapter, I thank Gloria Cuadraz, Micaela di Leonardo, Lynet Uttal, and six anonymous reviewers of *Frontiers*.

1. Shulamit Reinharz (1983) reviews the work of feminists who claim that feminist research has these and other characteristics, including "shar[ing] the fate of our subjects."

2. Shulamit Reinharz (1992) points out that contrasting perspectives on the relationship between the ethnographer and her subjects have a long history.

3. I spent fifteen months conducting field research during 1977–1978. The bulk of my data was life histories with twenty-four cannery workers and labor organizers, but I also did historical research on the canning industry and unionization by the International

Brotherhood of Teamsters, and did participant-observations in canneries and other public settings, such as union meetings. A few of the interviews were conducted in Spanish, in which my fluency is good but not excellent.

4. Limón provides a discussion of the origin of the term "Chicano," which has been traced to usage in 1911, and reports on surveys on ethnic identification where the majority of respondents preferred the terms "Mexicano" or "Mexican American," except in New Mexico.

5. Joseph V. Metzgar (1975) found that the use of "Spanish-American" had actually declined in use between 1962 and 1972, and that those who increased their use of "Chicano" were primarily age twenty and younger.

6. Ramón A. Gutiérrez (1991) investigated ethnic categories and identity in northern New Mexico, beginning in the eighteenth century after Spanish frontier society was firmly established. He documents that the overwhelming majority of the elites could not claim pure Spanish ancestry, yet they claimed an identity as Españoles to differentiate themselves from the Indians and claim honor. Mestizos, the ancestors of today's working-class Hispanos, socially constructed their self-designation as Spanish for their own ideological and material benefit. Even in Spain, there were so many interracial unions that it was impossible to reckon pure Spanish ancestry (Gutiérrez, personal communication).

7. Lamphere and Evans were the project directors, and Gonzáles and I were graduate student interviewers at the time, writing our own dissertations. We did a little participant-observation in public settings, but the research mainly drew from the interviews with eighty-nine people—thirty-eight worker couples and fifteen single mothers (in the end, two men were not interviewed)—of which I conducted many with the Mexican American women. Peter Evans interviewed plant managers as well.

8. Focusing on Chicago, Felix M. Padilla (1985) notes the importance of context for Mexican American identity: Encouraged by the division of labor in U.S. industrial society, which created common experiences of social inequality among Mexican Americans and Puerto Ricans, Chicano activists forged coalitions with other Latino groups and constructed a situational ethnic identity of Latinos.

9. Similarly, Jose Limón (1981) found that some Texans of Mexican descent have used "tejano" as a public referent, in part to distinguish between a Mexicano from Mexico and one from Texas.

10. In a survey of 370 respondents, Keefe and Padilla (1987) found that 25 percent had high Mexican cultural awareness and ethnic loyalty and were most likely to identify themselves as Mexicans; 74 percent were bicultural individuals who retained moderate or high ethnic identity. Only a small percentage were highly Anglicized and preferred "Americans of Mexican descent." In a survey of people of Mexican origin, Hurtado (Hurtado et al., 1992: 59; Hayes-Bautista et al., 1992) found that the first-generation respondents preferred "Hispanic" (88%), "Latino" (86%), and "Mexican" (76%); the second generation preferred "Hispanic" (83%), "Californian" (81%), and "American of Mexican descent" (78%); and the third-generation respondents preferred "Mexican American" (85%), "Hispanic" (83%), and "American" (82%), as well as "American of Mexican descent" (82%).

11. Based on interviews with advisory committee participants and political leaders, Laura E. Gómez (1992) argues that Hispanic represents the more "mainstream" political viewpoints of the participants, and became popularized during the 1980s.

12. Beginning with the 1980 census, the term "Hispanic" is a specially designated ethnic term that includes four subcategories: Mexican, Mexican American, Chicano; Puerto

Rican; Cuban; Other Spanish/Hispanic. For the state of New Mexico, there have been bipo-
lar self-designations, with the Mexican, Mexican American, and Chicano and the Other
Spanish/Hispanic making up the largest categories. Since it is unclear how many Iberians
reside in New Mexico, and since unlike other cities (like Miami, San Francisco, Los Angeles,
Washington, D.C., or New York), Albuquerque (the largest New Mexican city) is not a major site of Latin American immigrant settlement, we can only conclude that some Mexican
Americans are choosing "Other Spanish." Thus census data are particularly imprecise for
counting the Mexican American population in New Mexico.

13. Metzgar (1975: 55) claims that in the 1970s, "Hispano" was used almost exclusively
by scholars and professional writers to describe Spanish-speaking New Mexicans and did
not have widespread use in the barrios.

14. Ruth Frankenberg (1992) argues that the social construction of "white" carries several meanings—as distinct from "white ethnic," it means "spoiled by capitalism," so that
brand names like Wonder Bread connote blandness or processing and evocations of features of the body such as skin color. Micaela di Leonardo (1984) shows how late 1970s
white Italian-American women socially constructed their own sense of ethnicity, sometimes in racist terms.

15. Actually I said "mixed marriage." Thanks to Emma Perez (1993), who reminded me
that my use of a marriage analogy is a heterosexist formulation.

REFERENCES

Aguilar, John L. 1988. "Insider Research: An Ethnography of a Debate." In *Anthropologists
at Home in North America: Methods and Issues in the Study of One's Own Society,* edited
by D. A. Messerschmidt, 15–26. New York: Cambridge University Press.
Cannon, Lynn Weber, Elizabeth Higginbotham, and Marianne L.A. Leung. 1988. "Race and
Class Bias in Qualitative Research on Women." *Gender and Society* 2, no. 4: 449–462.
Cortera, Marta. 1980. "Feminism: The Chicana and the Anglo Versions, a Historical
Analysis." In *Twice a Minority: Mexican American Women,* edited by M. B. Melville. St.
Louis: C. V. Mosby.
———. 1977. *The Chicana Feminist.* Austin: Information Systems Development.
di Leonardo, Micaela. 1991a. "Habits of the Cumbered Heart: Ethnic Community and
Women's Culture as American Invented Traditions." In *Imagining the Past in
Anthropology and History,* edited by W. Roseberry and J. O'Brien. Berkeley: University of
California Press.
———. 1991b. "Introduction: Gender, Culture, and Political Economy: Feminist
Anthropology in Historical Perspective." In *Gender at the Crossroads of Knowledge:
Feminist Anthropology in the Postmodern Era,* edited by Micaela di Leonardo, 1–48.
Berkeley: University of California Press.
———. 1984. *The Varieties of Ethnic Experience: Kinship, Class, and Gender Among
California Italian-Americans.* Ithaca: Cornell University Press.
Fonow, Mary Margaret, and Judith A. Cook. 1991. *Beyond Methodology: Feminist
Scholarship as Lived Research.* Bloomington: Indiana University Press.
Frankenberg, R. 1992. *White Women, Race Matters: The Social Construction of Whiteness.*
Minneapolis: University of Minnesota Press.
García, Alma M. 1989. "The Development of Chicana Feminist Discourse, 1970–1980."
Gender and Society 3: 217–238.

García, Ignacio M. 1989. *United We Win: The Rise and Fall of La Raza Unida Party.* Tucson: University of Arizona Press.

García, John A. 1981. " 'Yo Soy Mexicano.' . . . : Self-Identity and Sociodemographic Correlates." *Social Science Quarterly* 62, no. 1: 88–98.

Golde, Peggy, ed. 1986. *Women in the Field: Anthropological Experiences.* Berkeley: University of California Press.

Gómez, Laura E. 1992. "The Birth of the 'Hispanic' Generation: Attitudes of Mexican-American Political Elites Toward the Hispanic Label." *Latin American Perspectives* 19, no. 4: 45–58.

Gómez-Quiñones, Juan. 1990. *Chicano Politics, Reality and Promise, 1940–1990.* Albuquerque: University of New Mexico Press.

Gonzalez, Nancy. 1969. *Spanish Americans of New Mexico: A Heritage of Pride.* Albuquerque: University of New Mexico Press.

Gonzales, Phillip B. 1992a. " 'Ethnic Diffidence' and 'Categorical Awareness': Aspects of Identity Among a Set of Blue Collar Spanish Americans." Unpublished manuscript.

———. 1992b. "The Political Construction of Ethnic Nomenclature in Twentieth Century New Mexico." Unpublished manuscript.

———. 1986. "Spanish Heritage and Ethnic Protest in New Mexico: The Anti-Fraternity Bill of 1933." *New Mexico Historical Review* 61, no. 4: 281–299.

Gonzalez, Sylvia. 1977. "The White Feminist Movement: The Chicana Perspective." *Social Science Journal.* 4: 65–74.

Gutiérrez, Ramón A. 1991. *When Jesus Came the Corn Mothers Went Away: Marriage, Sexuality, and Power in New Mexico, 1500–1846.* Stanford: Stanford University Press.

———. 1986. "Unraveling America's Hispanic Past: Internal Stratification and Class Boundaries." *Aztlan* 17, no. 1: 79–101.

Hammerback, John C., Richard J. Jensen, and José Angel Gutiérrez. 1985. *A War of Words: Chicano Protest in the 1960s and 1970s.* Westport, Conn.: Greenwood Press.

Hayes-Bautista, David E., Aída Hurtado, R. Burciaga Valdez, and Anthony C.R. Hernández. 1992. *No Longer a Minority: Latinos and Social Policy in California.* Los Angeles: Chicano Studies Research Center.

Hernandez, Patricia. 1980. "Lives of Chicana Activists: The Chicano Student Movement (A Case Study)." In *Mexican Women in the United States, Struggles Past and Present,* edited by M. Mora and A. R. del Castillo. Los Angeles: Chicano Studies Research Center Publications.

Hurtado, Aída, and Carlos H. Arce. 1987. "Mexicans, Chicano, Mexican Americans, or Pochos . . . ¿Que Somos? The Impact of Language and Nativity on Ethnic Labeling." *Aztlan* 17: 103–129.

Hurtado, Aída, David E. Hayes-Bautista, R. Burciaga Valdez, and Anthony C.R. Hernández. 1992. *Redefining California: Latino Social Engagement in a Multicultural Society.* Los Angeles: Chicano Studies Research Center.

Keefe, Susan E., and Amado M. Padilla. 1987. *Chicano Ethnicity.* Albuquerque: University of New Mexico Press.

Klein, Renate Duelli. 1983. "How to Do What We Want to Do: Thoughts About Feminist Methodology." In *Theories of Women's Studies,* edited by G. Bowles and R. D. Klein. London: Routledge & Kegan Paul.

Krieger, Susan. 1987. "Beyond 'Subjectivity': The Use of the Self in Social Science." *Qualitative Sociology* 8, no. 4: 309–324.

Lamphere, Louise, Patricia Zavella, Felipe Gonzales, with Peter B. Evans. 1993. *Sunbelt Working Mothers: Reconciling Family and Factory.* Ithaca: Cornell University Press.

Limón, José E. 1989. "Carne, Carnales, and the Carnivalesque: Bakhtinian Batos, Disorder, and Narrative Discourses." *American Ethnologist* 16, no. 3: 49–73.

———. 1981. "The Folk Performance of 'Chicano' and the Cultural Limits of Political Ideology." In *"And Other Neighborly Names": Social Process and Cultural Image in Texas Folklore,* edited by R. Bauman and R. D. Abrahams. Austin: University of Texas Press.

Méndez Negrete, Josie. 1991. "What Are You? What Can I Call You? A Study of Chicano and Chicana Ethnic Identity." Master's thesis, University of California, Santa Cruz.

Metzgar, Joseph V. 1975. "The Ethnic Sensitivity of Spanish New Mexicans." *New Mexico Historical Review* 49, no. 1: 49–73.

Miller, Michael V. 1976. "Mexican Americans, Chicanos, and Others: Ethnic Identification and Selected Social Attributes of Rural Texas Youth." *Rural Sociology* 41: 234–247.

National Association for Chicano Studies. 1991. *Noticias de NACS* 9, 3.

Nieto-Gomez, Ana. 1974. "La Femenista." *Encuentro Femenil* 1/2: 34–39.

Oakley, A. 1982. "Interviewing Women: A Contradiction in Terms." In *Doing Feminist Research,* edited by Helen Roberts. London: Routledge.

Padilla, Felix M. 1985. *Latino Ethnic Consciousness: The Case of Mexican Americans and Puerto Ricans in Chicago.* Notre Dame: University of Notre Dame Press.

Paredes, Américo. 1977. "On Ethnographic Work Among Minority Groups: A Folklorist's Perspective." *New Scholar* 6, no. 1/2: 1–32.

Pérez, Emma. 1993. "Speaking from the Margin: Uninvited Discourse on Sexuality and Power." In *With These Hands: Building Chicana Scholarship,* edited by Beatriz M. Pesquera and Adela de la Torre. Berkeley: University of California Press.

Pesquera, Beatriz M., and Denise A. Segura. Forthcoming. "With Quill and Torch: A Chicana Perspective on the American Women's Movement and Feminist Theories." In *Third Wave: Feminist Perspectives on Racism,* edited by N. J. Alarcon, S. Alexander, S. Day, L. Albrecht, and M. Segrets. New York: Kitchen Table Press.

Portes, Alejandro, and Robert L. Bach. 1985. *Latin Journey: Cuban and Mexican Immigrants in the United States.* Berkeley: University of California Press.

Reinharz, Shulamit. 1992. *Feminist Methods in Social Research.* New York: Oxford University Press.

———. 1983. "Experiential Analysis: A Contribution to Feminist Research." In *Theories of Women's Studies,* edited by Gloria Bowles and Renate Duelli Klein, 162–191. London: Routledge & Kegan Paul.

Riessman, Catherine Kohler. 1987. "When Gender Is Not Enough: Women Interviewing Women." *Gender and Society* 1, no. 2: 172–207.

Roberts, Helen, ed. 1981. *Doing Feminist Research.* London: Routledge & Kegan Paul.

Romano, Octavio I. 1968. "The Anthropology and Sociology of the Mexican American." *E. Grito* 2: 13–26.

Rosaldo, Renato. 1989. *Culture and Truth: The Remaking of Social Analysis.* Boston: Beacon.

Segura, Denise A., and Beatriz M. Pesquera. 1992. "Beyond Indifference and Antipathy: The Chicana Movement and Chicana Feminist Discourse." *Aztlan International Journal of Chicano Studies Research* 19: 69–92.

Sierra, Christine M. 1992. "Hispanos and the 1988 General Election in New Mexico." In *From Rhetoric to Reality: Latinos and the 1988 Election,* edited by Rodolfo O. de la Garza and Luis de Cippio. Boulder: Westview.

Stacey, Judith. 1988. "Can There Be a Feminist Ethnography?" *Women's Studies International Forum* 11, no. 1: 21–27.

Strathern, Marilyn. 1987. "An Awkward Relationship: The Case of Feminism and Anthropology." *Signs* 12, no. 2.

Thorne, Barrie. 1979. "Political Activist as Participant Observer: Conflicts of Commitment in a Study of the Draft Resistance Movement of the 1960s." *Symbolic Interaction* 2, no. 1: 73–88.

Wax, Rosalie H. 1979. "Gender and Age in Fieldwork and Fieldwork Education: No Good Thing Is Done by Any Man Alone." *Social Problems* 26, no. 5: 509–522.

Weston, Kath. 1991. *Families We Choose: Lesbians, Gays, Kinship.* New York: Columbia University Press.

Zavella, Patricia. 1989. "The Problematic Relationship of Feminism and Chicana Studies." *Women's Studies* 17, no. 1–2: 23–34.

———. 1988. "The Politics of Race and Gender: Organizing Chicana Cannery Workers in Northern California." *Women and the Politics of Empowerment,* edited by A. Bookman and S. Morgen, 202–224. Philadelphia: Temple University Press.

———. 1987. *Women's Work and Chicano Families: Cannery Workers of the Santa Clara Valley.* Ithaca: Cornell University Press.

Zinn, Maxine B. 1979. "Field Research in Minority Communities: Ethical, Methodological, and Political Observations by an Insider." *Social Problems* 27, no. 2: 209–219.

8

Reflections on Oral History: Research in a Japanese American Community

VALERIE MATSUMOTO

I CAME TO ASIAN AMERICAN HISTORY and women's history through curiosity about my own family's past. I plied my parents and grandparents with questions: How did Obaachan and Ojiichan meet? Why did they come to the United States? What was it like growing up in Oakland? How did Uncle Dewey learn to hypnotize chickens? Why was Auntie Ritsu sent to a finishing school in Japan? And then there were the questions about "camp," a major reference point for my parents and their Nisei friends from as far back as I could remember. It was an evocative word, used as shorthand for many experiences I could not then fathom, catching only glimpses of tar-papered barracks, bleak deserts, young people packing suitcases to go to New York or Chicago. We would sit up late after dinner, drinking tea with old friends passing through town, telling stories. "Camp," they would say, leaning back and shaking their heads, with a sigh. "Camp."

It was my mother who answered my questions, patiently explaining about the internment of Japanese Americans during World War II, recounting her family's trips, first to the Tanforan Assembly Center and then to the dusty Topaz Camp in Utah. How they could take with them only what they could carry; how after the war, they found that their stored belongings had been looted. I remember hearing about a woman who loved and rarely shared sweets, an expensive treat in camp. On some special occasion, she finally brought forth a box of chocolates she had been hoarding. When the box was passed around, everyone could see that the candies had become stale and wormy. Through my mother's shared memories, even this woman with the wormy chocolates became an engaging human linkage to the larger forces of history.

Recently I mentioned to my mother that a distant relative had expressed interest in hearing about her wartime experiences.

"Oh, it's too hard to talk about," she said.

"But you told me about it." I was surprised. "I didn't know you minded discussing it."

"You are my child, and you needed to know."

I preface my essay with this story because it underscores the kind of connection I have with a particular part of the U.S. past, the kind of gift oral history represents, and my own ignorance of the effort it took for my mother to share this with me. These kinds of lessons have been reaffirmed throughout the course of my research in Cortez, a small Japanese American farming community in central California. In addition to examining institutional records, local newspapers, and other primary documents, in 1982 I conducted more than eighty tape-recorded oral history interviews. They ranged in length from one hour to six hours.

Interviewing three generations of men and women raised many questions about feminist operating principles in the field. The process provided rich, sometimes humbling, insights into cultural and generational assumptions and necessitated frequent reassessment of my relations with individuals and the larger community. In this essay, I focus particularly on the issue of control in interviewing and on consideration of "insider/outsider" dynamics.

What feminism means to me as a researcher is not only the concern for equal rights and access for women but the effort to be mindful of the historical inequities and struggles that have shaped the material conditions of ourselves and our subjects, female and male. This includes for me, as a Japanese American scholar, attention to the complexity of race and interethnic relations, critical elements in the landscape I study. It also means trying to cultivate an awareness of social stratification and privilege and the ways in which they may affect the process of oral history interviewing.

In these aims I have been influenced by my training as a social historian. An outgrowth of the scholarly reassessment catalyzed by the social movements of the 1960s and 1970s, social history has broadened the panorama of the U.S. past to include people previously ignored as historical actors: women, racial ethnic groups, members of the working class. The language of social historians in the 1970s and 1980s included "uncovering" and "reclaiming" buried pasts, writing not only history but "herstory," acknowledging discriminatory structures while emphasizing "resistance" to them. To these ends, historians drew on an increasingly wide range of primary sources, from material artifacts to probate records and census data. Oral history interviews, long a staple method for anthropologists, proved particularly useful for gaining access to the experiences of people who left few personal written records. Such interviews lent texture and color as well as substance to the broader frameworks delineated by documentary materials such as newspapers, internment camp publications, and organizational records. In Cortez I found a wealth of primary sources, the richest and most varied of which was oral history.

The relationship between the Cortez community and me has in some ways been an unusual one. Because of the community's origin in 1919 as a planned colony and its strong constellation of institutions, its members have a deep-rooted sense of themselves as a community and of the importance of their collective history. Fortunately for me, they had already begun seeking a scholar to write their history when I started trying to locate a receptive Japanese American settlement, preferably rural, to be the subject of my dissertation. Although their plans to commission a researcher dissolved in an internal disagreement over the form (book, photo exhibit, documentary film) the completed project ought to take, they welcomed me into their homes, directed me to local institutional records, and generously shared their time and perceptions of the past.

Two families, one Buddhist and one Christian, helped me set up most of the interviews. I tried to interview at least one or two members of each Cortez family. In addition to conducting interviews with people now living in Cortez and in surrounding communities like Turlock and Atwater, I also talked with people who had grown up in Cortez but had later moved to the San Francisco Bay area. All of the surviving Issei (first-generation immigrants) met with me, as did fifty-six Nisei (American-born second generation), and nineteen Sansei (third generation). In my interviews with the nine Issei, I was fortunate to have the interpretive assistance of their children and friends; despite the limitations, these joint interviews afforded me not only a window onto community dynamics in the pioneering period of the 1920s and 1930s but also an opportunity to observe Issei-Nisei relations in 1982.

Because of the general interest in my project, many people were willing to be interviewed. Nevertheless, I encountered a fair number who felt nervous about the prospect. Even those who readily agreed often said, "Oh, my life isn't very exciting. I haven't done much. But you should talk to my neighbor, s/he's really got a lot to say." While jotting down the name of the friend with a lot to say, I hastened to explain why the interviewee's perceptions were indeed important to my gaining a full, balanced view of the community's development.

I tried to demystify the process of the interview and to give the interviewee as much control over it as possible. Because I was often introduced to potential interview subjects at community events like the Boy Scouts' fundraising pancake breakfast or a Japanese American Citizens League installation banquet, people usually had a chance to meet me first. I had prepared a set of questions (three pages, single-spaced) that I sent to everyone who expressed interest so they could see exactly what would be asked. The questionnaire followed a life-history format, tailored to include Japanese immigration, farm life, World War II internment, and gender role expectations. I told them that any questions they did not want to discuss would be omitted from the interview.

Some oral historians prefer not to give questions in advance, arguing that doing so lessens the degree of spontaneity and candor of the interview. I believe, however, that more individuals would have hesitated to talk with me had they not seen the questions. Reading the questions ahead of time, with veto power, not only alleviated anxieties but also gave people the opportunity to locate photograph albums and newspaper clippings and to verify dates and events with relatives. Actually very few asked to have any questions omitted. The subsequent interviews were generally relaxed and comfortable. Nearly all took place in the subjects' homes, with the crackle of an almond-wood fire in the background and hot green tea at hand.

In a reversal of roles, I got a taste of being interviewed myself at the outset of each session. Usually this mini-interview consisted of questions about my family, education, and interests. Although I wanted the people of Cortez to feel at ease with me and believed that I owed them information about my own history and goals, the question of how much to disclose caused me some reflection. The preliminary information established certain common ground; my telling them that my grandparents had immigrated from Fukuoka Prefecture, settled in Oakland and Orange County, California, and were interned in the Topaz and Poston Camps enabled them to place me within a Japanese American context to which they could draw connections. Indeed, one of the Cortez Nisei and I learned, after he pulled out his family genealogical tree, that we might be distantly related!

Sometimes I worried that they might censor themselves or unconsciously weight their responses to suit my perceived inclinations. Of course, the kinds of questions I asked, the fact that I was interested in women's experiences as well as men's, and my status as a Sansei woman pursuing a doctorate in history suggested certain things to them (e.g., that I might be politically liberal and inclined to feminism). I reasoned that anyone truly uncomfortable with me for this or any other reason would decline an interview, as a few individuals did. But I tried to convey my respect for the interviewees' opinions by my body language, verbal cues, and follow-up questions. On occasion, subjects would (inadvertently) begin to turn the interview into a conversation by asking my opinion of issues like gender role change or national politics. I tried to let them know that I would be happy to respond afterward, but that I wanted the interview to reflect their thoughts and concerns.

Some emotional outpourings occurred for which I was unprepared, being trained as a historian rather than a psychologist. Although I had tried to give the interviewees enough control to avoid topics they did not wish to discuss, I had not expected that certain seemingly innocuous questions might open the floodgates of painful memories. One Nisei woman, when asked, "What was it like growing up here?" suddenly began to describe the brutality of her father toward her mother and how she had felt as a child. Tears rolled down her cheeks and she started to sob, as the words continued to tumble out. I was aghast, unsure how the interview had taken this turn and what it meant. As I handed her tissues and turned off the tape recorder, my own eyes damp, I worried that I had, however unwittingly, dredged up dark memories that might haunt her even more. I suggested that we stop for the day and was surprised when she shook her head and went on speaking. When this happened again during an interview with another woman who had carried painful memories of abuse as a domestic servant for more than forty years, unspoken, I began to understand the force of the need to tell.

After both of these incidents, I worried that negative psychological repercussions might result from the opening of doors catalyzed by the process of the interview. (These revelations usually came in the middle of the interview, during discussions of childhood and adolescence, the periods when most individuals have the least control over their lives. The interviews, ranging from two to six hours in length, usually ended with positive reflections on the most memorable occasions or happiest times experienced.) It was somewhat reassuring to observe that, when each interview was finished, although I felt leaden and depressed, the women seemed lighthearted and cheerful, one of them whistling as she bustled around her house. I hope that the act of telling me their experiences provided some measure of relief. Given the parameters of my relationship with the Cortez people, I did not feel I could suggest to anyone that they seek counseling, nor was I certain that it would be appropriate.

What then, from this perspective, was my role as an interviewer with feminist concerns? I had to consider this further when I was asked to interview two individuals. This constituted another role reversal of sorts, because usually I was the one asking. In one case, an Issei man living in a nearby town had missed being interviewed for a project sponsored by his own community. His family knew that he felt bad about this and so requested that I speak with him. He gave me not only a useful perspective on the historical relations between his community and Cortez but also an expanded sense of the significance of being interviewed.

In the second case I was asked to interview someone whose relatives were concerned about the effects of the pent-up childhood suffering caused by the World War II internment. They felt that it might prove beneficial for the person to relate these experiences and thought that talking to a non–family member might be easier. Although I was willing to conduct the interview (and did), I felt nervous about what results they might expect and stated this. I was relieved to learn that they did not anticipate a miraculous transformation, although they did believe that the act of telling might in some way facilitate healing.

These two interviews particularly made me aware that others might have their own needs with regard to the interviews, and that the process might affect them in ways that I had not imagined but had to take into consideration. What made this less daunting was the fact that no one wanted me to be a counselor. Listening attentively was what I could do and what seemed to be desired. There were days on which I returned to my home base feeling something like a traveling confessional, drained by the intensity of the interaction. However, I also felt deeply grateful to be able to see the past through the eyes of others. To share in this wealth of experience was both heady and humbling.

Who is an "insider" in the context of such research? Who is an "outsider"? What does this status mean for the scholar? Carrying out interviews and documentary research in Cortez afforded a variety of vantage points from which I could consider these questions. From one perspective, I appeared to be an insider, as a third-generation Japanese American with rural roots and a grounding in Asian American history. I looked, sounded, and behaved very much like other

Sansei from the community, and on several occasions was in fact assumed to be a Cortez family member or relative by Japanese Americans from nearby towns.

The two families who generously hosted me during my research visits also treated me "like family," providing me with food, lodging, and emotional support as well as trying to tell me about the dynamics of various relationships within the community. The women especially offered cues and insights; their training in detecting the motivations and needs of others, and their keen observation of emotional undercurrents, greatly facilitated my research. They alerted me to the tensions in families, in addition to identifying which individuals had disagreed with each other over various community issues (e.g., whether to build a community hall or a swimming pool; draft resistance and military service during World War II). They particularly made me conscious of the tremendous amount of work involved in maintaining balanced, cooperative relations in a small, tightly knit community.

My being perceived as a species of insider, by virtue of ethnicity and family background, certainly made it easier for me to gain acceptance in the community. I think interviewees felt more comfortable, resting on common understanding. However, sometimes they assumed that I knew more than I did. Because my family had, in my distant childhood, been involved with row-crop cultivation, and the Cortez farmers have specialized in orchards and vineyards, the agricultural practices that were a matter of second nature to them seemed mysterious to me. This led to a great deal of backtracking and pleas for elaboration during interviews. Even when taken aback by my ignorance, they patiently explained the seasonal round of work.

Although in some respects I was an insider, of course I was also an outsider. I did not grow up in Cortez nor did I have any connection with the community before I began the research. I did not have to do farm chores as a child. My family lived in a town on the Arizona-Mexico border, where there were few other Asian Americans. The second language I studied was Spanish, and it was not until I went to college that I had a chance to learn even a little Japanese. Visits to my grandparents in California and Utah provided glimpses of involvement in ethnic community through their church activities, fishing trips with Issei buddies, the Japanese-language newspapers they read in the afternoon, and the tofu and fish they bought from a regular peddler. Because I had been for a number of years the only Japanese American child in a predominantly Mexican American town, the Japanese American worlds in which my cousins, aunts, and uncles were rooted appeared immensely attractive. Part of my interest in studying a Japanese American community stemmed from this naïve fascination with the workings of ethnic networks and their meaning for those who participate in them.

One of the key lessons I learned through interviewing was that I wasn't the only one experiencing the tugs of being both an insider and an outsider. Regardless of how others perceived them, many individuals—especially women who had come to Cortez through marrying local men—felt that in some ways they were outsiders as well as members. Their discussion of the groups (ranging from handi-craft clubs to civic organizations) to which they belonged, within and outside the community, and their place in the web of family ties made me conscious of the multiple affiliations they maintained. And I think my being from outside made it easier for them to talk about their relation to the larger group.

It is difficult for me to assess fully the impact of my own cultural upbringing on my interactions with the women and men of Cortez. On the surface, I possessed a degree of familiarity with certain aspects of food, commonly used Japanese words, the ongoing work of affirming ties and balancing obligation, and a shared history. This facilitated my exploration of their collective past. But it is harder for me to evaluate how much I responded to them as a Sansei woman seeking ap-proval (mostly from elders) and trying to "fit in."

Working within the community as a Japanese American, I tried to follow the practices of social grace as much as possible, within the constraints of a limited graduate student budget. For example, this meant finding ways to convey my ap-preciation, especially for the hospitality of the two host families with whom I stayed alternately for seven to ten days at a stretch, making trips back and forth between the San Francisco Bay area and Cortez. Because they were farmers with bountiful kitchen gardens, I did not feel I could bring those staple offerings of Japanese American gratitude, fruit and vegetables. Instead I baked cookies, which met the criteria of being a consumable and appropriate token gift. (Fruit, *manju*—a Japanese confection, and cookies were the offerings of choice for two other Asian American women I know who have carried out Japanese American oral history projects.) I did not make this decision as a researcher considering the expectations of subjects, but rather as a Sansei woman conscious of the generosity extended to her and desirous of making some acknowledgment, however small. For the majority of the people who helped me, feeding me with history and *okazu*, many thanks and the completed dissertation manuscript were the only re-turn I could make.

I have referred to myself as a "Sansei," because it was an important aspect of how I acted and was perceived within the community: as the grandchild of Japanese immigrants with a history much like that of the Cortez farmers. I also draw attention to my generational standing because it provides clues to my rela-tional perspective on the Issei and Nisei, as well as my blind spots. Like many Sansei, I am more familiar with the world of the Nisei than of their parents, the Issei. Although I knew the outlines of their patterns of work and settlement and understood that arranged marriages were the custom among them and that rela-tionships within the prewar family were in key ways different from those in the postwar period, conducting interviews in Cortez opened my eyes to generational differences I had missed.

One of the last questions in the interview particularly revealed the assumptions I had unconsciously made. I always ended a session with summing-up questions that reviewed the interviewee's life to date: "What was the happiest time in your life?" "If you had your life to live over, would you do anything differently?" "Is there anything I have not asked that you would like to add?" These questions seemed to work well. However, it became clear that one question to which Nisei responded readily posed problems of translation for the Issei: "What was the most exciting event in your life thus far?" The Nisei who translated for me struggled to ask this question. It became, "What was the most memorable event you experienced?" The fact that the question could not be asked in the same way in both languages made me aware of the nuances that I was missing in the Issei's responses, due to my lack of facility with Japanese. It also alerted me to differences in ways of perceiving and thinking about the world.

The responses to this question further underscored generational and cultural differences. Nearly all of the Nisei men and women said that getting married and the birth of their children were the most exciting events they had experienced. By contrast, the Issei did not cite these occasions. Instead, they talked about something that they had experienced alone, often linked with nature. For one Issei, it was a spiritual revelation; for another, it was seeing the sun setting behind Mount Fuji as his ship set sail for America. One woman described a night she still remembered vividly. She was working as a nursemaid for a Japanese consular official in Washington, D.C., from 1927 to 1930. Young and far from home, she felt lonely for her parents and familiar surroundings. One night when the diplomat and his wife were away attending a social function and all was quiet, she went outside by herself. She looked up and saw the beautiful full moon, and thought, "My mother and father in Japan may also be looking at the moon." Suddenly she felt connected to her family by the shining moon, and her loneliness disappeared.

For the Issei, whose marital partnerships were arranged by their parents, getting married meant crossing the threshold of adulthood but it did not include expectations of romantic love. Affection was viewed as an outgrowth of a relationship, not a prerequisite. The Nisei, however, who had giggled when their European American teacher gave a good-bye kiss to the husband who brought her to school, who had watched Clark Gable and Carole Lombard on the silver screen, had formed different hopes and dreams. Their attitudes about marriage reflected the norms of the larger U.S. society in the 1940s and 1950s. As a historian I understood and expected this, but somehow I was still surprised by the contrast in responses. I was much struck by how one generation chose events involving groups of people as "most memorable," and how another generation focused on individual experiences. Because there were so few surviving Issei, I was not able to proceed very far with this line of analysis, but it provided a salutary jolt to my thinking.

My relationship with the Cortez families did not end with the last interview. I have remained in touch with the two families—the Babas and the Yuges—who hosted me within the community; they have continued to keep me informed of local news. This has most often been, sadly, notification of the death of individuals I interviewed. These families have also served as intermediaries between me and the larger Cortez community, transmitting information back and forth.

I felt it was important for the community to have an opportunity to give feedback about the study. When I completed my dissertation in the fall of 1985, I sent several copies, bound and also looseleaf (so that people could easily make more copies). I told them that the manuscript would be further revised in preparation for publication and solicited their comments so that I could make changes. They were eager to see their history published and, with their usual efficiency, set up a network to facilitate the distribution of manuscripts for local review. A number of people sent tactful notes directing my attention to the misspellings of names and other such mistakes; two families returned helpfully marked copies. All of the suggestions I received related to the correction of factual inaccuracies (e.g., errors regarding maiden names and the number of miles between Cortez and Turlock). No one took issue with my interpretation; the only criticism that seeped back to me was someone's remark about how "scholarly" the dissertation was, which indicated, I think, that this person found the historiography a bit dry. The overall response was very encouraging. I am particularly grateful to the individuals who patiently read yet another draft.

As the manuscript progressed through revisions, and publication began to loom closer, like a long-awaited harvest, the Cortez families scoured their trunks and photograph albums for pictures that could be used as illustrations. Through another well-coordinated effort, they sent me nearly one-hundred photos of all sizes and ages, capturing community events and family milestones. Eleven were chosen for the book through a process of my indicating my wishes and the community's preferences to the production editor, who relayed these concerns to the press's art department, who then assessed the reproduction quality of the submissions.

Due to a series of factors including an auspicious coincidence and some delay in the publication of *Farming the Home Place: A Japanese American Community in California, 1919–1982*, a book party planned by the Cortez people for the fall of 1993 snowballed into a large community celebration in the spring of 1994. They decided, because 1994 would the seventy-fifth anniversary of the founding of Cortez, and because of the appearance of the book in 1994, to expand their annual community picnic into a reunion. Nisei and Sansei around the country responded enthusiastically; 600 people registered to attend the two-day event on April 30 and May 1, 1994. I was honored to be invited to be the guest speaker and to sign books (an academic author's dream).

I felt both excited and nervous as I drove through the San Joaquin Valley toward Cortez. It wasn't my first return trip, but I still worried: Would I recognize everyone I had met before? Would I remember names, and who belonged to which branch of which family? Would I feel like an awkward intruder at someone else's high school reunion? Insider/outsider anxieties resurfaced. I quickly discovered that many people returning to Cortez, or visiting it for the first time as inlaws and distant relatives, harbored similar uneasiness. My fears (and theirs, too, I think) soon evaporated in the warm outpouring of goodwill and affection. Nisei reminisced about childhood adventures and marveled at new farmhouses on short bus tours of Cortez. At the Japanese American Citizens League Hall, the community's all-purpose meeting place, parents and children clustered around an extensive photo exhibit, seeking familiar faces and telling stories. On the second day, families converged on the grounds of a local elementary school for the annual picnic. While Nisei and Sansei tossed horseshoes, played bingo, and watched a volleyball tournament, shrieking Yonsei (fourth-generation) children took part in games and races in which all participants won prizes. We ate hot dogs and beans. I happily signed many copies of *Farming the Home Place.* People I had heard about but never met came up to introduce themselves, providing more pieces for the sprawling historical jigsaw puzzle. The picnic ended with two traditional events: all children were issued water guns, with which they promptly and thoroughly drenched each other; and as parents carted away their dripping offspring, Nisei and Sansei men and women swiftly cleaned the grounds, packed up the food, and dismantled and hauled away tents, tables, and chairs. Everyone (including me) departed to continue smaller-scale family reunions throughout Cortez.

Doing research in the Cortez community taught me valuable lessons, as I emphasized in my speech at the evening banquet on April 30. The process made visible to me some of my own assumptions about generational perspectives, shaped as they are by gender, culture, and age. It gave me a chance to experience and observe the multiple layers of affiliation and difference that create insider/outsider identifications, and showed me how they vary according to context. Conducting oral history interviews caused me to reflect on the responsibility of the researcher to the subject, as well as on the meaning of being interviewed. And it has made me increasingly mindful of the gifts of trust and insight that sustain our work as scholars.

9

The Expeditions of Conjurers: Ethnography, Power, and Pretense

CINDI KATZ

TALK ABOUT GEOGRAPHICAL FIELD RESEARCH conjures up explorers, chart makers, and expeditions to far-flung lands. The geography of maps, charts, and terrae incognitae. When I was looking for dissertation funding in 1980, I was dazzled by the research budget of the National Geographic Foundation. My proposal for less than $10,000 to do an ethnography of children in rural Sudan was stacked up with (and unfavorably compared to) polar expeditions, space explorations, and ocean-floor mapping projects. I hadn't realized that "real" geography was a million-dollar enterprise. Romantic, expensive. Military.

Talk about ethnographic field research conjures up proper sweaty westerners "going native" in varying degrees of disarray. There was nothing urban, local, or domestic in the mythology of ethnography despite a history lasting several decades. Ethnography itself seemed a colony of anthropology, which continues to wage a losing battle to protect its disciplinary frontiers, in part by defining what proper ethnography entails. When I first went to the field, I felt free to ignore these codifications because of geography's loose affiliation with ethnography as such, and foundations funding ethnography, such as the Wenner-Gren Foundation and the Social Science Research Foundation, felt free to avoid me. My nontraditional approach was Janus-headed—I felt free to do an ethnography of the acquisition and use of environmental knowledge but was perennially insecure about what I was leaving out by not systematically addressing kinship patterns and the like.

Finally, talk of science, even social, even now, and research, even ethnographic, continues to conjure up a masculine presence. Despite a few star women in *the* field—indeed the name of Margaret Mead was virtually synonymous with anthropology in the lay imagination—it remained difficult to find women in *my* field who could serve as mentors or role models. And although this is changing, with many recent books celebrating the regendering of science and the academy, women remain marginalized in science, and our practices in the field (understood here both as discipline and as site of research) seem to require more negotiations than those of our male colleagues.

Talk of conjuring conjures up witches, jugglers, enchantments, and conspiracies. The possible worked out of the improbable. Under "conjurer," the *Oxford English Dictionary* offers the tantalizing, "professor of legerdemain"; for "legerdemain" it suggests "sleight of hand, the performance of tricks, deception, hocus pocus." In the crossroads of improbable possibilities and the performances of deception are some of the dilemmas of doing fieldwork. In this chapter I discuss the tightrope I walk between feminist geographer and "professor of legerdemain"; between the politics of fieldwork and fieldwork as politics.

I take as my starting point that social relations are ordered by the social construction of boundaries—political, economic, social, physical—over time and space; and contemporary social relations of production and reproduction, which are hierarchical and uneven, are oppressive and exploitative to most people in most places. The intersecting trajectories of these oppressions are well known. They include class, race, gender, nation, sexual orientation, and age. My political work, as a scholar and otherwise, is concerned with undoing these relations. Ethnographic work is a means of transgressing boundaries and thereby offers itself as a kind of politics. In this chapter I explore my efforts in this realm with an eye on their contradictory relation to the larger political project of transforming oppressive and exploitative social relations and suggest a direction for field research that offers the possibility of more direct political engagement. I begin by simultaneously tracing the projects in which I have been involved and the practical, theoretical, personal, and political dilemmas they have raised.

A Chronology, Some Confessions

In 1981 I conducted ethnographic field research in a village in central-eastern Sudan that had been included in a state-sponsored agricultural project a decade earlier. My focus in this project was the acquisition and use of environmental knowledge by children. This knowledge—of agriculture, animal husbandry, and the use of local resources—was central to the production and reproduction of everyday life in the village. I was interested in discovering not only what knowledge was passed on and by whom, but also in what ways its production and exchange were altered in the face of imposed socioeconomic and political-ecologic change. I was looking for resistance, possibly—as the song goes—in all the wrong places. The project was supported by a dissertation grant from the National Science Foundation. The grant included funds for my partner to document the children's activities of work and play on Super-8mm film.

The dilemmas of representation, "othering," and intent were raised by this work. These dilemmas were intertwined like the tightly wrapped braid I wore during much of the field research, and like that braid needed frequent unraveling, combing out, but ultimately rebraiding, in order to keep working. Like most ethnographies, the project was riddled with thorny questions of representation—who were we to go there to tell our stories in their names; how did our self-representations work for and against theirs? The project reiterates the uneven power relations between the United States and Sudan, between colonizer and colonized, that have become commonplace in the critique of ethnography, even as its intent was to undo these relations. As I have noted previously (Katz, 1992), I recognized the uneven power relations involved in doing this research in a rural setting of the so-called Third World, but I thought the meanings and practices of social reproduction would be more visible where they were threatened by the immediate impress of a transforming rural capitalism. As Marx suggested in a discussion of "the colonies" in volume 1 of *Capital*, the contradictions of capitalism may be witnessed more clearly at the margins. More importantly, I reckoned that if capital accumulation was a global process with multiple local forms, it was important to identify the range of oppositional practices to it. By investigating some of these local-global practices I thought that I might establish connections between them and help to build a politics that engaged capitalism in its multiple historical geographies. My sense was (and is) that "we" were already "there," and our presence created—perhaps even demanded—a space for anti-imperial ethnography.

This awareness and sense of mutual engagement in common problems differently experienced does not obviate the uneven power relations that are summoned and deployed in the enactments of such projects. It was, after all, I who went there and my research agenda that was carried out, and when I was finished I left. Such moves reflect power no matter what their broader intent is and no matter how deep are the feelings engendered in the process.

The politics was intensely personal, and my willingness to be untruthful for strategic reasons concerns and sometimes troubles me. How else can I understand my self-representation and the assumptions it made of the participants in my research? For example, I said I was married to my partner because I assumed our cohabitation would be interpreted as sinful and my work would be undermined. I, of course, was able to make relative moral judgments about their practices, but by my concealment I assumed that they were not capable of the same.[1] In a similar vein, as an anti-Zionist and an atheist Jew, I decided to pass as a Christian so as not to impede my research. I assumed that revealing I was Jewish to the uniformly Muslim and Arab-identified population of the area would create suspicions that I did not want to carry, especially given my deep and long-standing opposition to Zionism. Clearly I unfairly presumed a lack of subtlety on their part, but the strategy was also almost unforgivably lazy. In the United States I am willing to labor over the distinction between Jew and Zionist. Why not there? Again, I explained my choice to myself as strategic—just as I stopped being an always gracious host after a few weeks in the village (and got a kerosene, rather than charcoal, stove for when I was). I felt I did not have time both to engage in deliberations on Zionism *and* to get my research done. This was disingenuous. I feared that such self-disclosure might have undermined my work, and I was not willing to take that risk. The choice was surprisingly painful. Not only might I have had interesting political discussions with people in the village but I wasn't very good at being a Christian. I often felt sad because I could not talk about the many practices common to Judaism and Islam (especially when for many, these practices were more important than the political-economic relations I was so eager to discuss). Finally, I was evasive about the uneven economic relations between me and the people with whom I worked. My research grant was small, but was much larger than the average annual household income reported to me in my villagewide survey. There was keen interest in my financial affairs, and I often stumbled as I tried to explain that although I seemed to have a lot of money, I was a poor graduate student. The metric by which this was the case encapsulates the uneven power relations between me and the people in that village. All of these evasions and deceptions were strategic—to ensure the smooth operation of the research. Yet these were the very areas in which I expected people to be honest with me. Although my research did go well on many levels, I wonder how my strategic dishonesty undermined me and my project and whether it really did ease my way and facilitate the work.[2]

As I unraveled this braid of dilemmas I was determined not to be unraveled by them because of the larger political intent of my project. My intent was to uncover the practical responses to capitalism in the everyday practices through which knowledge was produced, shared, and used. As I have suggested, I saw myself engaged in similar oppositions and in this way connected my own work to those practices that were the focus of my inquiry. This connection seemed to undercut some of the exoticizing aspects of the project by locating me and the people in the village where I worked in an arena of struggle with some common ground. I do not underestimate our different stakes in that ground. But even this discovery raises a set of questions. I was concerned with resistance. I could not abrogate the fact that I defined the terrain of concerns and sought answers for myself in the practices of others. Moreover, while I think my concern with the practices of everyday life made sense to the people with whom I worked, I was caught up with uncovering resistance in the work knowledge parents shared with their children rather than where it might have been more readily located—in their religious teachings and practices. My insistence on finding particular patterns of resistance that might inform my own political practices probably blinded me to some of the more resilient—albeit discomfiting to me—sites of resistance.

In 1983 and 1984 I was back in Sudan working for CARE, a nongovernmental organization that was engaged in a reforestation effort intended to assist Eritrean and Ethiopian refugees. My task was to develop a program of social and agroforestry extension that would ensure the project goals for revegetation and livelihood assistance. I conducted ethnographic field research in the refugee settlements and their surrounds in order to ensure that extension activities addressed potentially conflicting political-ecologic needs and concerns among the major land use groups in the area, which apart from the refugees included Sudanese pastoralists, peasant farmers, and large-scale cultivators. I organized the program of research and carried it out with research assistants drawn from the refugee communities. The extension program itself was developed by my Sudanese counterpart, a rural sociologist with expertise in agricultural extension, and me, and was supervised over the five-year life of the project by him. My work in this project had ample funding and infrastructural support from CARE, and the experience of eliciting people's participation in the research with the promise of trees felt very different from the abstract promises of my doctoral research. Somehow the tangibility of the trees, which were almost a direct compensation for talking with me and my assistants, made the rhetorical promises of political solidarity that were part of my previous research seem that much more flimsy. The CARE project raised other concerns, and these had more to do with my practices as a scholar and professional. The project was considered a success by both participants and external evaluators. Part of its success was attributable to the intricate and labor-intensive extension program I developed. Yet I have never published anything about the work or other applied projects with which I have been engaged because this work lacks currency in the academy. The split between theory and practice and the privileging of theory are hallmarks of bourgeois and masculinist science. Our silence on such productive engagements in the field, then, is yet another dilemma of fieldwork that lets others define what counts.

When I moved to New York in 1986, I stopped working in Africa and was determined to work where I lived. I had several reasons for this: There were many problems in New York and my political commitments compelled me to address them; I was suspicious of my exoticizing impulse; and I was feeling fragmented by the distances between the multiple locales of my work. In 1987 I began mulling over the relation between the displacements suffered by children in rural Sudan and those experienced by working-class children in New York City. The consequences of capitalist agricultural development on the one hand and deindustrialization on the other appeared to have startlingly similar effects on children—including diminished prospects of meaningful work, dislocations of and depredations on sites of social reproduction, and deskilling leading to disqualification for all but the most marginal jobs. In one way or another this concern for children's displacement in its transnational guises has been at the heart of my work since 1987, and I have addressed it in New York while working on other projects. I have yet to undertake the long-term companion ethnography on children in New York I have promised myself and others I would do. The very dilemmas of fieldwork addressed in this volume have deterred me from completing this work. Without belaboring the point, these dilemmas include the fact that while I have moved the site of my research closer to home, it remains that most of my work in New York has been among working-class populations in central and East Harlem. I am not working class, Latino, or black, while most of those with whom I work are. I simultaneously question my decisions to keep the focus of my inquiries at some distance from my own identifications and understand them as appropriate, given the crises facing these groups and the need to build a broad-based political response to them. This, of course, puts me on the tricky borders attaching research, practice, advocacy, and activism.

In 1988 my colleague in the Children's Environments Research Group at the City University of New York was approached by the schoolyard committee of a school district in upper Manhattan to design an early childhood play environment. In a presentation that showed the kind of play environments our group has advocated and the participatory design strategies we favor, he convinced the committee to try to build a larger schoolyard that would provide an integrated play environment for children from preschool through sixth grade. Our group secured funding from the Aaron Diamond Foundation to develop a participatory design for the community schoolyard. We conducted a fairly spare ethnography of the schoolyard during and after school hours; elicited design ideas from almost all of the children in the school; debated competing design ideas over three-dimensional models of the yard among parents, teachers, administrators, staff, and children—separately and together—and presented the collective design in a kiosk on the street in front of the school so that community members and others could comment upon it. The design program generated through these participatory activities was used for an international design competition open to architecture and landscape architecture students. The winning design—selected by a committee that included the assistant principal of the schools in question and the deputy superintendent of schools in the district—was used as the basis for the design that only now, four years later, is about to be built.

Through the vicissitudes of working with overlapping bureaucracies, competing egos, and a long period of financial retrenchment in New York City we managed to develop a design that reflected the needs and desires of all involved. The research and design processes, together with their many compromises, were painstakingly negotiated. Yet here again I have barely published a word despite the value of this kind of work to the design professions, if not to social science as presently constituted. Apart from the dilemma of "what counts" for whom, this project raised more specifically the problems of advocacy, activism, and commitment in research. Although the schoolyard project was initiated by a school district committee and our approach was always participatory, I do not consider this project exemplary of action research. It was not community driven in its entirety, and its goal—a schoolyard—was predetermined, albeit by a local committee. Although the community voiced its support of schoolyard change as a priority, it is not clear whether if the work had been truly open-ended they would have chosen a schoolyard as the first project.[3] In addition, the project has been frustrating for all involved largely because of the relentless stonewalling by the Board of Education, which had to release funds and sign off on the project if the yard was to be built. I have been determined to see this project through to completion and have attended countless meetings and made modest donations of my own funds to that end. But I have often been inattentive in ways that at best slowed things down and at worst caused missed opportunities. Engaging in participatory community research directed at change is time-consuming and extremely frustrating. There are few rewards for these efforts in the academy and several punishments—years can go by without "results" and time that might be spent publishing is spent "perishing." The appreciation of my efforts by those at the school and in the community does not ease my conscience. My efforts are uneven and that—no matter what the reason—is inappropriate for committed research engagements.

The same year that the schoolyards project began, a group of cultural studies researchers at the City University of New York developed an alternative field project that became known as CAMEO (Community, Autobiography, Memory, Ethnography, Organization). Beginning in 1991, CAMEO members based at the university worked with community residents in East Harlem (El Barrio) in Manhattan and in Williamsburg in Brooklyn on issues of community concern using autobiography, memory, and ethnography as organizing strategies. We divided into two groups largely and (probably not) accidently along gender lines. Graduate students and community residents worked together as paid research partners, and research projects were developed collectively in each group. I was part of the El Barrio group in which, among other things, we collected several oral histories that wove together memories of everyday life in East Harlem and their connections to present concerns and practices; began an ethnography of children's everyday lives on a neighborhood block; worked on a place history of La Marqueta, which had been until a few years before a thriving market and focal point for the community and now was a struggling shell; and began to develop a social history of the Center for Popular Education. Some CAMEO participants also mounted a museum exhibit that highlighted local cultural forms and practices for the consumption of wider publics. After two years of sporadic engagement on my part I felt I had developed productive working relations with our research partner, who was a neighborhood community leader, and with some of the children who lived on her block. The graduate students in our group—all native speakers of Spanish—worked in the neighborhood more consistently and had developed closer working relations with more community residents and were also working as occasional teachers at the Center for Popular Education.

I had every opportunity to engage in an extended ethnography of the practices of children's everyday lives within the rubric of CAMEO, but I did not. This was only partly attributable to conflicting time commitments to other work. The reason has been mostly a nagging uncertainty about what was to be gained and for whom. Some of my concerns were raised by the first project in Sudan and do not find any easier resolution. In East Harlem I have addressed the theoretical and practical issues concerning the displacement and deskilling of children by the predations of a restructuring capitalism, but I have not done the detailed ethnography. Most of what would be gained by doing the fieldwork now has everything to do with my career and little to do with the communities where I work. I am skeptical of such productions of knowledge and fearful that they would expose the practices of those with whom I work to those who have an interest in controlling or surpressing them.

My work on this chapter has provided a path out of this dilemma. Rather than conduct the (long forestalled) ethnography of the children's everyday practices, I have concluded that the only viable project would be one of critical environmental education wherein the children's engagement in researching their own neighborhood would enable them to define the problems to be addressed and the means of addressing them. I would offer my skills as a geographer and a teacher to assist them in finding ways to address the questions of concern to them and in these ways would not only discover what issues are important to young people but would engage in a collective process that reworks science itself. My inspiration for this endeavor is drawn in part from the work of the Society for Human Exploration discussd below, which promulgated a notion of research as itself emancipatory.

The Politics of Fieldwork

Each of these endeavors raised a host of dilemmas; only a few of them are raised here, and they are never more than partially resolved. I participate in this critical self-reflection here and elsewhere to show that I am not sounding an anti-intellectual cry for ethnographic business as usual or that I have no guilt. Rather, I want to suggest that the ethnography of ethnographers is reaching an unproductive internal vanishing point. It is time to live and work with and against the contradictions rather than employing self-confession as a barrier against them. Social scientists who engage in field research must find noninnocent (self-reflexive and clearly positioned) ways to work in the world such that we can at once uncover common bonds and recognize differences. If scholars and other practitioners committed to social and economic change promising greater equity and social justice retreat only to speak about themselves or otherwise self-consciously undermine their projects, there will be little hope for the development of new forms of engaged critical scholarship.

This book, and other recent books, surveys critically the politics of fieldwork (Wolf, Chapter 1). My colleagues have addressed many of these issues with great integrity and insight. Here I want to question the politics of fieldwork more closely and explore the possibilities of moving toward a more explicitly politicized research practice. In this task I am multiply positioned as a geographer, feminist, social scientist, and activist. I focus on a small, distinguished, but insufficiently recognized part of the history of geographical field research, the Detroit and Toronto Geographical Expeditions of the late 1960s and early 1970s, because they suggest inspiring, if problematic, strategies to rework committed field research.

Geographic research has long been associated with imperial interests and military conquest (Godlewska and Smith, 1994; Livingstone, 1992). In the United States, if not in Europe, its field practices were traditionally concerned with surveying, charting, and resource assessment more than with social practice. When the latter was the focus, the trajectory of research was often descriptive, environmental determinist, or, more recently, concerned with how people adjusted to environmental challenges such as way-finding, spatiotemporal constraints, or drought. A fieldwork tradition concerned with the sociospatial practices of people's everyday lives, or with people's productions of space, place, and nature as constitutive of social life, has developed in U.S. geography largely since the 1970s. It remains relatively unusual to engage in ethnographic field research in contemporary geography, although of course it was a staple of the European imperial traditions. Whereas anthropologists engage in relentless autocritiques of the practices of ethnography, ethnographically inclined geographers must still defend these methods within the discipline at the same time as they guard against the naïve appropriation of this problematic methodology from anthropology. As a geographer I not only confront a legacy of field research that I want to stand on its head, but I also engage in peculiar intra- *and* interdisciplinary politics concerning ethnographic methods and the nature of qualitative research.

In neither task am I alone. In recent years there has been a spate of articles on the problems and questions raised by qualitative research, as well as a number of conference sessions and journal sections devoted to questions raised by feminist research practices (*The Canadian Geographer,* 1993; *The Professional Geographer,* 1994). This work explores such issues as self-reflexivity, intersubjectivity, representation, positionality and epistemic privilege, and the uneven power relations of research (Eyles and Smith, 1988; Pile, 1991; Keith, 1992; McDowell, 1992; Dyck, 1993; Rose, 1993; Gilbert, 1994; Kobayashi, 1994; Nast, 1994). Yet this increasingly lively and sophisticated discussion remains a minor discourse in geography, and those deploying a qualitative analysis and/or ethnographic strategy in their research are often asked to defend or explain their strategies in journals, at conferences, and elsewhere. Thus there is an internal politics of fieldwork within geography as a discipline over critical issues such as voice: who gets to speak and how; epistemology: how knowledge is constituted and by whom; and method itself. Given these stakes, it is hard to call this struggle "purely academic." It has everything to do with power/knowledge, and those engaged understand that their victories and losses shape the contours of the field—the way it looks from the outside and the way it feels from within. Its outcomes determine employment, publication, promotion, funding, and practitioners' attractiveness to students—that is, the tenor, power, and fulfillment of everyday life in the academy. But there are broader issues to which this contest is connected.

In geography there is an interesting, if short, history of work concerned with producing "emancipatory geographies." The Detroit and Toronto Geographical Expeditions, arguably the most notable of these, sought self-consciously to turn the notion (and intent) of "the expedition" on its head. Replete with explorers, survival themes, discovery, and base camps, the two expeditions, carried out intermittently between 1968 and 1975, were anti-imperial, land reclaiming, and folk-empowering projects.

The Geographical Expeditions were the vision of William Bunge, a U.S., white, middle-class, male geographer who had the notion that the skills of geography could be democratized and used by people to alter the oppressive conditions of their lives. In a piece reflecting on the first years of the Detroit Expedition, Bunge (1977) noted that (traditional) explorations were always vital to the societies that undertook them, and that these quests for resources, wealth, and power were commissioned at the highest levels of authority, which were—not coincidentally—their main beneficiaries. By interpreting the social vitality and political-economic consequences of exploration democratically, Bunge and his colleagues offered a radical notion of exploration whose purpose was to help "the human species most directly" (35). They attempted to rid exploration of its exotic and imperial impulses. The point of their Expeditions was that people should explore their home terrains in order to reclaim and restore them. As Bunge suggested, the purpose of exploration would no longer be a search for paradise but a search within the self, a means to develop "a more appropriate base map for our times" (33).

Lacking the panache (and military-industrial rationale) of space explorations and the like (*Field Notes*, 1971; Bunge and Bordessa, 1975), these "subaltern geographies," as we might now call them, and "maps of the human condition" were not funded by the National Geograhic Society.[4] As Bunge noted, the Expeditions were neither "nice" nor "status quo" geographical enterprises. Indeed their essence was an engagement in oppositional geographical practices—the very antithesis of a traditional expeditional foray. In both Expeditions "explorers" were drawn from the neighborhood as well as the university (Stephenson, 1974). Although the academic geographers made their skills available to particular communities, the definition of problems to be addressed rested with the community as a matter of principle. Stephenson (1974) notes that over half of the research problems addressed by the Toronto Expedition, for instance, were defined by the "community,"[5] and that throughout the life of the Expedition, these research areas had priority over others originating elsewhere. Expedition participants made much of the fact that they were invited into "the community," and stayed only as long as they were welcome by its members. Full-time participation in the enterprise was essential to the Expedition ethos. Some suggested that this level of commitment distinguished an expedition from (mere) fieldwork (Stephenson, 1974).

Explorers established a "base camp" in the neighborhood where they worked, and lived there at least for the duration of the expeditions—which generally took place over the summer months. The explorers worked in teams to research issues such as children's survival and open space, traffic, highrise construction; hidden spaces and cultural expression; rats and garbage; and "urban nationalism." The overarching structure was an analysis of the spaces of nature, mankind, and machines at five scales, the neighborhood, the metropolis, the nation, the continent, and the planet (Bunge and Bordessa, 1975).

Despite their democratic rhetoric, the Expeditions apparently retained hierarchical tendencies. Stephenson (1974) notes, for example, that Bunge was the

Expedition "theoretician," and he took the problems identified by fieldworkers and produced a "theoretical manual" casting them in a broader structure—complete with hypotheses to be tested in the field. Stephenson called this "the most essential role in the Expedition." Theorizing not only expanded the scope of the work, but gave it a coherence that prevented it from "degenerat[ing] into a series of interesting studies" (1974: 99–100). Drawing on the research manuals, the team leaders, explorers, and part-time explorers collected data in the neighborhood, analyzed it in relation to the hypotheses, and developed proposals for improving the conditions they addressed. Hypotheses were proven or disproven in action through monitoring changes in the community. There seems to have been no internal critique of this highly positivist procedure, although Expedition members occasionally point to the hierarchical presumptions of those outside (e.g., Warren, 1971). My retrospective sense, however, is that this resilient hierarchialization of work must have been inimical to the radical democratic intent of the Expeditions themselves.

The Geographical Expeditions were deeply embedded in their own history and geography. With the U.S. civil rights and antiwar movements came a flowering of socially committed research and radical experiments with action research strategies. These strategies were given greater urgency following the uprisings in many U.S. cities in the late 1960s. The unprecedented withdrawal of capital from Detroit and the riots that followed ravaged the city and were an extraordinary impetus to Bunge, other radical scholars, and the Expeditions.

But the Expeditions also have roots in the geographical practices or inspirations of an earlier time. Among their antecedents was the nineteenth-century Russian anarchist geographer Kropotkin's work on environmental learning. Kropotkin emphasized a kind of environmental learning that fostered people's abilities "to organize their lives cooperatively, reject externally imposed designs for living, and become active agents for change" (Breitbart, 1992: 80). As the feminist geographer Myrna Breitbart notes, one of the keystones of Kropotkin's alternative pedagogy entailed community study as "a critical and emancipatory process," whereby children and others might examine the social relations embedded and perpetuated in the physical environment as a means of understanding and confronting the forces of dominance in their lives. Kropotkin promulgated the notion of "direct community and workplace exploration" that drew on the expertise of people who lived and worked in these environments, and saw this as a strategy of social and environmental change (Breitbart, 1992: 80; Breitbart, 1981). The similarities between Kropotkin and the work of the Geographical Expeditions are clear. Not only was the Society for Human Exploration committed to precisely these sorts of critical explorations of the community, but much of its emphasis was upon education, especially sharing the skills of academic geography with community members and students of all ages who could use them to design strategies for change. They seem to have enacted an inspiring form of praxis that encompassed teaching, learning, researching, and work toward change.

The Society for Human Exploration remained active from 1968 to 1975. During that time they launched major Expeditions in Detroit and Toronto that produced a wealth of data relevant to those engaged in emancipatory projects of urban social and geographical change. Their maps, charts, and diagrams are still provocative, and the problems they examined remain, tragically, on the agenda. Most of these problems, such as children's access to the outdoor environment, children's exposure to environmental hazards, urban disinvestment, and the conflicts between cities and their suburbs, have only gotten worse. The Expeditions were exemplary in engaging community residents in projects that focused their anger and empowered them to change conditions that were oppressive. Among the projects of the Detroit Expedition, for instance, was an atlas of human needs that identified areas that lacked health services and included maps of children's injuries from traffic accidents and maps of people who lived alone. Children produced neighborhood maps that showed, among other things, the location of trees (living or dead), rubbish, and streetlights. Some of the documents were written by community members, who often attacked academic elitism as well as racial and other social structures of dominance. The axis of power/knowledge they expressed and revealed remains extraordinary and makes the withering of the Expeditions all the more regrettable.

There were problems. As my references to species, humanity, and the planet suggest, the Expeditions tended to naturalize and essentialize social difference and experience. Their language and actions were often tainted with traces of racism, sexism, and nationalism: the responsibility of "thinking and telling," Bunge says at one point, "is dangerous work, manly work, like sand hogging or coal mining." They were often macho, even militaristic, and simultaneously self-aggrandizing: "If there are any dirty or dangerous or doubtful experiences to be faced, the geographers go first, and the leader of the Expedition goes very first" (Bunge, 1977). And the heterosexism of the Expeditions was completely unquestioned. Their rhetoric was explicitly survivalist and its Darwinian overtones sometimes led to naturalized rather than socially wrought strategies for change.

The Expeditions would invert as much as undo the binary relations of power that structure social life under capitalism and patriarchy, leading to a predictable paternalism. For example, the voices of black residents were privileged consistently by the (white, male, bourgeois) leadership, not only because they experienced the most oppressive and dominating social relations in Detroit or Toronto, but *because* they were black. Women were praised and privileged as mothers, with little sense that children and mothers were anything but biologically given units. However salutory and liberating they were in the early days of a political movement (McDowell, 1992), such essential inversions tend to harden the positions they oppose. An overall lack of reflexivity characterized the Expeditions' writings.

For all its problems, the Society for Human Exploration and its Expeditions were largely community driven and activist oriented and sought a radical socialization of science. Without much theoretical fanfare their work bored right into the heart of what is now framed as power/knowledge and reworked detached notions of science to produce a scientific practice that was as much about organization as about knowledge. My criticisms (with the benefit of hindsight) trace a range of dilemmas that recur in field research, and like my own dilemmas, are only provisionally resolved. Among the lessons of feminist, antiracist, and postcolonial scholarship in recent years have been a clear understanding of the constructed and mobile nature of social categories and a critical awareness of how constructions of difference serve uneven ends. As Audrey Kobayashi (1994: 78) suggests, echoing a central dilemma facing ethnography, this politics of difference highlights the problem of "speaking for" others, and this in turn raises how difficult it is "to move unheralded into just any field situation and become an effective part of its struggle for change just because we believe in its political ends." That kind of engagement stakes out the borders and negotiates difference, identity, and change in an ongoing manner. In reading the texts of the Society for Human Exploration we see that the Expeditions foundered precisely on this point. Like most explorations, they were more concerned to stake out the boundaries and examine the goings-on within them than to live on the borders and understand their multiple positionings around them. A reinvigorated geographical expedition would need to constantly rework this delicate task.

When I reflect, not on the dilemmas of fieldwork alone, but on the serious dilemmas of social change and the relation of my work to them, I am drawn to the vigor and commitment of the Expeditions, despite their considerable blemishes. They offer a welcome corrective to the often paralytic and self-serving musings that forget the larger dilemmas of social change to focus on the blemishes alone. The urgency of these concerns requires that as variously positioned feminist scholars, we keep conjuring up ways—however problematic—to transgress and renegotiate the boundaries that stop us from working toward meaningful social change. A little enchantment might help, but it will take more than legerdemain.

NOTES

1. See Wolf, Chapter 1. Such "white lies" (a revealing term) are not made in a vacuum. While in the field we planned to get married, after years of living together and telling similar lies to landlords. My dissertation adviser had the astute insight that having lied to strangers at the start, we felt that we had been dishonest with family by the end. In some way we felt compelled to get married to make good on the lie. I still have not told that branch of "my family" that we are divorced.

2. By focusing on my own deceptive self-representations, I do not mean to suggest that I think the people who participated in my research were transparently honest. They were, of course, engaged in representation of their own. I have discussed these questions of representation elsewhere (Katz, 1992).

3. This, of course, begs the question of what is meant by "community." There were multiple communities within the neighborhood. These groups often had competing interests despite the fact that they had overlapping constituencies.

4. The work of the Detroit Geographical Expedition and Institute was given modest support by the Association of American Geographers, who in 1969 noted the significance of the DGEI in drawing students from outside of academia and providing them with the research skills and tools to meet their needs, and in pioneering the use of "the geographic method" with a citizen action group (Field Notes 3). Reading the "Field Notes" and the AAG Committee's report on the DGEI made the 1960s seem like another planet, one worthy of exploration.

5. As is often the case with such work, "the community" was not well-defined. As I suggested above, the term remains a kind of catchall that suggests but does not guarantee democratic participation.

REFERENCES

Breitbart, M. M. 1992. "'Calling up the Community': Exploring the Subversive Terrain of Urban Environmental Education." In *Words That Ring Like Trumpets,* edited by J. Miller and P. Glazer. Amherst, Mass.: Hampshire College.

———. 1981. "Peter Kropotkin: The Anarchist Geographer." In *Geography, Ideology, and Social Concern,* edited by D. R. Stoddart. Oxford: Basil Blackwell.

Bunge, W. 1977. "The First Years of the Detroit Geographical Expedition: A Personal Report." In *Radical Geography,* edited by J. R. Peet. Chicago: Maaroufa Press.

Bunge, W. W., and R. Bordessa. 1975. *The Canadian Alternative: Survival, Expeditions, and Urban Change.* Toronto: Department of Geography, Atkinson College, York University. Geographical Monograph 2.

Canadian Geographer, The. 1993. "Focus: Feminism as Method." 37: 48–61.

Dyck, I. 1993. "Ethnography: A Feminist Method?" *The Canadian Geographer* 37: 52–57.

Eyles, J., and S. Smith. 1988. *Qualitative Methods in Human Geography.* Cambridge, England: Polity Press.

Field Notes. 1971. "The Geography of the Children of Detroit." Detroit: The Detroit Geographical Expedition and Institute. Discussion Paper 3.

Gilbert, M. R. 1994. "The Politics of Location: Doing Feminist Research at 'Home.'" *The Professional Geographer* 46, no. 1: 90–96.

Godlewska, A., and N. Smith. 1994. *Geography and Empire.* Oxford: Basil Blackwell.

Katz, C. 1994. "Playing the Field: Questions of Fieldwork in Geography." *The Professional Geographer* 46, no. 1: 67–72.

———. 1992. "All the World Is Staged: Intellectuals and the Projects of Ethnography." *Environment and Planning D: Society and Space* 10, no. 5: 495–510.

Keith, M. 1992. "Angry Writing: (Re)presenting the Unethical World of the Ethnographer." *Environment and Planning D: Society and Space* 10, no. 5: 551–568.

Kobayashi, A. 1994. "Coloring the Field: Gender, 'Race,' and the Politics of Fieldwork." *The Professional Geographer* 46, no. 1: 73–80.

Livingstone, D. 1992. *The Geographical Tradition.* Oxford: Basil Blackwell.

McDowell, L. 1992. "Doing Gender: Feminism, Feminists, and Research Methods in Human Geography." *Transactions of the Institute of British Geographers,* n.s., 17, no. 4: 399–416.

Nast, H. 1994. "Opening Remarks on 'Women in the Field.'" *The Professional Geographer* 46, no. 1: 54–66.

Pile, S. 1991. "Practising Interpretive Geography." *Transactions of the Institute of British Geographers,* n.s., 16, no. 4: 458–469.

Professional Geographer, The. 1994. "Women in the Field: Critical Feminist Methodologies and Theoretical Perspectives." 46: 54–102.

Rose, D. 1993. "On Feminism, Method, and Methods in Human Geography: An Idiosyncratic Overview." *The Canadian Geographer* 37: 57–61.

Stephenson, D. 1974. "The Toronto Geographical Expedition." *Antipode* 6, no. 2: 98–101.

Warren, G. 1971. Director's Annual Report. *Field Notes: The Geography of the Children of Detroit.* Detroit: The Detroit Geographical Expedition and Institute. Discussion Paper 3.

10

Situating Locations: The Politics of Self, Identity, and "Other" in Living and Writing the Text

JAYATI LAL

> *[As] Ethnography is moving into areas long occupied by sociology, . . . It has become clear that every version of an "other," wherever found, is also the construction of a "self," and the making of ethnographic texts . . . is the constant reconstitution of selves and others through specific exclusions, conventions, and discursive practices.*
>
> —James Clifford, *Partial Truths*

THE VERY NOTION of what it means to do research on gender and development in the contemporary historical arena has been urgently called into question by recent critical discourses on anticolonialism. For instance, debates on postcoloniality have interrogated the excavation of the Third World as a resource for Western theory. Additionally, feminist discourses on difference and universalism have challenged the construction of the "Third World woman" as an essentialized Other. And finally, methodological writings in sociology and anthropology have also articulated a deep skepticism about methodological vantage points that colonize, or objectify, the subjects of one's research. The common theme that underlies these strands of questioning is their collective interrogation of the foundationalism that is embedded in much extant social science research, which rests on an essential division between "Self" and "Other," or between the knowing subject (the researcher) and the known, or soon-to-be-known, object (the researched).

In this chapter, I look at the politics of representation and the epistemologies of locations in attempting to articulate a nonuniversalizing feminist methodology that goes beyond colonialist representations of "Third World women." In so doing, I bring together anthropological discourses on rethinking the project of ethnographic fieldwork and the politics of ethnographic writing, feminist discourses on, and critiques of, canonical ways of knowing and dominant epistemologies, and sociological discourses on feminist methodologies and critiques of malestream social science research. Despite the overlapping areas of concern in these disciplinary discourses, they have by and large not been involved in an interdisciplinary dialogue that, I argue, could be very productive.[1] In developing my arguments, I draw on my experiences of fieldwork—a term that I will attempt to deconstruct as I proceed—in a mixture of writing genres. Utilizing narrative, interpretive, and reflexive modes, I examine fieldwork encounters and my own background for their theoretical and epistemic implications.

Postmodern Disjunctures

In the postmodern era of intensified globalization, the international movements of capital, labor, and commodities shape not just the objects of our academic inquiry—factories and finance capital, workers, and products—but critically determine the forms that such inquiry and the discourse surrounding it takes. In the first instance, these international circuits mark us as individual scholars and locate us in a complex web of lived material realities that shape our notions of ourselves, our identities, our politics, and our writing. Furthermore, the subjects of our research on the globalization of the economy increasingly inhabit locations that do not fit our historically derived theoretical expectations of where they might be. Although the "native" subject might be increasingly likely to inhabit the privileged world of the First World anthropologist, many Third World scholars who immigrated to the United States for higher studies are also increasingly dislocated when they return "home."

There is a growing body of literature that acknowledges this historical moment in the disciplinary fields of anthropology and, to a lesser extent, in other social science disciplines. A generation of Third World scholars returning home have foregrounded epistemological concerns raised by scholars studying their own cultures within the West, particularly those studying "Third World" cultures and communities within the United States.[2] These concerns have coalesced with those stemming from a paradigmatic movement that is informed by poststructuralist concerns regarding representations of the Other and the author/ity of the researcher-ethnographer and ethnographic texts. Issues of nativity have once again come to the fore in analyses of non-Western and "Third World" societies, but it is now the nativity of the *researcher* rather than the research subject that is problematized.[3] This "return of the native" in recent anthropological debates specifically problematizes the assumption of an authentic insider (Narayan, 1993), arguing instead for the recognition that we all occupy multiple and fluid locations—a theme that I will pursue in more detail later.

This chapter situates the researcher-in-practice by addressing the multiple locations in the production of my identity as a Third World woman and U.S.-

based graduate student returning home from the academy to conduct research on women. Exploring my construction as a researcher around the multiple locations and positionalities that constitute the politics of self and identity—Third World woman in the United States, scholar and graduate student in the academy, feminist, middle-class researcher in India—I will explore the epistemological implications of such multiple locations and positionalities in the political practice of fieldwork. I will therefore examine the *politics of locations* in living the text in the field. In particular, I will examine the implications of these locations for the author/ity of the text in light of academic discourses on epistemic privilege and the authenticity of native accounts. Secondly, I explore the *politics of representation* in writing the text by examining how engaging with research subjects' agency and resistances to ethnographic authority provides their own (less partial) account through self-presentations. In conclusion, I suggest that our texts have potential for *pedagogical empowerment,* which is an important avenue for political activism within the locational setting that assumes particular salience in contextualizing my identity at this juncture: the academy.

In developing this analysis, I draw on my own locations both within and outside of the academy to ground my arguments. In so doing, I seek to explicate the manner in which my positionalities within those locations is implicated in the account that I provide or, in other words, that "the problem of *voice* ('speaking for' and 'speaking to') intersects with the problem of *place* (speaking 'from' and speaking 'of')" (Appadurai, 1988: 17; emphasis mine).

The feminist dilemmas in and of fieldwork that are referred to in the title of this anthology are thus broadly conceived in this discussion. My focus is on identity and (inter)subjectivity as they crosscut the boundaries of the dualisms of home:work, field:academy, and personal:professional. I thus attempt to erase the boundaries that mark the domains of private:public in my life while simultaneously writing within them as they have been constituted, demarcated, and redrawn in the process of the encounters and intersections of my history with the history of various disciplinary developments and the history of Others. More specifically, my focus in this discussion is on the research/reading/writing that extends beyond that narrowly demarcated period of being in the field.[4] This reconceptualization of what constitutes the field has been a powerful contribution of a poststructuralist ethnography, because it foregrounds the authorial role in constructions and representations of the subject—rendering positivist depictions of social scientists in the "researcher-as-detached-observer" mode obsolete.

Questions That Ensue from the Fieldwork

My discussion draws on the experiences of eighteen months of research in Delhi with women workers and their employers and managers in fourteen garment firms and seven television firms. In the course of this fieldwork, I visited the factories, workshops, sweatshops, and homes where the production-related work of these firms was conducted. With the help of two research assistants, I conducted interviews with 196 workers (of whom 90 percent were women), and 57 managers and owners. I conducted all the interviews with the managers, owners, and contractors, and sixty of the worker interviews. The episodes that I relate in this paper are drawn from the interviews I conducted, and the quoted statements that I reproduce here are from transcripts of these interviews. Additionally, I relied on nonparticipatory ethnographic methods of observation, the analysis of firm records, and archival research. The goals of my research were to examine processes of gendered class formation and factory-level gender politics that undergird the widely noted feminization of the workforce in these industries under new conditions of globalization.

My primary sources of information were structured and semistructured interviews which lasted from one and a half hours to three hours, depending on the respondent and the location of the interview. Although the bulk of interviews were conducted on the firms' premises, interviews of domestic workers and of workers in one firm where on-site access to workers was denied were conducted in the homes of workers or coworkers. There were additional opportunities for meeting with workers outside the formal interview situation—especially during tea and lunch breaks, which I spent with workers, and during the brief mingling that occurred after work hours and while commuting.

In the process of doing this research, I encountered several dilemmas that have made me deeply skeptical of our ability to realize feminist methodologies in practice—especially in light of the prescriptive methodological guidelines, canonical texts, and authorizing forms of discourse that have been put forth in this literature (Lal, 1993). In this chapter, I address three closely related sets of questions that were suggested by my experiences in my research and which bear on current debates on representation and reflexive methodologies that are in evidence across the social sciences.

The first question, broadly conceived, involves the issue of the authority of my voice. I am concerned with the epistemological question, "How do I know?" specifically as it is premised on my particular history and identities. In examining this issue, I attempt to initiate a move away from an identity-based epistemology that rests on a self-conceived identity as a native or Indian woman to an epistemology that is based on an engagement with one's politics of location in articulating partial perspectives based on "situated knowledges" (Haraway, 1988a). The second question is, What do research subjects' actions and responses tell me about the construction of ethnographic authority? How do subjects assert their agency and shape their own representations? How does this inform endeavors toward postcolonial ethnographic representations? The third question is, How and where can I effect change? That is to say, from which site—among the multiplicity of sites that I currently inhabit—can I practice my feminist politics: in the field, in the academy, or both? In this context I examine the limits on praxis in Third World industrial settings and the limits of a postmodern ethnography in which the possibilities for politics are often limited to *textual* practices. In what follows, I do not aim to provide answers to these questions so much as to reintroduce and reframe these issues into ongoing and well-established debates.

Situating Identities: Locating Self and Other

Disciplinary Conjunctures

The issue of disciplinarity is perhaps the most important determiner of how one defines a research area and what methods one chooses to study it. Although feminist anthropologists have attempted to address the challenges posed by postmodernism to ethnographic writing and responsibility quite seriously,[5] debate about these issues seems curiously lacking in methodological writings on qualitative fieldwork in sociology, although there are some recent important exceptions to this.[6] My training as a sociologist left me unprepared for the complex concerns that surfaced during my fieldwork around issues of representation and identity.

Reflecting on the historical moment of my graduate training, I realize that I am in between a new generation of scholars who have had exposure to a variety of methodologies within the social sciences and courses that are explicitly labeled "feminist methodologies" and previous generations of scholars who are now turning their experiences of trial and error in the field into interdisciplinary feminist course offerings. Clearly, these generational differences reflect the paradigmatic developments and disjunctures experienced within various disciplines. Yet epistemic shifts are never uncontroversial: Kuhn (1970) and Foucault (1984) both recognized the power of defining/defending the paradigm/canon. Within the social sciences this canonical construction of appropriate research and adequate proof has often meant the outright rejection of ethnographic approaches, based on the concern for a "statistically significant sample size." My point here is that those who are relatively powerless in the academy—students—rarely have the ability to choose approaches that do not fit the desired model for appropriate research designs.[7]

Issues of disciplinarity are further complicated within the interdisciplinary field of women's studies. Not only is doing ethnographic fieldwork looked upon skeptically within dominant constructions of appropriate sociological research, often hegemonically constructed through the availability of computerized survey data files as hypothesis-driven number crunching, but in addition, feminist work is still likely to be viewed with suspicion even within more openly constituted sociology departments. These politics, once again, translate into special difficulties for those who are relatively powerless within the academy: students and untenured junior faculty, particularly in the arena of defining and defending intellectually appropriate research projects that go against the grain of disciplinarity and hegemonic neopositivism. In articulating my research design, I felt these tensions and pressures quite strongly. As I worked through these issues and progressed into the research, I moved further and further away from my initial design of interview surveys and relied increasingly on ethnographic observational techniques.

In/Essential Identities (Native, Indian, Woman)

What is the nature of reality that is presumed in the construction of a researcher's identity that has stable boundaries? Who is the assumed historical subject in such a construction? How have such constructions undergirded the critical political practices of representing of Third World subjects? In other words, what happens when the traditional boundaries between the knower and the known begin to break down, are reversed, or are crosscut with mixed and hybrid identities? What are the implications of this for the politics of field-based research? Unavoidably, the many locations that shape my identity and notions of self influenced my choices, access, and procedures in research and also permeate the representation of research subjects in my writing. Among these is the subjective construction of my identity as an Indian woman.

Living and growing up in a very sheltered nonurban university town setting in India for most of my childhood, I had and have a very definite sense of myself as "Indian," even though my Yugoslavia-born, naturalized American immigrant–citizen, relocated-to-India-by-marriage mother stood out in this small and cloistered community. In such a construction of my mother as "Other," I do not mean to naturalize my father's "Indianness": as with most Indians of his generation, his travels to the West (for education in both the United Kingdom and United States) were deeply implicated in the larger postindependence, postcolonial relations of exchange, immigration, and return.

My speaking English at home and attending an English-medium convent school made Hindi a language I was never completely comfortable in, and I struggled with Hindi throughout high school with the help of a home tutor. Although my poor Hindi subjected me to humiliating taunts in high school, in college, Hindi as a "Modern Indian Language" was something that I just had to pass, and I was immediately less marked as different. In college, my incapacity in Hindi did not define me as inferior but as westernized, and hence, in the neocolonial mentality of postcolonials, as exotically different.[8] Upper-middle-class Indian culture, floating as it does above the Indian reality of the masses, is constituted as a complex hybrid mix of East and West—the latter embodying both British and American cultures. Within such a scenario, being marked as different because of a white mother did not construct me as Other. In many ways I was as "Indian" as all my urban college classmates, who were just as out of touch with Indian reality.

Perhaps equally unremarkable for my generation of Delhi University students was my lack of sustained political investments in ongoing events and a relatively underdeveloped sense of myself as a feminist. In India, my relatively cloistered middle-class existence (both at home and away from home) had not really allowed for the development of a feminist consciousness. Like many upper-middle-class women, I took for granted class privileges—such as a good college education—

that crosscut gender boundaries. Feminism was an encounter that unfortunately was, and sadly continues to be, primarily defined through academic debates and theories. Mary John, in examining her transformations toward becoming a post-colonial feminist in the United States, makes a similar observation. She notes that it was her dislocation from a sheltered middle-class Indian environment to the United States, with its "refined technologies of gender," that led to the espousal of an explicitly feminist politics (1991: 17).

Furthermore, it was only after relocating to the United States for graduate studies that I began to develop a political sensibility and a sense of myself as "Other"—both in the immediate sense of everyday interactions that situated me as such and in my growing awareness of myself as a member of a minority—as a South Asian/Third World woman of color in the United States. As Lata Mani (Frankenberg and Mani, 1993: 297) has noted, this process of Othering, of definition of oneself as Third World, often *begins* within the racialized context of contemporary United States immigrant relations and begs differentiation from the situation of those Others who are native within the United States.

In historically locating myself within the geographical context that I did my research in, I have tried to disrupt the notions of power and difference that are assumed in discussions of nativity. Prevailing relations of power define what constitutes Other (unacceptably different) and what remains within the boundaries of acceptably different. "Inauthentic natives" can circumvent the status of Other through the privilege of class and its attendant forms of cultural capital which, although culturally and historically specific, are often manifested within postcolonial contexts though idealized/idolized Western trappings. My privileged and secular upper-middle-class Indian background situates me *within* this class less as Other than as Self/same, while simultaneously demarcating Us from the "real" Others outside our class. Furthermore, I have sought to bring out the ways in which I am constituted as a historical subject, deeply imbricated in the larger postcolonial relations of exchange of commodities, labor, and capital between East and West. That my labor power is realized in the West is, of course, the thorniest issue of all; for it is the fact that our sites of enunciation center in the West that is the most problematic, and potentially most compromising, aspect of a postcolonial feminist critique (John, 1991).[9]

On Fieldwork (or, "Going Home?")

After a six-year stay in the United States pursuing graduate work, I returned to Delhi for my dissertation research, to a city where I had spent five critical years of my life as a college student. Yet in many ways, I entered a world that was completely foreign to me. I was traveling to factories in the industrial districts and zones in and around the city that were surrounded by working-class neighborhoods and squatter slums; I was searching for addresses of fly-by-night operations in the narrow *galis* of neighborhoods that few people knew existed—areas that can best be characterized as villages within the city. These communities were often nestled cheek by jowl alongside more affluent communities that were on the map of my familiar. I was a "native" returning to a foreign country.

I will never forget the sense of excitement that I experienced when I walked into my first "real" factory, a large garment manufacturing unit. This sense of discovery was repeated when I visited the fabrication units to which work was sent out. "These are *sweatshops,*" I thought to myself, appalled at the filth, dingy lighting, and cramped quarters of the fabrication units. I thought excitedly of all the great theoretical, historical, and comparative possibilities that this would generate. After these initial moments of recognition and several hours spent talking to workers and contractors, observing their work and relationships to firms, I moved quite naturally to seeing the fabrication units as more complex lived realities and not as mere manifestations of theoretical constructs. Immersion in the field provides its own corrective. As we begin to develop "nativised selves" (Karim, 1993: 248) we see phenomena that we explore more from the perspectives of those who *live* those realities rather than from our imperialist academic vantage points, ever ready to appropriate the experience of others into our preordained theoretical categories (Smith, 1987; Hale, 1988). Furthermore, when writing the text, exploring the interpellation of the local social phenomena that we investigate into larger global histories also serves to denaturalize and de-exotify their existence, to work against a romanticization of Third World phenomena as somehow existing outside of history (Jordan, 1991).

Just how invested are we in locating exploitation? While doing and writing our research, we must vigilantly question our own investments in looking for the exotic—that truly paradigmatic theoretical subject of our disciplines. In crossing the class barriers of my upbringing and moving into the arena of industrial manufacturing in Delhi, I was confronting that Other for the first time. For a first-time fieldworker, self-consciousness about our (trained) tendencies to represent the Other comes quickly, and it is a self-consciousness we must strive hard *not* to let subside once we return from the field into that other field of representation—the academy—because it is in the academy that we feel the pressure to reproduce colonizing discourses on the Other most strenuously. As Ganguly (1990: 76) notes, "the best way to make a 'splash' in ethnographic circles is still to write about something exotic." In moving from living to writing the text, then, we can work against reproducing colonizing discourses if we assiduously maintain the perception of the academy as just another field location and of writing as a continuation of "fieldwork."

Nonparticipant Urban Industrial Fieldwork: The Researcher as Outsider

In many ways my marginality in Indian society fueled a preoccupation with my identity, especially in the initial stages of the fieldwork. As an Indian returning home, I had assumed that I would not face many of the difficulties that an outsider might, because of our partially shared histories as Indian women. Yet because of my privileged class background, I also realized that our differences were much more significant than our similarities. Coming to grips with these differences made me realize my dislocation even within that space that I had thought of as home (Martin and Mohanty, 1986). In the actual practice of research, of course, one is faced with the need to constantly negotiate *between* the positions of insider and outsider, rather than being fixedly assigned one or the other subject position. More important than a sameness that might be assumed in my possible identity as an insider are the power differentials and class inequities that divide those insiders and the divisions between the researched and researcher that are created by the very act of observation.

While initiating contact with firms, I was never sure of what conditions would be provided for the worker interviews. Although these varied greatly from firm to firm, all television manufacturers were much more reluctant to let me on to the shop floor. Most garment worker interviews were conducted on the shop floor, with us sitting on the floor in quiet corners of particular production departments. In these cases, I often interviewed women as they were doing their work—checking garments, thread cutting, or embroidering. In the television factories, I was typically assigned a private space to conduct the interviews—a manager's office, an office worker's desk, or a guest room. These differences in the provisions for my setup speak directly to differing forms, and intensities, of labor control within firms. In smaller garment-manufacturing firms, there is close and personal supervision of work and hence contact between workers, managers, and owners. In these largely paternalistically run firms, my close contact with workers during interviews was therefore not seen as disruptive of larger factory-based class configurations, since managers and owners themselves rely heavily on informal, personal, and direct forms of control.

Larger firms, which included most television firms and one garment firm, rely on hierarchical and formal systems of control and regulation. In these firms, the provision of a clean and private space (such as an office) that was provided for my interviews clearly served to protect my class privileges. But in protecting my class privileges, firms also acted to maintain the class boundaries and hierarchies within the firm and to reinforce the hierarchical factory regime upon which production itself was predicated. The spatial locations in which the interviews were conducted thus provide a vivid mapping of class and gender hierarchies within the factory and set the boundaries within which my desired subject location (as researcher) could be positioned.

The research situation often places the researcher in an overtly powerful position vis-à-vis research subjects, and this inequality is exacerbated by the researcher's often necessary relationship with access providers who may have control over other research subjects. This is an especially likely outcome of nonparticipatory industrial ethnographic research, where the researcher does not have unmediated or immediate access to the research subjects. In my research, managers and owners of firms were simultaneously research subjects and access providers, making for a contradictory power imbalance in my relationships with them. Thus, while clearly flattered at being interviewed, managers were often quick to (re)establish their authority over me and also took every opportunity to demonstrate their authority over the workers. Most often this would be done while I was attempting to schedule interviews with workers, such that "this department is too busy today" or "you will have to come back tomorrow" were lines I came to read not just as simple statements of fact.

Gaining access to firms with the consent of managers and owners often meant that women were called to a room that was assigned to me for interviewing, without knowing why they had been called upon. This situation was understandably seen as extremely threatening by some of the women, who sometimes assumed that I was a *sarkari* (government) employee and hence someone to be wary of. This was especially true for those women who were not in stable jobs. After I explained the research project and the nature of the interview to each prospective interviewee, not a single woman who was approached refused to participate.

This does not suggest that participation in the project was voluntary, since women who were summoned to the room allocated for the interviews most likely perceived this as an order from management and hence did not see themselves as having a choice about whether they would be interviewed. Because they also saw that I toured production facilities accompanied by the owner, the manager, or the supervisor, this tended to place me in a powerful and potentially authoritative position merely by association. Often this was evidenced in the questions that they posed once outside the factory premises, while we walked to a common bus stop, or while we commuted in a company bus at the end of the workday. Word about the study would spread after the first interview on the first day, and subsequent interviewees were clearly more comfortable as women came to them in the context of information provided by previous interviewees.

The following example highlights—through the curious juxtaposition of researcher, interviewee, and potential interviewee that ensued—the incredibly paradoxical position that one might be forced to adopt as a researcher seeking to minimize her power and distance from her research subjects. This conversation was extracted from an interview with the production manager of a large garment-manufacturing firm, who was responsible for hiring all production workers in the factory. The manager's objectification of women workers, although not directly caused by me, was indirectly the result of my interviewing him. I asked him how he recruited new workers.

He responded, "For production jobs we never advertise. That's only for clerical or typists' jobs, for office jobs. We just tell the girls. If someone comes to the gates looking for a job . . . if she's a good *phurti* [smart, agile, prompt] girl, we'll take her. We don't advertise on a board outside the factory gates either. No, it is not hard finding people for production jobs in this industry. For one vacancy I sometimes get up to twenty applicants. So then we see which ones are educated, agile . . . like eighth [grade] or tenth pass, we'll take them. So I'll take those who look like they are quick. I look for *phurtipan* (*Mein phurtipan dekhta hu*), that's what I look for . . . that they are quick and agile in their work. I can tell that by just looking at them. Someone who can work fast, that's more important than an education."

I have trouble understanding his use of the word and want him to be explicit about what he means, to clarify the concept so I ask him, "What exactly do you mean by *phurtipan*?" He turns to the contractor for "pressmen" (men who iron the garments prior to packing), who had been sitting in the room during our interview, and tells him to bring a particular person into the room. I am puzzled, because I'm not sure what this is leading up to. He says, "I'll show you what I mean. I'm calling this girl, and you will see for yourself truly what I mean, you will understand immediately upon looking at her."

At this point the woman who was summoned enters the room. She is young, around twenty years old, neatly dressed, and does not appear to be intimidated as she comes into the room. "You called for me, Sir?" she asks him. "Like her, she looks active, doesn't she?" He directs this question to me, pointing to her as he does so. Then he dismisses her and asks her to send another person to his office, whom he refers to by name. He turns to me and says, "Now I'll show you what I mean by a *dhila* [loose, lethargic] person."

I am very embarrassed by this and, now that I know what he is about to do, try to dissuade him from calling on anybody else. I tell him that I have understood what he means by *phurtipan*, but he insists on calling the second woman in, arguing that the workers won't object to it as they are not very busy. He wants to prove to me that *phurtipan*, his sole criterion for hiring women or at least for their placement within the band, is a tangible quality that can be seized upon and discerned in the few seconds that the women he had called were in his office. In response to his second summons, an older Nepalese woman who looks quite tired and is easily forty years old comes into the room a little diffidently and looks at him questioningly, not saying anything. "You see?" He says to me, "Now this is what I mean by 'dead weight,' just look at her, you see what I mean?"[10]

He dismisses the woman after saying this to me while she is in the room. Despite my attempts to dissuade him from calling upon "examples" of alert and lethargic women, the manager was proud to display what he felt was a clever and keen ability on his part to distinguish between the two on the basis of this very important characteristic and predictor of future productivity—*phurtipan*. The episode clearly located me (along with the manager) in a position of power over the two women who were called upon to exhibit the meaning of *phurtipan* through their physical appearances. Demonstrating his power over the women who worked under him in this fashion could be seen as a deliberate attempt on his part to minimize the incongruity of the class- and gender-based power relations between us as middle-class female researcher and working-class male production manager. Although it may have narrowed the distance between us in his eyes, it had the reverse effect on me. Moreover, this episode only served to distance me even further from these two women and possibly from all the workers on the shop floor at that time who witnessed the women being called into the production manager's office.

These contradictions constitute an essential component of the process of doing social science research in the "real" world. Because social science research is always "a social interaction in its own right" (Stanley, 1990: 8), it unavoidably reflects the social world in which it and we are situated. And if the social world that is being investigated is a sexist and hierarchical one, the process of research is sure to become a sexist and hierarchical social interaction. Moreover, if the men one is researching have power over other female subjects and they assert that power in the context of the research situation—either as a means to impress the foreign-returned female scholar and hence reclaim an inverted gender hierarchy created by the research dyad, or as a means to innocently illustrate responses to queries— then they act to undermine and subvert a researcher's goal of nonhierarchical and nonobjectifying relationships.

Despite my intention to minimize the distance between me and the women I interviewed, I was not able to avert episodes such as this one. Furthermore, my research choices and entrée into factories inevitably located me well before I was able to proceed to the stage of interviewing workers. This is because within the factories, I would first conduct the interviews with managers, owners, and contractors. This served the purpose of providing background information on the firms, such as on the distribution of workers by departments, work that was subcontracted out, and so forth. Clearly, the methods of nonparticipatory industrial ethnography and interviewing worked to shape my position as an outsider within the factories. Yet, given the overdetermined configurations of class within a factory setting, and within the larger societal configurations in contemporary India, I am not convinced that other methods would enable a researcher to transcend the boundaries of "outsider."

In examining the range of assigned subject positions available to me as a researcher within different factory settings, it would seem that I was constituted as a powerful outsider. Yet I have been simultaneously working *against* this construction of the "researcher as outsider." This is because I found myself deeply implicated in the very class hierarchy that I was investigating through my construction as Other *within* local factory class configurations. This clearly reduces the utility of an insider-outsider distinction, because with each threshold of an insider boundary that one crosses, there would seem to be another border zone available for one's definition as outsider. What is it, then, that one is ultimately inside of (Aguilar, 1981: 25)? I have been constantly shifting the connotation of insider in my discussions thus far—as insider to India, to women, to factory, to workers—to highlight the problematical nature of such a distinction. Within such a configuration of locations, it is only someone who is not Indian, not a woman, and not a fieldworker who can mark me as an insider.

One's identity within the research context is thus neither fixed nor predetermined.[11] The degree to which others and the research situation itself manipulate one's identity (Narayan, 1993: 674) would seem to suggest that identity is not a useful site for the exploration of one's positioning into the research situation, because one is constantly being situated into it by the micropolitics of the research interactions and the macropolitics of societal inequality. To expect a researcher to become an insider is to demand that she transcend these politics, to escape the differences that are embedded in the everyday life that we examine. The feminist injunction for nonhierarchical research relations can thus only be met by an *escape* from reality—it is a search for positionality "outside the text"—a position that is politically irresponsible, empirically impossible, and epistemologically indefensible.

Toward a Postcolonial Methodology

I'd like to briefly explore the epistemological implications of my multiple locations in terms of debates on epistemic privilege—a notion that is fraught with difficulties for feminists—and feminist methodologies. Within feminist methodological and epistemological debates, the issue of representations has been largely contained within a discussion of the notion of a *feminist standpoint,* which privileges the experiences of women as a vantage point for developing knowledge (e.g., Hartsock, 1987; Smith, 1987). Much like Hegel's slave who, from her subjugated standpoint, has a less partial view than the master, oppressed women's vision in patriarchal settings is argued to have greater power and objectivity because of its subjugated status (see Harding, 1986: 26, 158). Notions of epistemic privilege that derive from a feminist standpoint were argued to essentialize women, and later reworkings of the idea of women's standpoints have attempted to account for differences among women, while still privileging particular perspectives (see Collins, 1991).

Ironically, acknowledgment of the critique of universalism leveled against feminist theory by women of color on the grounds of the exclusion of their perspectives has led to two paradoxical outcomes. On the one hand, it has resulted in the widely noted trend for women's studies scholars to make the obligatory pronouncements of their positioning into the analysis without ever actually contending with these differences *in* the analysis (John, 1991: 2–3; Rao, 1992: 41); toward a mere invoking of what has been called the "mantra" of self-positioning vis-à-vis the axes of race-sex-class-sexuality (Patai and Koertge, 1994: 68). This lip service to difference does not inform an assessment of how such positionings are implicated in one's analysis, and as such it is a politically disengaged response.

On the other hand, in the corrective epistemological project of working against hegemonically universalist subject positions available in dominant modes of theorizing, subjugated epistemological standpoints have had a special appeal.

Notwithstanding Harding's (1987: 185) careful enunciation of a feminist stand-point as something that is *achieved* through political struggle rather than by merely claiming it, this epistemological privileging of marginality has resulted in special claims to knowledge by Third World women, based on the "authenticity of their personal experience of oppression" (Martin and Mohanty, 1986: 199). It has also resulted in widespread expectations of, and demands for, Third World women to speak *from* the location of their authentic otherness (Minh-ha, 1989).

I do not contest the fact that notions of epistemic privilege play an important political role in accounting for the implications of categorical aspects of identities (such as race, gender, nativity, or ethnicity) in the production of knowledge. But if the representations are assumed to be innocent, authentic, and natural outcomes of this identity, then they lead to the epistemological equivalent of identity poli-tics, or "identity epistemology" (Patai and Koertge, 1994: 60).[12] Positing privi-leged epistemic standpoints from the specific ontological location of the op-pressed thus downplays the very real possibility that such representations can be colonialist, while simultaneously obscuring the possibility of noncolonizing rep-resentations emerging from nonsubjugated standpoints.[13] Clearly, both responses (i.e., mere mantralike evocation of identities and standpoint epistemologies) err in being excessive; one is irresponsibly disengaged and the other is so deeply en-gaged that it questions our ability to see from nonsubjugated standpoints.

The problems associated with standpoint epistemologies are paralleled in the presumed epistemology of the native insider. Both constructions are essentialist and reduce either the native or the Third World woman to an assumed homoge-neous entity. Both suggest subjectivist, ideographic methodologies on the as-sumption that experience is the basis for knowledge. Both reduce the politics of location to the experience of (a presumed homogeneous) identity. Furthermore, such constructions have the unintended effect of reinforcing the very distinctions that they are supposed to erase. This is because the construction of subjugation, nativity, and insiderness, as privileged epistemic standpoints from which to counter the universalism of Western theory, are all premised on maintaining the same borderlines between Us and Them, Self and Other, and Subject and Object that they wish to question in the first place. In other words, reversing the binaries does not go far enough in questioning the grounds for *either* epistemology—subjectivist-insiderism or objectivist-outsiderism; both rely on a "naïve empiri-cism" (Aguilar, 1981: 23). As Lennon and Whitford (1994: 14) note, "we must be wary of making a fetish of 'otherness,' simply reversing the hierarchy of the origi-nal categories. The danger here is that the binary structure remains intact, divid-ing the world along pre-determined faultlines, attributing a spurious homogene-ity to the categories."

These binaries are deeply embedded in conventional research practices that rely on realist epistemologies, such as traditional ethnography and sociological fieldwork methods (e.g., participant-observation). They are founded on the as-sumed division between the researcher as observer and the researched as observed, between a knowing subject and a research object, and between research in the field and writing it up in the academy.[14] Since these dualisms have provided the grounding assumptions for foundationalist epistemologies, most conventional social science methodologies rest on these assumptions.

There have been several recent attempts to theorize from the locations of multiple and hybrid identities.[15] Because these identities are not easily transcribed into either separate halves or synthetic composites that fit into one or the other end of the locational poles provided by realist epistemologies, they have worked against the reductionism and essentialism of the nativist epistemologies depicted in the positions of Native and Insider. The dis/locations of these mixed, or multiple, identities serve to highlight the point that there is no easy or comfortable in-between location that transcends these dualisms.

In the examination of my histories, I have indicated how the identity "Indian woman" is deeply divided by class privileges, among other differences, thereby disrupting the essentialism of an assumed universalist vantage point of the Third World woman. Furthermore, my own inhabitations of, and positionings within, the class-specific location of upper-middle-class Indian woman were sharply demarcated by my divergent political and epistemic projects before and after I had lived in the United States as an adult. As a middle-class Indian and a Western-educated feminist researcher, I was clearly able only to partially access the lives and worlds of working-class women in Delhi.[16] I have examined the constitution of my subject positions in order to argue that an epistemology of locations cannot spring out of an a priori ontological location.

I have thus been working to denaturalize the stability in the boundaries that are assumed in the binary pairs of oppositions and dualisms immanent in realist conventions of ethnographic and sociological research that rest on foundational epistemologies. But in displacing this boundary, I do not mean to suggest that the postcolonial intellectual has the ability to surpass these dualisms.[17] In other words, I am arguing against the possibility of a unique synthetic position, which surmounts the dialectic embedded in these terms. Rather, I would suggest that *all* of us live in contradictory locations, and not just those of us who are perhaps involuntarily placed into those contradictions. There can be no blood count that determines postcoloniality. As a politics it is a feminist and anticolonial intellectual location that we choose to position ourselves into, rather than being assigned into it on the basis of our gender, class, race, ethnicity, sexuality, nationality, or other identity-based ontological categories.

There is, however, the very real danger of creating a new fetish—hybridity as the new site of epistemic privilege—which we must actively resist. The postcolonial intellectuals' dislocation as a historical site is merely a useful starting point from which we can begin to enunciate and theorize a "postcolonial methodology." But it does not have to be this. In fact, I have borrowed this phrase from Jennifer Robinson who, as a white South African attempting to study the Indian community in South Africa, refuses to be constrained by an epistemology of identity, "It is within the postcolonial idiom that I find some of the most useful pathways through—though not solutions to—this relationship [between researcher and researched]" (Robinson, 1994: 218–219). It is this sense of an imagined community of postcolonial intellectuals that rise above national, racial, and gendered boundaries in the articulation of politically responsible representations that I have been working to explicate in this chapter.

Articulating this as a methodology has the advantage of shifting our gaze from questions of identity and experience to those of "positioning," which Donna Haraway posits as the "politics and epistemologies of location" (1988a: 589). It is only an examination of our politics and accountability, in questioning where and how we are located, that will get us out of mere reversals of the dualisms of native: non-native and insider:outsider positionings and on to a more productive engagement with the nature of our relationships with those whom we study and represent, on to questioning the nature of our insertion into the research process and its resultant representations, in ensuring that the "object of knowledge be pictured as an actor and agent, not as a screen or a ground or a resource" (Haraway, 1988a: 592). A postcolonial methodology then, enjoins us to "examine the hyphen at which Self-Other join in the politics of everyday life" (Fine, 1994: 70), and to work against inscribing the Other.

The Politics of Representations

Let us be clear of the silences that are initiated by the focus on a reflexive mode, clearly evidenced thus far in this discussion: the voices of the subjects of my research (with the exception of a manager) are conspicuously absent. Although my focus has been on reflections prior and subsequent to the actual fieldwork, this marginalization of the subjects of my research, whose voices were *not* heard here, is a problematic result of reflexive accounts. As even a cursory reading of the literature on experimental ethnography indicates, although the discussion regarding the *representation* of the anthropological subject that is so central to this movement is sensitive to textual practices that serve to undermine and distance the Subject, the undeniable effect of the discourse is to displace her (Balsamo, 1990). As a textual strategy, self-reflexivity gives voice to the already-speaking author. As a rhetorical device to foreground this silencing, in the previous section I sought to concentrate primarily on my own experiences and subjectivity, rather than deploying the strategy of both narrative and reflexivity.

I now recount an example of the conversations and dialogues that arose during my interviews with women workers in a consciously reflexive mode. Such "ethnographic encounters" (most often narrated through a conversation between researcher and researched) serve to illustrate some of the difficulties one faces in doing industrial ethnography: for example, in negotiating the stereotypical representations of Indian women workers voiced in numerous managers' interviews, or even those that come from workers' own interviews. These encounters also serve to bring alive the processes of confrontation and acceptance that occurred between me and the women I interviewed—as researcher and researched, as women, as Indians, as Self and Other—and the ways in which we "worked the hyphen" (Fine, 1994). Yet one must also wonder to what extent such a narrative serves to whet the readers' or audiences' desire to know, and the narrator's need to prove, that one really was "There!" In a reflexive mode, there is thus always a danger that "the people studied are treated as garnishes and condiments, tasty only in relationship to the main course, the sociologist" (Richardson, 1988: 205).

I am therefore uneasy about the strategy of calling on my research subjects' voices selectively to buttress my arguments, ever aware that feminist and anticolonial discourses "are engaged in this very subtle and delicate effort to build affinities, and not to produce one's own and another's experience as a resource for another closed narrative" (Haraway, 1988b: 111). The issue of how one works against the tendency to appropriate another's experience while making the connections remains a productive source of tension that is perhaps never resolved.[18] Writing the text thus becomes a key arena in which the authorial Self confronts and inscribes the Other as a "captive" object: an object that we capture via new technologies of inscription: tapes, surveys, interviews, word processing. Conceiving of writing as an extension of fieldwork foregrounds this process of inscription, a process that deserves much closer scrutiny than it typically receives.

I have examined how the configuration of factory-level class politics overdetermined my position within the factory. Yet I would also like to suggest that in the microdynamics of the interview, these hierarchies are easily displaced, although we may often fail to see that this has occurred. How one reads into the conversation can just as easily place the research Subject *back* into her location as Object, even though she actively tries to claim the space of Subject. As Kaplan suggests, "scrupulous attention to the micropolitics of the 'elicited situation,' the context of interviewer and interviewee, raises critical questions about how women's subjectivity is formed, reported, and interpreted" (1992: 125). Let us examine one example of my interactions with women workers, which suggests that subject-object relations within the interview context are easily displaced.

Representing Sunita's Self-Presentations

Sunita is a married garment worker aged between thirty-six and thirty-eight, who works in a small garment factory that is located behind South Extension Market and has been working there for approximately three years. She travels for about an hour and takes two buses to get to the factory from her home in Meherauli. She has been working off and on for the last ten years, and has lived in Delhi most of her life. All but one of the jobs (her first) have been in the garment industry. Her first job was with an informal *masala* (spice) packing company. Sunita first started to work after she was married, when her three children were between the ages of two and six. Before she started this job she quit work for about two years because her children had started fighting a great deal with each other, so much so that they were getting complaints from their neighbors that her children were spoiled and troublesome.

She left one of her previous jobs, also at a garment factory, because of the oppressive conditions of work and the often involuntary overtime that workers were subjected to, including enforced overnight stays. Her husband would not allow her to stay overnight at the factory after the first time that this happened (when they were unable to make special arrangements for her to be picked up from work). After this episode, she left that job as soon as she could find another one. The next job was as a temporary worker without benefits or minimum wages. She worked at that job until she found her current one, which is permanent and pays minimum unskilled wages, although as a garment checker, she is performing semiskilled work.

The factory where she works is owned and operated by a woman. It is a small business, a family-run affair that is actually run by her alone, with only about twenty workers on the premises, excluding contract workers. The atmosphere is cozy, friendly, and all the women know and talk to one another. The owner does require overtime, but makes arrangements to drop the workers off at their homes in a van when she needs them to stay late at night. Both of the contractors to whom work is sent out (and who bring contract workers into the factory) are women. Sunita says that her husband has met "Madam" (the owner) and is very happy that she is working here. The owner tells me that she makes a point of meeting the families of workers—the familial and m/paternalistic disciplining of workers is thus readily in evidence in this firm. Many of the workers tell me that they feel like "daughters."

Sunita came across as a very strong and confident woman. She has managed to get her younger sister a job in the same factory and tells me that she first began working partly because they needed the money and partly because, as she told me, "If everybody else is going out to work, then why not me?" She also enjoys the opportunities for friendships outside her family that work gives her, and the very extrafamilial experience that work provides, "It's good to get out; by coming out one has one's friends . . . [and] one learns to do various things." There was a mixture of shyness and eager curiosity in her manner with me that characterized her interview. I have this written in the notes that I wrote after the interview: Several times during the interview she asked me, "Is it over yet?" But this wasn't out of impatience or boredom, because when I was interviewing someone else after my interview with her, she came repeatedly to where we were sitting to see how we were doing and what we were talking about. After my second day of intensive interviews with the workers, several of us were talking about garment "export" work and the perceptions that other people and the workers themselves have about it.

My interest in generating such conversations was to contrast conditions and definitions of work, and discourses about them on television and in the garment industry. I discovered that definitions of export work as "cheap" rest primarily on the looser regulation of work conditions and sexuality in dispersed, informal, and fragmented garment production. The workers told me about the bad working conditions, the late nights, and about how it is looked upon as unseemly and questionable work. Sunita says:

> Yes, many people think this (and some husbands don't like it either)—that these girls are characterless, they work in factories and so on. But not in our house, because they know that we go to work, and work in a nice place. They have even come here and seen the place. Among our neighbors, not everyone knows that we work in factories, and we don't tell everybody that we are working in exports; they just know that we are working. So if other people get to know, it won't be very nice. So our names should not appear anywhere and our photographs should not come out anywhere, OK? If my family saw it, *Meri bejti ho jati* (I would be shamed) . . . because we have never done anything like this before: had our picture taken or our interview; this is the first time that someone has interviewed me. So if my husband heard that my photo was printed in a newspaper or in a book, then he'd be upset and wouldn't like it.

Although a complex discussion of the range of intersecting discourses that situate Sunita's statement—and of the interesting issues that it raises about the interrelationships between gender and class—is outside the scope of this discussion, let us examine the available referents in the limited information that I have provided here to see how they might impact a possible interpretation and representation of Sunita. The ambivalence and contradictions regarding her "work" identity are indicative, I think, of the way in which work in this particular factory has been contained within, and defined through, "home." This is expressed, for example, in statements such as, "She [the owner] is like a mother to us"; "we are like daughters to her." That is, it is expressed through readily available gendered identities constituted through the idiom of family. The class anxieties expressed in these statements are thus articulated primarily through gendered idioms.

Rather than constructing this as an instance of a "nonfeminist, non-western other," as a "failure to achieve modernity" (Ong, 1988: 80) it might help to look at the play—the active juggling—between the idioms of worker and wife that are expressed in her voiced wish "not to get found out" by "society." As Sunita *tells me* how to represent her, I see Sunita's ambivalence regarding her gendered status as a "worker" as an attempt to actively work through the contradictions of "modernity" and "tradition." Although it would be easy to try to impose our own narrative of liberation onto her experience of work (an approach that would inevitably see this as a "lack" of a modern work identity), this would erase completely her creative use of the work opportunities provided by this "modern" factory (relative to her previous work experiences) to suit the construction of her gender identities. This firm provides women workers access to "good femininity" through a regime of labor discipline that is at best paternalistic (or more appropriately, maternalistic). This allows her to continue to work, which she needs to do for the sake of her family and which she *enjoys* doing. In fact, as she tells me, it is work that allows her to "get out" from her household.

To represent her concerns with her public work identity as a co-optation of the "liberating aspects of work" would be to buy into the narrative of modernization where capitalism is seen to improve women's status vis-à-vis traditional patriarchy, and would completely obscure the active renegotiation with patriarchy that is occurring. Yet this is certainly a dominant representation of Third World women in the literature on gender and development. As Aihwa Ong (1988: 86) notes, " 'Non-western woman' as a trope of feminist discourse is either nonmodern or modern, she is seldom perceived as living in a situation where there is a deeply felt tension between tradition and modernity."

If we are to be truly open to what our research subjects tell us, we must be willing to read against the grain and yet within the larger contexts that situate their responses. Although partial truths are an inevitable outcome of research that is situated and constructed around specific locations, this should not necessarily lead to, or be an excuse for, distorted representations (Birth, 1990). There is always a need to situate responses into larger historical and societal contexts that can frame a meaning, in order to avoid the risk of either giving voice to stereotypes (Bhavnani, 1993) or perpetuating stereotypes *about* one's research subjects.

Other instances of respondents' silences and misinformation that they gave during interviews also indicated the degree to which research subjects shape their own self-presentations. For example, I interviewed another garment worker, Prema, whose husband worked with her in the same firm where she was employed. In order not to be perceived as a childless couple, both husband and wife lied to me about how long they had been married, which I learned coincidentally through another coworker. This example highlights a fact that often gets underplayed in the discussion of ethnographic responsibility in feminist and anthropological discussions about the politics of representation. The fact is that our subjects are often not just responding to our agendas and to our questions, but they are also always engaged in actively shaping their presentations to suit their own agendas of how they wish to be represented.

Moving away from the subjective mode of analysis deployed earlier, in this discussion I have drawn on interactions with workers during interviews and casual conversations. These encounters illustrate the way subjects actively responded to, and resisted, the interview process and particular inquiries and requests that I made. Sunita told me how I could and could not represent her, which *must* be read against the grain if we are to avoid stereotyping her as an "unliberated" Third World woman. Prema's silences in response to specific questions and her conscious misrepresentation of herself in other responses also signal an active process of self-presentation and empowerment (Bhavnani, 1988). Researchers contributing to debates in feminist methodology and experimental ethnography point to strategies of polyvocality and suggest giving research subjects a voice in a move to decolonize the subject, yet we often fail to take account of the challenges to modes of representation and contestations for meaning by research subjects who provide their own self-presentations. We need to acknowledge this agency, to treat the researched as subjects with whom we are engaged in a *mutual,* though unequal, "power-charged social relation of 'conversation'" (Haraway, 1988a: 593). In other words, we must develop the art of "listening to" and (not just) "talking with" if we are to avoid the "rape of the scientists' 'looking at'" (Tyler, 1986: 139–140). Otherwise we risk getting into the trap of just giving voice to subjugated positions, which, as we well know, are never innocent. As Sherry Gorelick (1991) has effectively argued, just "giving voice" is not enough. Unreflexive attempts to get beyond the binarisms of Self and Other, through tactics deployed by poststructuralist ethnographers—such as voice giving and polyvocality—can thus end up *reconstituting* them (Ganguly, 1990: 74) unless they are deployed critically.

Academic Politics and the Pedagogy of Empowerment

Whereas the reflexive methodology employed in this chapter clearly derives from postmodernism's focus on the multiple and fragmented self, a focus on identity often elides politics, thereby circumventing the intent of such analyses (Hutcheon, 1989; Birth, 1990). Furthermore, a focus on textuality has also displaced politics to matters of stylistic conventions, away from real-world interventions (Rosenau, 1992). Although postmodern ethnographers avowedly seek "evocation" rather than presentation or representation (Tyler, 1986: 123), the point, as Birth (1990) has pointed out, is not just to evoke understanding but also to provoke action. This "retreat into the politics of textuality" (Said, 1989: 209), although an interesting and necessary intervention, cannot adequately support the feminist project of revisioning and reshaping the canon.[19] As feminists demand new subject positions within the academy, we need to think through the ways in which we can "organize collectively for 'doing academia' differently" (McKenna, 1992: 127). We cannot allow the text to serve as a *pretext* for not seeking a political moment of engagement with either our research subjects or our readers.

Searching for an avenue within which this reflexive methodological practice can serve a political end, I would argue that *pedagogical praxis* can be one important means by which our research becomes feminist, thereby erasing the boundaries between theory, methodology, and practice, and between the field and home. What I have in mind is an approach in which we explicitly employ the practice of deconstructing our fieldwork experiences, thereby rendering them nontransparent. Given the commonplace dislocations of feminist researchers within the field and the academy, this practice has tremendous value in its potential for the pedagogical empowerment of a new generation of feminist scholars within social science disciplines.[20] It also introduces a new dimension of power into feminist discussions of power relations in research, for it posits the empowerment, not (just) of research subjects, but also of fellow and future social science researchers. This is an especially meaningful avenue for critical interventions for me, given my First World location and relative powerlessness within the Third World industrial/factory field setting in which I did my research.

I am keenly aware that a focus on self-reflexivity and on the politics of representation that is in currency in overlapping debates on feminist and anticolonialist research has tended to displace and obscure the research subject and instead place the *researcher* at the center. Yet I am unhappy with attempts to bring research subjects into the analysis in what I perceive to be a necessarily incomplete and exploitative fashion in an attempt to redress this power imbalance. My response to a critique of self-absorption, then, has been to use these analyses of Self and Other, and Self-Other dynamics, as part of my rationale for making the point that these academic discourses *must* be put to political use because of their pedagogical value to other scholars and new entrants into critical and feminist ethnography and fieldwork.

This tendency to silence the subjects of our research is made even more disturbing in light of the fact that the conditions under which we produce and labor as intellectuals tend to push us into being more accountable to The Academy than to the communities we study. That the relations of production within the academy are more constraining for younger and untenured academics than for established scholars is perhaps the reason for the widely noted fact that reflexive pieces often follow the substantive work rather than preceding it. The politics of the academy also makes students more accountable in the legitimate appropriation of new writing genres than those with more power (see Marcus, 1994).

Despite the powerful critique against foundationalist discourses and positivist epistemologies, I am reluctant to forgo completely the all-important political work that remains to be done in the arena of empiricist reconstructions. The *feminist empiricist* project thus continues to be an arena within which we must direct academic political action. Contributions by academics to the 1991 Indian census redefinition of what constitutes "work" are a good example of the type of project that must not be abandoned (Krishnaraj, 1990). Such reformulations have an impact not just on policy but also on our discursive constructions and representations of Indian women workers.[21]

Conclusions

Within the current theoretical movement toward deconstruction and critiques of representations, when we have thrown out our "technoscience booster literature" (Haraway, 1988a: 576), what do we have left in the way of writing new technologies of the subject? In this chapter, I have tried to articulate new modes of writing the text. I have attempted to do this by disrupting the boundaries between Self and Other in three primary ways.

First, I have attempted to destabilize the notion of the field, as well as several other dualisms that accompany the construction of the field as the Third World. In articulating the academy as a site for feminist politics in the conduct of research, I have also tried to expand our vision of where the field lies and where we practice empowering methodologies. Second, in locating myself as a political and historical subject and as part of the same forces that shape my research subjects, I have attempted to break down the divisions between subject and object. For example, I argued that our labor power in the academic mode of production can be fetishized as a product of difference—epistemic privilege—a division of labor that should be resisted on political and epistemic grounds. In both of these respects, then, I have been viewing the researcher as Object, or the Self as Other. Third, I have argued that examining the self-presentations, silences, and resistances of research subjects in the ethnographic encounter also works to disrupt this binary. Here the researched Other acts as Subject, and the Other is transformed into the knowing, acting, self.

We must, however, be wary of the potential paralysis of analysis that ensues from the reflexive mode of analysis and concentrated attentiveness to the authorial strategies and powers of representations, especially when situated within the context of the current postmodernist theoretical moment, which is characterized by "the contemporary crisis of representation, the profound uncertainty about what constitutes an adequate depiction of social 'reality'" (Lather, 1991: 21). As Lather notes, "In an era of rampant reflexivity, *just getting on with it* may be the most radical action one can make" (p. 20; emphasis mine). We cannot allow reflexivity to become an end in itself—another academic fad that is pursued for its own sake. A reflexive and self-critical methodological stance can become meaningful only when it engages in the politics of reality and intervenes in it in some significant way. Otherwise, we risk the charge of self-absorbed navel gazing or "soul searching" (Harding, 1987: 9). Within the current moment, then, and especially in the context of the relativist politics that can ensue from some versions of postmodernism, the task before us is to critically engage in "passionate scholarship" (DuBois, 1983), where we "work the hyphens" between Self and Other (Fine, 1994) rather than reproduce the tensions between Us and Them.

N O T E S

Field research for this article was made possible through grants from the American Institute for Indian Studies and the Graduate School and Mario Einaudi Center for International Studies at Cornell University. This is a condensed version of a paper presented at the 1995 Spring Colloquium of the Program on Gender and Global Change at Cornell University. The discussion held at this presentation and other presentations where portions of this paper were presented have been very useful in writing this chapter. Uma Narayan provided a careful reading and detailed commentary on some of the issues raised in this chapter. I am grateful to Diane Wolf for her patience, kindness, and suggestions for readings which have helped me in this project. I am deeply indebted to Lourdes Beneria for her constant support of my work and her inspiring and exemplary pedagogical praxis. My biggest debt of gratitude is to Neelam Bhatnagar and Alka Narang, my two research assistants, without whose help this research could not have been accomplished.

1. For example, "giving voice" is an issue that comes up in each of them in varying ways: in the literature on feminist methodology, giving voice to research subjects is one way of breaking down power relations between the researcher and researched. Similarly, in anthropology there is an attempt to create "polyvocal texts" to disrupt the authority of the ethnographer. Feminist epistemological articulations of a subjugated "standpoint epistemology" and recent attention in Indian historiography to subaltern perspectives also indicate parallel moves to attend to marginalized perspectives.

2. See, for example, the collected essays in Messerschmidt (1981), Fahim (1982), and Harrison (1991), which provide some examples of anthropological work being done in one's own society. This focus is relatively recent, given anthropology's project of studying Other, which necessitates a focus on authenticity and subjectivity (hence the focus on getting close to the natives and relying on native informants, without "going native"). The discipline of sociology, on the other hand, has historically been premised on studying self and hence obsessively concerned with creating and maintaining distance rather than on undermining it.

3. I use the terms "native," "home," "Third World," and "non-Western" advisedly and work to deconstruct these terms as I proceed in this chapter. Critical students of development as well as scholars influenced by postmodernism clearly suggest the problematical constructions of specific countries as Third World in the unstated assumptions of a master narrative of development that might indeed be replicated outside of the historical experience of the West. Although later references to these terms will be without quotes, the reader should always read them critically.

4. Other researchers have also argued for a reconceptualization of what we conceive of as the field and question this separation between the field and the academy, or home. See D'Amico-Samuels (1991), Harrison (1991), and Ganesh (1993).

5. The challenge of postmodernism, in its broadest sense, refers to the deep skepticism posed to "epistemological foundationalism," where knowledge and representations are assumed to mirror reality and approximate Truth. Postfoundationalist epistemologies (postmodern epistemologies) focus rather on the politics of representation and the necessarily incomplete and distorted representations of reality that circulate in knowledge, by asking the questions: Whose representations prevail? Who is silenced? Postmodern epistemologies thereby undermine claims to Truth and the possibility of complete or nonpartial representations (see Fine, 1994; Yeatman, 1994).

6. The essays in Denzin and Lincon (1994) and recent special issues of two journals, *Current Perspectives in Social Theory* and *Current Issues in Symbolic Interaction* provide examples of such recent work. Although the literature on feminist methodologies is large and diverse, it has only recently begun to engage with the postmodern critique (Olesen, 1994).

7. I recall having gone into the field with the words of one of my advisors ringing in my ears, that I had better come back with some "real data." This powerlessness is carried into the writing of ethnographic research. For example, the editor of a recent anthology has argued that most of the contributors to the collection were established scholars in the field, because junior and marginal scholars could not afford the luxury of reflexivity currently in fashion in anthropology (Clifford, 1986: 21). It is interesting that an alternative reading of this statement could well define it as a form of gatekeeping in the process of defining a new canon within the discipline (Gordon, 1988).

8. It should be clear from this discussion that I am critical of the term "postcolonial" inasmuch as it signifies the closure of a historical period of dependence and the consequent erasure of neocolonial power relations. Despite these problematic connotations, I re-

tain the use of "postcolonial," because it helps to foreground the methodological arguments that I make later in this chapter for a politics of postcoloniality.

9. By "sites of enunciation" John is referring to the fact that for many postcolonial feminists, our audience and locations are the First World: "What might it mean for me—a third world feminist whose current institutional home is in the first" (John, 1991: 2) to examine this? For an insightful reading of Gayatri Spivak's (1990) site of enunciation as perhaps an unresolved issue in this critical postcolonial feminist's work, see Ray (1992).

10. The reference to "dead weight" is to a phrase that he coined earlier in the interview. He refers to the majority of women in the production department who are working in low-skilled jobs as "dead" labor, to which he assigns mostly married and older women, "this is dead labor . . . [I am] giving them a salary for free. . . . I call them "dead" because even if they don't work, things still go on." The analysis of the ways in which women are constructed as cheap labor on the shop floor and in the labor process cannot be dealt with here. I examine these issues at length in my dissertation (Lal, 1996).

11. Even outside the specific research situation, one's identity needs to be denaturalized. Sociologists working on issues of identity have made this point about the social construction (and contestation) of identity quite emphatically: "identity is not simply imposed. It is also chosen, and actively used" (Pettman, 1991: 191).

12. The problematic nature of this assumption can be illustrated quite simply by examining the potentially different political positions that one may hold while inhabiting same-space locations within categorical axes of identity: Black women may be for or against the Nation of Islam, whereas Jewish women might be either for or against Palestinian nationhood. For a nuanced discussion of the range of political options open to those who occupy positions of potential epistemic privilege, see Uma Narayan (1989).

13. I do not intend to imply that standpoint epistemologies completely close out these possibilities. For example, Uma Narayan (1988) argues that the concept of epistemic privilege does not preclude the possibility that oppressed groups can have distorted perceptions and that nonmembers can gain knowledge of the oppressed. For an insightful discussion of colonialist representations of their own communities by insiders, see Jennifer Robinson's discussion of Fatihma Meer's construction of Indians in South Africa. Robinson argues that Meer "is clearly presenting a picture of Indian people for outside consumption . . . the 'outsider within' sociology, [who] constructs Indian people through a lens of exotica and 'sameness'" (Robinson, 1994: 215–216). My point here is simply that we should not be closed to these possibilities purely on ontological grounds.

14. Further examples of such dualisms might include global-local, modern-primitive, First World–Third World, author-object, represented-represented, self-other, outsider-insider, and so on. Although not all these oppositions may be assumed in the actual practices of research, listing them together in this fashion serves the function of making us more self-conscious about the assumptions that guide our research, especially in the field of gender and development. Dogmatic constructions of the field as synonymous with the Third World have been disrupted by recent feminist questioning of the role of the native researcher (Abu-Lughod, 1991; Narayan, 1993; Visweswaran, 1994). Postmodern ethnography has also explicitly called such dualisms into question.

15. Various terms have been used to describe these (dis)locations within the boundaries that are produced in foundationalist discourses. Some of these are "outsider within" (Collins, 1991), "native informant" (John, 1988 and 1991), "postcolonial intellectual" (Robinson, 1994), "multiplex identity" (Narayan, 1993), "inappropriate other" (Minh-ha,

1988 and 1989), "postfoundationalist intellectual" (Yeatman, 1994), and "nativised self" (Karim, 1993). In my discussion, I have used the term "inauthentic native" to disrupt the boundaries between inside-outside, native-other, and self-other.

16. I do not wish to normalize the subject location of upper-middle-class, Western-educated, Third World researcher. Certainly immigrant academics from working-class backgrounds have also returned home for research. Even within such a trajectory, discrepant locations in the politics of fieldwork are likely.

17. There is some slippage in my use of the term postcolonial that the reader should be alert to—between referring to a historical subject such as myself, whose personal history is shaped by a geographic region with a colonial history, on the one hand, and a political subject who is committed to the politics of anticolonialism regardless of her personal history, on the other. This slippage may result in some confusion, but the context should help the reader locate my meaning. Furthermore, this conflation reinforces the point that I am making here: that postcoloniality is a politically engaged location that we may all choose to position ourselves into, regardless of our individual histories and particular identity configurations.

18. Although the strategy of selective presentation of my subjects could serve to *exacerbate* the unequal power that I hold vis-à-vis my research subjects, it is also clearly the case that the encounters that I recount here illustrate workers' resistances to my authorial power. I would note that just as it is possible to select examples that reflect rather than challenge dominant discursive constructions of Third World women as victim and oppressed, it is also possible to err in the construction of overly agentic representations. This intellectual romance with resistance (Handler, 1993; Abu-Lughod, 1990) has potentially damaging results in that it can lead to a form of blaming the victim, when, for example, subaltern agency cannot inadequately "resist" the structures of colonialism.

19. For example, it is disturbing to me that for Visweswaran (1994), important issues of betrayal and resistance get displaced by the textual style that she deploys in reading this as a play in three acts (see chapter 3). The textuality of the text thus serves to direct attention to the politics of representation, but one must wonder, along with Birth (1990: 555), whether such textual experimentation serves its purpose, for "When highly trained, intelligent people—that is, informed readers—have trouble reading an article, . . . [this] writing subverts its own primary purpose—changing the reader." This issue becomes especially problematic in a pedagogic context.

20. It must be noted that this approach is already being adopted in narrative ethnographies and reflexive texts. Losing the transparency of the mechanics of doing research also contributes to what Harding (1992) refers to as 'strong objectivity' within a postpositivist, feminist framework.

21. Although there is a tendency to devalue the feminist empiricist project as an early phase in the development of feminist epistemologies—which is argued to have been superseded by standpoint and postmodern epistemologies (Harding, 1991)—I think that it is a process that we must *continually* engage in. This is a form of feminist realpolitik: as long as censuses continue to be important means of identifying segments of populations for providing state social services and protection, this project must remain an ongoing part of a larger feminist project of revisioning the grounds and challenging the assumptions of malestream science and knowledge. In my own work this has translated into a carefully detailed empirical analysis of women's work histories, which provide a useful window into the inadequacies of the Indian census data on women's work.

REFERENCES

Abu-Lughod, Lila. 1990. "The Romance of Resistance: Tracing Transformations of Power Through Bedouin Women." *American Ethnologist* 17(1): 41–55.

———. 1991. "Writing Against Culture." In *Recapturing Anthropology: Working in the Present,* edited by Richard G. Fox, 137–162. Santa Fe, N.Mex.: School of American Research Press.

Aguilar, John. 1981. "Insider Research: An Ethnography of a Debate." In *Anthropologists at Home in North America: Methods and Issues in the Study of One's Own Society,* edited by Donald Messerschmidt, 15–28. Cambridge: Cambridge University Press.

Appadurai, Arjun. 1988. "Introduction: Place and Voice in Anthropological Theory." *Cultural Anthropology* 3(1)(February): 16–20.

Balsamo, Anne. 1990. "Rethinking Ethnography: A Work for the Feminist Imagination." *Studies in Symbolic Interaction* 11: 45–57.

Bhavnani, Kum-Kum. 1988. "Empowerment and Social Research: Some Comments." *Text* 8(1-2): 41–50.

———. 1993. "Tracing the Contours: Feminist Research and Feminist Objectivity." *Women's Studies International Forum* 16(2): 95–104.

Birth, Kevin. 1990. "Reading and the Righting of Writing Ethnographies." Review Article. *American Ethnologist* 17: 549–557.

Clifford, James. 1986. "Introduction: Partial Truths." In *Writing Culture: The Poetics and Politics of Ethnography,* edited by James Clifford, and George Marcus, 1–26. Berkeley: University of California Press.

Collins, Patricia. 1991. "Learning from the Outsider Within: The Sociological Significance of Black Feminist Thought." In *Beyond Methodology: Feminist Scholarship as Lived Research,* edited by Mary M. Fonow and Judith A. Cook, 35–59. Bloomington: Indiana University Press.

D'Amico-Samuels, Deborah. 1991. "Undoing Fieldwork: Personal Political, Theoretical and Methodological Implications." In *Decolonizing Anthropology: Moving Further Toward an Anthropology for Liberation,* edited by Faye V. Harrison, 68–87. Washington, D.C.: American Anthropological Association.

Denzin, Norman K., and Yvonna S. Lincon, eds. 1994. *Handbook of Qualitative Research.* Thousand Oaks, Calif.: Sage Publications.

DuBois, Barbara. 1983. "Passionate Scholarship: Notes on Values, Knowing and Method in Feminist Social Science." In *Theories of Women's Studies,* edited by Gloria Bowles and Renate D. Klein, 2–29. London: Routledge and Kegan Paul.

Fahim, Hussein, ed. 1982. *Indigenous Anthropology in Non-Western Societies: Proceedings of a Burg Wartenstein Symposium.* Durham, N.C.: Carolina Academic Press.

Fine, Michele. 1994. "Working the Hyphens: Reinventing Self and Other in Qualitative Research." In *Handbook of Qualitative Research,* edited by Norman K. Denzin and Yvonna S. Lincon, 70–82. Thousand Oaks, Calif.: Sage Publications.

Foucault, Michel. 1984. *The Foucault Reader,* edited with an introduction by Paul Rabinow. New York: Pantheon Books.

Frankenberg, Ruth, and Lata Mani. 1993. "Crosscurrents, Crosstalk: Race, 'Postcoloniality' and the Politics of Location." *Cultural Studies* 7(2): 292–310.

Ganesh, Kamala. 1993. "Breaching the Wall of Difference: Fieldwork and a Personal Journey to Srivaikuntam, Tamilnadu." In *Gendered Fields: Women, Men and Ethnography,* edited by Diane Bell, Pat Caplan, and Wazir Karim, 128–142. London: Routledge.

Ganguly, Keya. 1990. "Ethnography, Representation, and the Reproduction of Colonialist Discourse." *Studies in Symbolic Interaction* 11: 69–79.

Gordon, Deborah. 1988. "Writing Culture, Writing Feminism: The Poetics and Politics of Experimental Ethnography." *Inscriptions,* no. 3/4: 1–7.

Gorelick, Sherry. 1991. "Contradictions of Feminist Methodology." *Gender and Society* 5, no. 4: 459–477.

Hale, Sylvia M. 1988. "Using the Oppressor's Language in the Study of Women and Development." *Women and Language* 11(2): 38–43.

Handler, Richard. 1993. "Anthropology Is Dead! Long Live Anthropology!" Review Article. *American Anthropologist* 95(4): 991–999.

Haraway, Donna. 1988a. "Situated Knowledges: The Science Question in Feminism and the Privilege of Partial Perspective." *Feminist Studies* 14 (3): 575–599.

———. 1988b. "Reading Buchi Emecheta: Contests for Women's Experience in Women's Studies." *Inscriptions,* no. 3/4: 107–124.

Harding, Sandra. 1986. *The Science Question in Feminism.* Ithaca: Cornell University Press.

———. 1991. *Whose Science? Whose Knowledge? Thinking from Women's Lives.* Ithaca: Cornell University Press.

———. 1992. "After the Neutrality Ideal: Science, Politics, and 'Strong Objectivity,'" *Social Research* 59, no. 3: 567–587.

Harding, Sandra, ed. 1987. *Feminism and Methodology: Social Science Issues.* Bloomington: Indiana University Press.

Harrison, Faye, ed. 1991. *Decolonizing Anthropology: Moving Further Toward an Anthropology for Liberation.* Washington, D.C.: Association of Black Anthropologists, American Anthropological Association.

Hartsock, Nancy C.M. 1987. "The Feminist Standpoint: Developing the Ground for a Specifically Feminist Historical Materialism." In *Feminism and Methodology: Social Science Issues,* edited by S. Harding, 157–180. Bloomington: University of Indiana Press.

Hutcheon, Linda. 1989. *The Politics of Postmodernism.* London and New York: Routledge.

John, Mary. 1988. "Postcolonial Feminists in the Western Intellectual Field: Anthropologists *and* Native Informants?" *Inscriptions* 5: 49–73.

———. 1991. "Discrepant Locations: Feminism, Theory and the Post-Colonial Condition." Ph.D. dissertation, University of California, Santa Cruz.

Jordan, Glenn H. 1991. "On Ethnography in an Intertextual Situation: Reading Narratives or Deconstructing Discourse?" In *Decolonizing Anthropology: Moving Further Toward an Anthropology for Liberation,* edited by Faye Harrison, 42–67. Washington, D.C.: Association of Black Anthropologists, American Anthropological Association.

Kaplan, Caren. 1992. "Resisting Autobiography: Outlaw Genres and Transnational Feminist Subjects." In *De/Colonizing the Subject: The Politics of Gender in Women's Autobiography,* edited by Sidone Smith and Julia Watson, 115–138. Minneapolis: University of Minnesota Press.

Karim, Wazir J. 1993. "Epilogue: The 'Nativised' Self and the 'Native.'" In *Gendered Fields: Women, Men and Ethnography,* edited by Diane Bell, Pat Caplan, and Wazir Karim, 248–251. London and New York: Routledge.

Krishnaraj, Maithreyi. 1990. "Women's Work in Indian Census: Beginnings of Change." *Economic and Political Weekly* 25 (48–49), Dec. 1–8: 2663–2672.

Kuhn, Thomas. S. 1970. *The Structure of Scientific Revolutions.* Chicago: The University of Chicago Press. Second Edition, enlarged.

Lal, Jayati. 1993. "Can There Be a Feminist Methodology: Reflections on the Impediments to 'Doing' Feminist Research in a Third World Context." Unpublished manuscript, Department of Sociology, Cornell University.

———. 1996. "Of Televisions and T-Shirts: The Making of a Gendered Working Class and the 'Made in India' Label." Ph.D. dissertation, Cornell University, forthcoming.

Lather, Patti. 1991. *Getting Smart: Feminist Research and Pedagogy with/in the Postmodern.* New York: Routledge, Chapman and Hall.

Lennon, Kathleen, and Margaret Whitford. 1994. "Introduction." In *Knowing the Difference: Feminist Perspectives in Epistemology,* edited by Kathleen Lennon and Margaret Whitford, 1–16. New York and London: Routledge.

Liebow, Elliot. 1967. *Tally's Corner: A Study of Negro Streetcorner Men.* Boston: Little, Brown.

Marcus, George E. 1994. "What Comes (Just) After 'Post'?" The Case of Ethnography." In *Handbook of Qualitative Research,* edited by Norman K. Denzin and Yvonna S. Lincon, 563–574. Thousand Oaks, Calif.: Sage Publications.

Martin, Biddy, and Chandra Mohanty. 1986. "Feminist Politics: What's Home Got to Do with It?" In *Feminist Studies, Critical Studies,* edited by Teresa de Lauretis, 191–212. Bloomington: Indiana University Press.

McKenna, Kate. 1992. "Subjects of Discourse: Learning the Language That Counts." In *Unsettling Relations: The University as a Site of Feminist Struggle,* edited by H. Bannerji et al., 109–128. Boston: South End Press.

Messerschmidt, Donald, ed. 1981. *Anthropologists at Home in North America: Methods and Issues in the Study of One's Own Society.* Cambridge: Cambridge University Press.

Minh-ha, Trihn T. 1988. "Not You/Like You: Post-Colonial Women and the Interlocking Questions of Identity and Difference." *Inscriptions* 3, no. 4: 71–77.

———. 1989. *Woman, Native, Other: Writing Postcoloniality and Feminism.* Bloomington: Indiana University Press.

Narayan, Kirin. 1993. "How Native Is a 'Native' Anthropologist?" *American Anthropologist* 95: 671–686.

Narayan, Uma. 1988. "Working Together Across Differences." *Hypatia* (Summer).

———. 1989. "The Project of Feminist Epistemology: Perspectives from a Non-Western Feminist." In *Gender/Body/Knowledge: Feminist Reconstruction of Being and Knowing,* edited by Alison Jaggar and Susan Bordo, 256–272. New Brunswick: Rutgers University Press.

Olesen, Virginia. 1994. "Feminisms and Models of Qualitative Research." In *Handbook of Qualitative Research,* edited by Norman K. Denzin and Yvonna S. Lincon, 158–174. Thousand Oaks, Calif.: Sage Publications.

Ong, Aihwa. 1988. "Colonialism and Modernity: Feminist Re-presentations of Women in Non-Western Societies." *Inscriptions,* no. 3/4: 79–93.

Patai, Daphne, and Noretta Koertge. 1994. *Professing Feminism: Cautionary Tales from the Strange World of Women's Studies.* New York: Basic Books.

Pettman, Jan. 1991. "Racism, Sexism and Sociology." In *Intersexions: Gender/Class/Culture/Ethnicity,* edited by G. Bottomley, de Lepervanche, and J. Martin, 187–202. Sydney: Allen and Unwin.

Rao, Brinda. 1992. "Dry Wells and 'Deserted' Women: Gender, Ecology, and Agency in Rural India." Ph.D. dissertation, University of California, Santa Cruz.

Ray, Sangeeta. 1992. "Shifting Subjects Shifting Ground: The Names and Spaces of the Post-Colonial." *Hypatia* 7, no. 2: 188–201.

Richardson, Laurel. 1988. "The Collective Story: Postmodernism and the Writing of Sociology." *Sociological Focus* 21(3): 199–208.

Robinson, Jennifer. 1994. "White Women Researching/Representing 'Others': From Antiapartheid to Postcolonialism?" In *Writing, Women, and Space,* edited by A. Blunt and G. Rose, 197–229. New York: Guilford Press.

Rosenau, Pauline M. 1992. *Post-Modernism and the Social Sciences: Insights, Inroads, and Intrusions.* Princeton: Princeton University Press.

Said, Edward W. 1989. "Representing the Colonized: Anthropology's Interlocutors." *Critical Inquiry* 15 (Winter): 205–225.

Smith, Dorothy E. 1987. "Women's Perspective as a Radical Critique of Sociology." In *Feminism and Methodology: Social Science Issues,* edited by S. Harding, 84–96. Bloomington: Indiana University Press.

Spivak, Gayatri Chakravorty. 1990. *The Post-Colonial Critic: Interviews, Strategies, Dialogues,* edited by Sarah Harasym. London and New York: Routledge.

Stanley, Sue. 1990. "Feminist Praxis and the Academic Mode of Production: An Editorial Introduction." In *Feminist Praxis: Research, Theory and Epistemology in Feminist Sociology,* edited by L. Stanley, 3–19. London: Routledge.

Tyler, Stephen A. 1986. "Post-Modern Ethnography: From Document of the Occult to Occult Document." In *Writing Culture: The Poetics and Politics of Ethnography,* edited by James Clifford and George Marcus, 122–140. Berkeley: University of California Press.

Visweswaran, Kamala. 1994. *Fictions of Feminist Ethnography.* Minneapolis: University of Minnesota Press.

Yeatman, Anna. 1994. "Postmodern Epistemological Politics and Social Science." In *Knowing the Difference: Feminist Perspectives in Epistemology,* edited by Kathleen Lennon and Margaret Whitford, 187–202. New York: Routledge.

11

Afterword:
Musings from an Old Gray Wolf

MARGERY WOLF

As I ENTER MY SIXTIES, I find two of the academic practices that have provided me with the greatest intellectual excitement—feminism and ethnography—under attack, both from within and without. In a book I published a few years ago (Wolf, 1992), I argued with some of the critiques made (by what I then labeled "postmodernism") of ethnography, both as fieldwork and as text, as well as the response of feminism to those critiques. Diane Wolf (no relation, honest) has asked me to return to some of these thoughts as I encounter them in the work of the fieldworkers in this volume. She suspected that I might have clarified or changed my position on some of the issues that concerned me then and that continue to engage the social scientists writing here. In truth, I am not sure that I have, but I find myself worrying more now about where the greatest danger to the feminist agenda is positioned. Perhaps it is within. Perhaps we are letting interesting critical positions from outside feminism weaken our confidence in our work; perhaps we are taking too seriously the criticisms of our process by those who have never experienced it.

Because of my lack of academic credentials, in the first part of my career I was very much an "outsider within," in current usage (Collins, 1991), or perhaps an intellectual halfie (Abu-Lughod, 1991), to abuse another concept. China was the area in which I did research, not because of my passion but because it was the choice of the student I married. I have no regrets about doing fieldwork in and writing ethnography about Taiwan and China. I felt then and still feel that what I wrote was more helpful than harmful, but I will not deny that I went about it with fewer sensitivities than would now be acceptable, even to me. I operated with a rudimentary feminism that I could not yet label properly but about which I nonetheless could and did get quite exercised on occasion.

215

In my early fifties, I became an insider with a tenured position at a midwestern university full of students who were aware of the ferment going on in anthropology and in feminist studies but not sure what it meant. Over the next few years, as is so often the case, my students unwittingly pushed me toward defining more carefully my own position in the whirl of feminisms and critiques of anthropology, and I began at the same time to ease out of the China field and find my own geographic area. On the one hand, the new path I have taken is somewhat safer in that I am doing a historical ethnography in the United States, thus freeing myself, at least for now, of some of the very problems discussed in this volume; but on the other hand, my enthusiasm about the new directions in my own work keeps me even more passionately engaged with the issues that concern feminist social scientists, wherever they work.

Some very sensible people have seriously considered giving up on field research altogether—some because they now believe it to be unethical under any circumstances and some because they no longer feel that they, as individuals, can ethically continue. I could not disagree more. What would happen if feminist researchers cut themselves off from all lived experience in an/other setting? Probably not much at first. Nonfeminists, men and women, would continue to do their work as they had before. Our critiques of their methods and epistemologies would become strictly theoretical—those of armchair anthropologists. In time what progress we have made would fade, and we might again find ourselves reading ethnographies about women, or worse, the experience of women would be represented only through the filter of their menfolk's accounts. If as feminists we still hope to reform our disciplines from within, then we must not give away the authority to speak from our own experience. As we struggle to find less exploitative methodologies, even the most outraged positivist occasionally sneaks a glance at what we are doing. More importantly, however, our students, male and female, have begun to take for granted a set of responsibilities in fieldwork that they often no longer recognize as coming out of feminism. But we cannot influence this next generation if we stop doing it ourselves, and if we don't influence the next generation, we will be back near where we started. Under these circumstances, how could there be any question about where our feminist responsibilities lie?

So if giving up on fieldwork is *not* a responsible position for feminist scholars, how do we deal with some of the very real dilemmas we face in the field? In this chapter, I am not going to suggest specific methods for doing feminist fieldwork—my own experience was too long ago, in a setting that no longer exists, to be useful. Rather, I want to address head-on what I think is troubling many feminists as they contemplate fieldwork, namely, power differences and how disruptive they are for feminist notions of proper working relations. Some of the thoughts I express here go against the current tide, but I know I am not the only feminist thinking them and that a few others are beginning to voice them. Subaltern studies, postcolonialism, and searching out new examples of orientalism have become a major academic industry on which many careers rest. Without a question, their products have been valuable to us all in identifying our frailties and reanalyzing our representations. However, if we allow these critiques to paralyze us, and far too many scholars have, then we are failing in our political responsibilities.

I think it is time we move beyond the churning of these issues. I am not suggesting that we forget them—indeed, it is a healthy, if uncomfortable, tension that we must live with. But let us now try to find some practical use for this tension. For example, a young fieldworker who comes from a demonstrably long line of working-class ancestors may have trouble handling the privilege her nationality and race gives her when she begins her first field project somewhere in Asia. She may either be unaware that she has it or she may recognize it and fail to understand how dangerous it is. To call her a neocolonialist accomplishes nothing; helping her figure out (before she gets to the field) how to use this power as an effective tool to benefit her project and the people she is studying benefits everyone. Mutual respect of difference is essential, but this respect should not pretend an equality of power that does not exist. Eventually, it will lead to resentment on both sides of the field encounter.

Exploitation happens, but it needn't happen because there is a power differential. Exploitation occurs when the fieldworker uses her advantage to gain her goals at a real cost to the women she is studying. I suspect that even a carefully situated feminist methodology could not totally eliminate the unequal outcome of a fieldwork encounter in individual terms. However, the feminist researcher will use the information obtained from her informants to—at some level—analyze structures of inequality, analyses that we must assume that one day will benefit many more women than the residents of the small area in which she worked. Obviously, she will also enhance her own career in so doing. If asked, her informants no doubt would prefer that the fieldworker use her power to provide them with something that would improve the quality of their immediate everyday lives. I cannot help but believe that spending years of one's life in a small community doing great good for a very few is a waste of feminist resources if those same resources could be put to use to benefit all women. If we have so little faith in our agenda, then maybe we *should* abandon the whole feminist project. But I don't really think that is the issue here.

I am not suggesting that we "grab the data and run." I am suggesting that we act practically as well as responsibly. We can do a lot for our informants as individuals and for their communities, but we cannot erase the differences between us. In truth, we would not be there doing research if there were not differences; our findings would be neither interesting nor important. One of the partial solutions suggested (I have done so myself) to this dilemma is to encourage the education of women from the countries or in the ethnic groups in which we ordinarily work to do the research themselves. Which leads me back to the concepts I borrowed to introduce myself at the beginning of this chapter. Patricia Hill Collins gave us the wonderful concept of being an outsider within. Clearly it resonated with many feminists, and in one version or another comes up in nearly every chapter in this book. Particularly in the papers here, the idea is shown to be more complex and perhaps to have implications Collins had not anticipated. I suspect that Collins did not think of it as a form of standpoint theory, and this is not the place to sort out the differences between them, but the chapters in this book, without explicitly addressing standpoint theory, point to some of the analytic failings of that theory, as well as to the complexity of doing research as an outsider within.

Patricia Zavella's paper is a particularly apt example. She shows how labeling (Chicana/o, Hispanic, Spanish, Spanish American, Mexicana/o, Mexican American) can be enormously important politically in organizing around identity. She also shows us how she, the insider in one interview, becomes an outsider in another interview in the same community. Basically, we are all outsiders and insiders, and what is or should be part of the feminist agenda—the circumstances that let an outsider in and the circumstances that turn an insider into an outsider—too often nowadays seems to get sidetracked as we fret over who is more oppressed than whom. From the fieldwork perspective, Patricia Zavella, an insider by most research definitions, found herself redefined in some but not all of her interviews. Her analysis of why is very informative but must be dismaying to those who truly believe that one must be one to understand one. Zavella did not speak directly to her place in the power differentials in this community, but the existence of a political hierarchy in the community was clear and the labeling was relevant.

Carol Stack's work with the return diaspora in the South is equally informative on the problems of power and identity that go with the insider/outsider status, but not in this case the power of the researcher. Her subjects told her that they felt very constrained politically by the social circumstances of life in the rural South. To avoid losing the support of their rural kin and friends for their progressive agendas, they had to take on the externals of home girl and home boy. Many of them worried that in time they would become "insiders" and lose the perspective that had brought them back determined to make changes. Again, the special insights of the insider depend on the insider's having been outside, and it is from these insights that the outsiders in this instance (and most others?) acquire power.

The implications of this for fieldworkers are multiple. Insofar as locally born field researchers are educated in a Western tradition, are they not just as clearly outsiders as white American researchers when they ask about things that local people do not ordinarily ask one another about? And when they risk their insider status by behaving as outsiders, their advantages over outsiders weaken. Ping-Chun Hsiung returned to do work in Taiwan's small factories, where the feminism she had acquired with her U.S. education left her intolerant of the sexism that is basic in Taiwan, and she was indignant when she was sexually harassed herself. Her response was not that of an insider woman, and although it may have been informative for the Taiwanese women observing her, it did not exactly enhance her field situation.

Günseli Berik's research situation was even more constrained. Because she was an insider, people assumed that she could not herself be the researcher—no decent Turkish woman would be wandering around the countryside alone—so she had to elevate her accompanying husband to the position of researcher in order to get entry for herself into female space. Even in her relations with her father and husband, she found herself required to assume a subordinate role (quite different from their normal egalitarian relationships) that left her both uncomfortable about the deception involved but confident that it was worth it for the sake of the project. Clearly, in this case the power rested not with the researcher but with the researched. They could be and obviously were prepared to simply say no. And this is not that unusual in fieldwork these days. Power is no longer a simple one-directional factor in field relations.

In sum, what I am suggesting here is that the insider/outsider concept and standpoint theory have real methodological limitations that contributors to this volume have, consciously or unconsciously, laid out, and that in most instances these problems are related to a misreading or a very clear reading of differences in the ability to manipulate a fieldwork encounter, that is, differences in power. Although I am on considerably less stable grounds, I also want to suggest that standpoint theories and the privileging of insider perspectives are *not* necessarily the most insightful or the most useful analytically because they deny agency to the subordinated and imply more wit to their oppressors than is merited.

If we assume that African Americans in the rural South and women in Taiwanese factories understand (not experience but understand) their oppression more clearly than their oppressors, we are making some very negative assumptions about them as agents. For example, the women that Hsiung talks about don't analyze their oppression in terms of a global economy or even of a patriarchal society, but neither are they helpless victims of it. They have developed mechanisms for coping with the sexism in their society that are inventive and functional. Without that recognition by an outsider, these women might seem like pawns in the hands of a misogynist hierarchy that is consciously aware of its capacity to manipulate them.

Speaking more directly to the insider/outsider concept, it sometimes appears—and I am not referring to Hsiung's careful research here—that some of the old anthropological chestnuts may still have meat in them. Certainly, objectivity and "keeping one's social distance" look silly in the light of contemporary theory and field situations, but I am not convinced that the advantage of being a native-born researcher always outweighs that of the foreigner who casts a fresh eye on a scene that to the native-born is so familiar that it is invisible. In the 1960s, Taiwanese anthropologists found the study of their own society totally without interest, preferring to focus on the newly exoticized aboriginal populations, sometimes researching questions similar to those that the foreign anthropologists took to the Han population. Or a better example, the illumination of "orientalism" did not come from a white American intellectual but from an outsider (who is of course now very much an insider).

But where then does all this lead us? I began by claiming that much of our angst as feminists doing fieldwork comes from our discomfort over power differences, or put more bluntly, our lack of experience with the possession of power. Whatever our ethnicity, we are more commonly less powerful than our nearest associates—even if we are white women. In our work as feminists, many, but not necessarily all of us struggle to create nonhierarchical workplaces and domestic relations. Feminists who enjoy the luxury of separatism have better opportunities to level power structures (but are not always successful; see Weston and Rofel, 1984). Those of us who integrate often find our attempts to rule by committee and make decisions by consensus put us at a disadvantage in academia and in the marketplace. Ask any women's studies program that refuses to give a vote to a dean unless or until it is a consensus decision, or is faced with a dean who appoints an ad hoc chair from the program's steering committee because he (usually) wants a "responsible party."

I am not suggesting that we abandon these important parts of our feminist practice, but I do suggest that we get more realistic about using the power we have. Sending young feminists into the field prepared to interact with factory women in India or middle-class white families in Central City in the same way as they do with their colleagues in women's studies will not do them or our feminist goals much good. I am reminded of a young woman who spent six months not long ago in an isolated field site and came out overwhelmed with feelings of guilt and of anger. The women she was working with berated her daily for not giving them enough money, for not having her rich family (not true by anyone's standards) send them televisions, and so forth. These women quickly recognized that they had a salable product and a very inexperienced buyer in their hands. They proceeded to set such a high price on their goods that the young fieldworker was soon out of money and out of the field. She was well prepared to be nonexploitative, to share her limited resources, and to try to use her project to directly benefit the women with whom she worked. She was not prepared to defend herself against exploitation, blackmail, and the enormous sense of guilt that these contradictions can inflict. Her extraordinary advantages were useless to her, and in the long run to her informants, because of her feminist scruples. Not long after she left, some less-fastidious male scholars arrived on the scene and abruptly carried away the documents of the women with whom she had been working.

The second point I wanted to make in this chapter concerns unity and respecting difference. The oppression competition is tiresome: the assumption that a white face has a colonialist mentality behind it is Lamarckian, but how many of us are willing to question that in public? None of the chapters in this book are marred by this kind of ugliness, and that is why I have felt emboldened, even as a white woman, to question the continued usefulness of the insider/outsider concept, standpoint theories, and their role in epistemic privileging. At times, to be honest, these approaches seem like patronizing attempts to empower members of a subordinate group—who by and large don't need to call on their "special position" to enhance the merit of their analyses of women's experience. Special knowledge is another matter—by virtue of growing up in a particular community one knows more readily some facts that a newcomer would not know—but I don't think I would be alone in insisting that the color of my skin and my ethnicity do not determine my ability to understand knowledge acquired through another person's experience. If one has never had a toothache, one cannot totally appreciate the physical agony of one, but one can analyse the causes and work toward a solution of the problem. I am not as convinced as I once was that the visceral experience of oppression is essential to understand it and oppose it, whether it is in the form of racism, classism, or sexism.

I have far overstepped Diane Wolf's charge to me. I hope that I have not offended those who disagree with any of my comments, but I also hope that they will encourage others to move on past this critical period with a lighter load of guilt and a stronger commitment to changing the way we work—both in the field and with each other.

REFERENCES

Abu-Lughod, Lila. 1991. "Writing Against Culture." In *Recapturing Anthropology: Working in the Present,* edited by Richard G. Fox, 137–162. Santa Fe, N.M.: School of American Research Press.

Collins, Patricia Hill. 1991. *Black Feminist Thought: Knowledge, Consciousness, and the Politics of Empowerment.* Boston: Unwin Hyman.

Weston, Kathleen, and Lisa Rofel. 1984. "Sexuality, Class, and Conflict in a Lesbian Workplace." *Signs* 9, no. 4: 623–646.

Wolf, Margery. 1992. *A Thrice Told Tale: Feminism, Postmodernism, and Ethnographic Responsibility.* Stanford: Stanford University Press.

About the Book

Fieldwork poses particular dilemmas and contradictions for feminists because of the power relations inherent in the process of gathering data and implicit in the process of representation. Although most feminist scholars are committed to seeking ethical ways to analyze women and gender, these dilemmas are especially acute in fieldwork, where research often entails working with those who are in less privileged positions than the researcher. Despite attempts by feminist scholars to conduct more interactive and egalitarian research, they have rarely been able to disrupt the hierarchies of power.

This book offers an interdisciplinary exploration of the kinds of dilemmas feminist researchers have confronted in the field, both in the United States and in Third World countries. Through experientially based writings, the authors unravel the contradictions stemming from their multiple positions as "insiders," "outsiders," or both, and from attempts to equalize the research relationship and, in some cases, to ameliorate the situation of those studied. The introductory essay includes an extensive review of the literature.

About the Contributors

GÜNSELI BERIK is assistant professor of economics and women's studies at the University of Utah. She authored *Women Carpet Weavers in Rural Turkey* (ILO, 1987) and articles on the effects of paid work on rural women's well-being and household status, and on gender inequalities in manufacturing employment in Turkey. She is engaged in a comparative study of gender in the industrialization and structural adjustment processes in Brazil, Korea, Taiwan, and Turkey and is part of a group of feminist economists attempting to integrate gender into macroeconomics.

CARMEN DIANA DEERE is professor of economics, director of the Latin American studies program at the University of Massachusetts, Amherst, and past president of the Latin American Studies Association. She has written extensively on gender and agrarian relations in Latin America. Her books include *Household and Class Relations: Peasants and Landlords in Northern Peru* (University of California Press, 1990). In recent years, she has been conducting research on the agrarian transformation in Cuba.

PING-CHUN HSIUNG is assistant professor in the Department of Sociology at the University of Toronto, Scarborough College. Her book, *Living Rooms as Factories: Class, Gender, and the Satellite Factory System in Taiwan* (Temple University Press, 1995), analyzes how Taiwan's "economic miracle" comes about in a local and daily way through the work and family lives of married women. Her current research is a comparative study of women's issues in Taiwan and China.

SUAD JOSEPH is professor of anthropology at the University of California–Davis. She founded the Association for Middle East Women's Studies and its bulletin, AMEWS NEWS, and the Middle East Research Group in Anthropology and its bulletin, MERA FORUM. She has conducted research in her native Lebanon since 1968, with comparative work in Iraq. She has published on Muslim-Christian conflicts, family systems, women's visiting networks, and the cultural construction of personhood, and most recently, "Brother/Sister Relationships: Connectivity, Love, and Power in the Reproduction of Arab Patriarchy" in the *American Ethnologist* in 1994.

CINDI KATZ, a geographer, is associate professor in environmental psychology and women's studies at the Graduate School of the City University of New York. She is the editor (with Janice Monk) of *Full Circles: Geographies of Women over the Life Course* (Routledge, 1993). Her research addresses children's environmental knowledge in the context of political-economic and cultural-ecologic transformation, the ways global economic restructuring dislocates and disqualifies children similarly in urban "First World" and rural "Third World" settings, political ecology and the critique of development, gender and spaces of everyday life, and the practices of ethnographic research.

JAYATI LAL is completing her Ph.D. in sociology at Cornell University. Her next project will be an analysis of the cultural construction of factory women in India, which she will incorporate into a book based on her dissertation, "Of Television and T-Shirts: The Making of a Gendered Working Class and the 'Made in India' Label." She will also be editing a volume entitled *Critical (Re)Constructions of "Third World Women": The Politics of Gender, Culture, and Representation in Cross-Cultural Research,* based on two panels she organized at the Fourth NGO Conference on Women in Beijing.

VALERIE MATSUMOTO is associate professor in history and Asian American studies at the University of California–Los Angeles. Her book *Farming the Home Place: A Japanese American Community in California, 1919–1982* was published by Cornell University Press in 1993. She is now researching Japanese American women artists and writers of the 1930s.

CAROL B. STACK is professor of women's studies and education at the University of California at Berkeley. Her books include *All Our Kin* and *Call to Home: African Americans Reclaim the Rural South.* She is completing "Why Work? The Meaning and Dignity of Work in the Lives of Minority Youth" (with K. Newman). She has collaborated on a book entitled *Breast Cancer? Let Me Check My Schedule.*

BRACKETTE F. WILLIAMS is associate professor of anthropology and African American studies at the University of Arizona. She has conducted fieldwork in Guyana, South America, and various regions of the United States. She recently published "Classification Systems Revisited: Kinship, Caste, Race, and Nationality as the Flow of Blood and the Spread of Rights" in *Naturalizing Power: Essays in Feminist Cultural Analysis* (Routledge, 1994). Currently, she is editing a volume on gender and nationalism.

DIANE L. WOLF is associate professor of sociology at the University of California–Davis. She coordinates a Ford Foundation grant to the Gender and Global Issues group at U.C.-Davis that brings four Third World women activists to campus for one academic quarter every year. Her book *Factory Daughters* (University of California, 1992) is based on fieldwork in Java, Indonesia. She is currently researching recent Filipino immigrants in California.

MARGERY WOLF is professor of anthropology at the University of Iowa. Her past research focused on women and family in Taiwan and China. She no longer works in either place, and her theoretical interests now are more concerned with the construction of ethnography. Currently, she is doing research for a project entitled: "Coyote's Land: A Historical Ethnography of Several Cultures and One Landscape."

PATRICIA ZAVELLA, an anthropologist, is professor of community studies at the University of California–Santa Cruz. Along with Louise Lamphere, Felipe Gonzales, and Peter B. Evans, she has coauthored *Sunbelt Working Mothers: Reconciling Family and Factory* (Cornell University Press, 1993). Her current research examines gender, race, and poverty in the Santa Cruz area.